T0355792

The World Made Meme

The Information Society Series

Laura DeNardis and Michael Zimmer, Series Editors

Interfaces on Trial 2.0, Jonathan Band and Masanobu Katoh

Opening Standards: The Global Politics of Interoperability, Laura DeNardis, editor

The Reputation Society: How Online Opinions Are Reshaping the Offline World, Hassan Masum and Mark Tovey, editors

The Digital Rights Movement: The Role of Technology in Subverting Digital Copyright, Hector Postigo

Technologies of Choice? ICTs, Development, and the Capabilities Approach, Dorothea Kleine

Pirate Politics: The New Information Policy Contests, Patrick Burkart

After Access: The Mobile Internet and Inclusion in the Developing World, Jonathan Donner

The World Made Meme: Public Conversations and Participatory Media, Ryan M. Milner

The World Made Meme

Public Conversations and Participatory Media

Ryan M. Milner

The MIT Press
Cambridge, Massachusetts
London, England

This book was set in Stone Sans and Stone Serif by Toppan Best-set Premedia Limited. Printed and bound in the United States of America.

Library of Congress Cataloging-in-Publication Data

Names: Milner, Ryan M., author.
Title: The world made meme : public conversations and participatory media / Ryan M. Milner.
Description: Cambridge, Massachusetts : The MIT Press, [2016] | Series: The information society series | Includes bibliographical references and index.
Identifiers: LCCN 2016010239 | ISBN 9780262034999 (hardcover : alk. paper)
Subjects: LCSH: Memes. | Memetics. | Culture diffusion. | Mass media.
Classification: LCC HM626 .M553 2016 | DDC 302—dc23 LC record available at https://lccn.loc.gov/2016010239

10 9 8 7 6 5 4 3 2 1

Contents

Acknowledgments

This book, like the texts at its heart, is a collective endeavor. It wouldn't exist without years of help and support from the people closest to me. From the earliest iterations of this research, the insight and sacrifice of my mentors and friends have proven invaluable. In many ways, this book began when I first wandered into Nancy Baym's graduate seminar on digital media at the University of Kansas a decade ago. I was a dazed M.A. student who wasn't quite sure why he was there, but Nancy's years of guidance shaped me into the scholar I am today, and I can only hope this work honors that profound influence.

The same could be said for the professors who guided parts of this project at the University of Kansas. I spent my graduate education crowding the offices and struggling through the seminars of Jay Childers, Dave Tell, Yan Bing Zhang, Ben Chappell, and many others, grappling with half-formed ideas along the way. They helped walk those ideas closer to fruition. My time in Lawrence, Kansas, was also defined by some of the finest friends I could hope for. My fellow graduate students Mike Anderson, Evan Center, Chelsea Graham, Vince Meserko, John Vilanova, and Clare Echterling spent years generously lending me their eyes and ears—and on a few nights, their couches. As this project comes to a close, I have not forgotten them.

As I left the University of Kansas, the help and support did not wane. Mentors like Jean Burgess and Limor Shifman, as well as colleagues like Kate Miltner, have provided substantial insight. Whether sitting right next to me at a conference panel or trading ideas with me from halfway across the world, these mentors and colleagues have been instrumental. In particular, Whitney Phillips has been astounding in her support, camaraderie, and kindness. This book is the better for her feedback and friendship, and I'm a better scholar for both. As I have struggled to refine the perspectives that became this book, I am grateful I have not had to do it alone.

I have many people to thank from my time at the College of Charleston as well. Leigh Moscowitz, David Moscowitz, April Bisner, Paul Anderson, Max Kovalov, Carl Wise, Kaitlin Reiss, Bea Maldonado-Bird, and Abby Steere-Williams have all opened their homes, offered their insight, and—most importantly—provided their friendship, shaping this project along the way. Among my friends at the College of Charleston, David Parisi and Jacob Steere-Williams have proven ever more invaluable with every article shared, every class co-taught, and every happy hour toasted. Without the community of friends and scholars around me, this book would still be a half-hoped dream.

At home, Sarah, Sophia, Gabriel, and Pearl have endured more than their fair share of long workdays and forcibly quiet rooms. And they've responded with nothing but love, esteem, and giant hugs every time I walk through the door. Back in Kansas City, mom and Eric have kept close even as their son and brother moved across the country. My family has stayed right here with me, celebrating my every success and commiserating my every worry through every step of this project. I wouldn't be me without them, so this book wouldn't exist without them.

From its earliest conception to its final days with the stellar team at the MIT Press, the collective that wrote this book is too vast to list. I am grateful for every reviewer, editor, panel chair—every student, mentor, and friend—who has shaped the pages to follow. I am also grateful for the innumerable constellations of participants creating, circulating, and transforming memetic media. Every hashtag, every mashup, every Photoshop; this book wouldn't be anything without any of them. So thank you.

Introduction: The Rise of Memetic Media

The Memetic Tapestry

This book is about emerging patterns in public conversations, and about the social participation essential to those conversations. It focuses on internet memes—the linguistic, image, audio, and video texts created, circulated, and transformed by countless cultural participants across vast networks and collectives. Internet memes take the form of pictures captioned on Reddit, puns hashtagged on Twitter, and videos mashed up on YouTube. They can be widely shared catchphrases, Auto-Tuned songs, manipulated stock photos, or recordings of physical performances. They're used to make jokes, argue points, and connect friends. The concept has risen in prominence over the last twenty years, emerging from the esoteric forums and message boards where participants first linked Richard Dawkins's (1976, 1982) theories of cultural replication to shared in-jokes, catchphrases, and signature texts.

As the years have worn on, the scope and reach of this connection has widened. In the past half-decade, memes such as "Binders Full of Women," "The Harlem Shake," "Pepper Spray Cop," "We are the 99 Percent," "Double Rainbow Guy," "Grumpy Cat," "Ridiculously Photogenic Guy," "Planking," "Kanye Interrupts," "Rickrolling," "Slenderman," "Hands Up, Don't Shoot," "Black Lives Matter," "Yes All Women," and "The Ice Bucket Challenge" have become cultural touchstones. The sites where memetic media are often shared—Twitter, YouTube, and Reddit, among many others—have also grown in public interest and significance. In 2015—the year this manuscript was written—it's hard to imagine a major pop cultural or political moment that doesn't inspire its own constellation of mediated remix, play, and commentary.

In this environment, mediated expression and debate consistently occur through and around an ever-growing collection of populist memetic texts. Memetic media are premised on participation by reappropriation, on balancing the familiar and the foreign as new iterations intertwine with established ideas. In this way, small strands weave together big conversations that are increasingly prominent, vibrant, and instantaneous. This book is about those small strands and the big conversations they inspire, as—moment after moment, representation after representation, dialogue after dialogue—public participants memetically make their world.

This memetic participation is larger than any individual image, video, or tweet. Memetic media are aggregate texts, collectively created, circulated, and transformed by countless cultural participants. They're innumerable—as dense as they are vibrant—and understanding their implications for public conversation requires understanding intertextual connections, even when assessing singular texts. The weaving metaphor that persists throughout this book therefore casts individual participatory media texts as strands that intertwine into threads of interaction, eventually forming whole tapestries of public conversation. This process is memetic; it's premised on new commentary being crafted by the mediated circulation and transformation of ideas that have come before.

When everyday members of the public contribute their small conversational strands to the vast cultural tapestry, they are memetically making their world. The cultures we inhabit have always come from the intertwine of these small strands, but this intertwine is even more powerful in our contemporary media ecology. Our cultural tapestry is more vibrant because of the wide spectrum of hashtagged status updates, remixed photos, and mashed-up videos that dominate participatory media. Our public conversations are bigger and louder than they've ever been. There are more voices in the air, even if age-old limitations and marginalizations persist in the midst of this vibrancy. By amplifying these voices, memetic media evidence creativity and contribution that push us further away from simple "top-down" understandings of media influence. The participatory media world is made—is brought into existence and sustained—through messy memetic interrelationships. It exists in the space between individual texts and broader conversations, between individual citizens and broader cultural discourses.

To assess these interrelationships, I focus here on *memetics* as a set of social practices, instead of focusing exclusively on *memes* as individual texts. For this reason, I often choose to invoke the adjective and adverbial forms of *meme*—*memetic* and *memetically*—to emphasize the social processes essential to the creation, circulation, and transformation of collective texts, regardless of the individual text itself. It's an easy shortcut to call a solitary image we scroll past on Twitter or Tumblr a *meme*, as if the term is synonymous with "a quirky little JPG from the internet." However, it takes memetic processes to turn an individual text into a memetic one. The examples that opened this introduction—from "Rickrolling" to "Black Lives Matter"—are not static, self-contained texts. Instead, they resonate because of intertwining collective contributions. An individual tweet or image or mashup or video isn't in and of itself a *meme*, though it may be *memetic* in its connection to other tweets, images, mashups, and videos, and it may *memetically* spread along with others in kind. In this connection and spread lies the true significance of memetic media.

The argument anchoring this book—that memetic media are significant as individual strands in vast tapestries of public conversation—has developed as I've grappled with the concept over the last half-decade. I've been researching internet memes since late 2010, and—fortunately for me—this time has coincided with a rising wave of scholarship on memetic media and the collectives creating, circulating, and transforming them. Whitney Phillips's *This Is Why We Can't Have Nice Things* (2015b), Adrienne Massanari's *Participatory Culture, Community, and Play* (2015), Limor Shifman's *Memes in Digital Culture* (2014), Karine Nahon and Jeff Hemsley's *Going Viral* (2013), and Henry Jenkins, Sam Ford, and Joshua Green's *Spreadable Media* (2013) precede this book in their assessment of memetic media. And this is saying nothing of the ever-expanding catalog of scholarly and popular articles assessing memetic media across social and cultural contexts. Building on this body of scholarship, I argue that the social processes underscoring memetic media are essential to the contemporary media ecology, and that our public conversations are made more vibrant by the popularization of these media.

To that end, I present here an analysis based on a corpus of media texts and popular commentary that I have been building since late 2010. I recognize that any situated textual analysis comes with limitations. Because the memetic media cataloged here are loosely bound between 2010 and 2015, each of the examples in the chapters to follow carries the risk of becoming dated by the time it's read. Furthermore, the analysis here is almost entirely situated in Western contexts, most specifically English-speaking contexts within the United States.[1] In these ways, this work is a geographically and historically positioned product of a specific cultural moment. A reader picking up this book in twenty years—or one picking it up outside of the West—may be unfamiliar with the individual examples at the heart of this analysis. As cultural practices and technological affordances shift, so too, inevitably, does what people share.

However, with these limitations in mind, I'll argue throughout this book that memetic logics persist beyond individual examples. Even as individual strands and threads fade from public use, the tools for making the tapestry persist. Participatory media facilitate vast constellations of individual expression, which intertwine into collective commentary, even as specific texts rise and fall. For better or worse—and this book will highlight a bit of both—the memetic creation, circulation, and transformation of mediated messages has given shape and texture to contemporary public conversations, and will continue to do so in the future.

As the following chapters will illustrate, these public conversations—the worlds that are created through participatory media—are memetically made. They're made when new cultural contributions emerge from the mediated remix, mashup, and reappropriation of texts and ideas that have come before, which themselves are their own remixes, mashups, and reappropriations. By assessing how social worlds are memetically made, we can better understand the contours—the affordances and the limitations, the shortcomings and the potentials—of contemporary mediated conversations. We can better understand the logics that are essential to the good, bad, and in-between of collective public participation. Memetic media have risen to prominence; this book assesses how they work and what they mean.

Chapter Organization

The chapters to follow are broken into two parts. Chapters 1 through 3—Logics, Grammar, and Vernacular—address the formal and social dimensions of memetic media, asking what underpins interaction in a media ecology made memetic. Chapters 4 through 6—Antagonism, Voice, and

Conversation—assess the implications of memetic media for public participation, unpacking how memetic media simultaneously facilitate both empowerment and marginalization. Following these two parts and the conclusion, the appendix provides an account of this project's methods. It also discusses the ethical and representational tensions inherent to analyzing the ambiguously public media texts essential to this book. Across this book's two parts, its six chapters are designed to move from a focus on foundational memetic logics, through a focus on situated social interactions, and then out to a focus on massive cultural conversations. In a media ecology that weaves strands into threads into tapestries, understanding the *micro*, the *meso*, and the *macro* dimensions of that ecology is essential. Across these layers of mediated interaction, public participants connect and converse, debate and antagonize, consume and contribute. This book is organized to chart these layers.

Part I's first chapter, Logics, introduces the fundamentals of memetic media. It traces the (imperfect) connections between Richard Dawkins's (1976, 1982) conceptualization of memes as cultural replicators and the mediated texts that have come to bear the name in pop cultural parlance. It then outlines five fundamental logics central to memetic participation. Memetic media are unique for their multimodality (their expression in multiple modes of communication), their reappropriation (their "poaching" of existing texts), their resonance (their connections to individual participants), their collectivism (their social creation and transformation), and their spread (their circulation through mass networks). These logics are central to the chapters that follow.

Chapters 2 and 3, Grammar and Vernacular, work in tandem to assess how memetic logics are employed as participants weave individual texts into social interactions. Chapter 2 focuses on the complex multimodal reappropriation at the heart of memetic media. It addresses the tensions between imitation and transformation in this process. Chapter 3 focuses on the social dimensions of these practices, arguing that memetic participation depends on the interrelations of fixed premise and novel expression. It then outlines the creativity required in this process, emphasizing the collective standards guiding that creativity. Ultimately, these chapters argue that memetic media are a lingua franca, a shared "common tongue" for mass participation.

In part II, chapters 4 and 5, Antagonism and Voice, work in tandem to examine how memetic logics, grammar, and vernacular facilitate both exclusion and empowerment during public conversations. Chapter 4 focuses on the everyday antagonisms that are perpetuated through memetic participation, specifically regarding race and gender identities. However, it also argues that memetic participation can be employed for the counterpublic contestation of those same antagonisms. Chapter 5 argues that memetic media carry the potential for public voice, even in the midst of the everyday antagonisms outlined in chapter 4. Focusing on mediated conversations surrounding the Occupy Wall Street movement, it addresses tensions between populism and pastiche when popular culture is part of public commentary. Ultimately, these chapters argue that memetic media afford polyvocality—the participation of many voices—even in the midst of persistent inequality.

Chapter 6, Conversation, argues that memetic participation complicates the culture industries that remain at the heart of public life. It assesses the ambivalent relationship between collective participation and individual expression, especially when age-old gatekeepers intertwine with new means of sharing information. It focuses on the complex relationship between collectivism, publicity, and fame in memetic media, as well as on concerns about commercialism and credibility in a seemingly open media ecology.

In all, this book demonstrates that memetic media bring with them a mix of new potentials and old tensions. In this interrelationship, individual expression intertwines with cultural precedent. This mediated intertwine connects participants spread across great distance, but also can normalize problematic perspectives. The chapters to follow assess this intertwine, as strands of small expression memetically thread into vast social worlds.

Part I Media Made Memetic

The first half of this book argues that memetic media are a lingua franca for digitally mediated participation, a common tongue allowing geographically dispersed participants to connect and share. Chapters 1 through 3 focus on the micro formal layers and the meso interactional layers of memetic media, articulating how participants express and engage across those layers. Tapestries of conversation are crafted when individuals tie their unique contributions to texts and ideas that have come before. Participatory media accelerate the memetic dimensions of this vast process, a media ecology where it's relatively cheap and easy to make a statement, remix a text, or spread an idea. Understanding this ecology requires understanding the logics, grammar, and vernacular that underpin memetic media. The first half of this book therefore assesses the fundamentals of how memetic media work. The more macro assessment of civic and public conversation in part II would not be possible without the foundation in part I.

From one perspective, the argument in part I about the ubiquity of memetic media is easy to accept. After all, it's being made at a time when memetic media are more prevalent, prolific, and powerful than ever. This hasn't always been the case. When I started my Ph.D. dissertation on internet memes in late 2010, many people I talked to about the project had scant knowledge of the term. During a job interview in 2011, a dean listened, head cocked, as I explained my work, stared at me afterward, and finally said, "With most candidates I have some idea what they're talking about; I have no idea what you're talking about." I had to pull out my iPad and flip through my collection of "funny internet photos" before we shared enough common ground to continue the conversation. In 2015, the term is much more integrated into popular parlance. It doesn't take much to connect even the least-invested listener to the prevalence and significance of the shared images, videos, and hashtags that emerge from nebulous collectives on sites like Reddit, YouTube, and Twitter. Even NPR's website is running stories highlighting the political implications of its "#MemeOfTheWeek" (see Sanders 2015). Given the growing ubiquity of this lingua franca, its particulars—its logics, grammar, and vernacular—are worth assessing in depth.

From another perspective, though, this ubiquity has different connotations. For some, 2015 may not signal the triumph of memetic media, but rather a moment when internet memes have been "done to death." To the participants who spent the last decade active on a few esoteric forums and message boards, *internet meme* came to label a specific—if ever-expanding—set of niche texts, in-jokes, and practices. Emerging out of sites like 4chan, Something Awful, and YTMND in the early to mid 2000s, these initial exemplars found their way to Reddit, Tumblr, and beyond as collective attention grew. This niche lineage of memetic participation is knotted up with the unwieldy chimera that is "internet culture," a contested label for a loose set of discursive practices and a loose canon of texts that emerged sometime during the last twenty years.

From this framing—one tied to moments like the ROFLCon internet culture conference that ran between 2008 and 2012—the narrative about internet memes often centers on a once-thriving "subculture" corrupted by "mainstream" attention. No doubt at least a few readers of this book will have become familiar with internet memes through this lineage, and may therefore wonder about the utility of assessing memetic media in 2015. After all, ROFLCon closed its doors in 2012; 4chan's founder, Christopher "moot" Poole, sold the infamous message board earlier this year; and NPR is now writing headlines like "#MemeOfTheWeek." Given these shifts, it might be tempting to see this book as an analysis of the texts and tropes central to a waning subcultural moment.

But the argument here is larger than that subcultural moment, even if it draws from that moment. The formal and social analysis at the heart of part I is not centered solely on internet memes as a relatively narrow set of texts that rose to prominence sometime between 2002 and 2012, and may or may not be trite in 2015. Instead, it centers on the logics, grammar, and vernacular essential to memetic media, which are more persistent than any individual exemplar. Part I will address the "subcultural corruption" narrative (chapters 2 and 3 in particular will complicate this perspective), and the whole book will assess conversations occurring in relatively niche corners of sites like 4chan, Reddit, and Tumblr. That said, the memetic logics introduced in chapter 1 are fundamental to mediated cultural participation above and beyond the relative few sites and relative few years that carried the term *internet meme* into public prominence. The systems supporting this lingua franca are significant to a wide array of conversations, spanning platforms, eras, and degrees of mediation.

Yet another perspective—one steeped in the fields of cultural studies or anthropology—might question the utility of using the memetic lens to assess public conversation. Richard Dawkins's (1976, 1982) theory describes the spread of ideas by using the metaphors of genetic inheritance and viral infection, but those metaphors can deny the individual agency of social actors. From this deterministic lens, memes propagate as they leap "from brain to brain" through behavioral imitation. Given the limiting nature of this paradigm, there's cause to question the value of an argument that more thoroughly tangles up Dawkins's determinism with mediated expressions and conversations. Instead of tying the complex tapestry of culture to a simplistic theory of viral spread, it may be better to diminish the connections between Dawkins's argument and participatory media. We may have the term *internet meme* because an errant idea from the biological sciences happened to resonate on 4chan a decade ago, but there's no guarantee that the memetic lens tells us anything new about mediated conversation. Likewise, a study of mediated conversation may not necessarily tell us anything new about memetic theory.

But the argument here is larger than Dawkins's theory, even while drawing from it. As such, parallel to its complication of the "subcultural" dimensions of memetic media, part I will also complicate the "memetic theory" dimensions of memetic media, assessing its theoretical baggage and its utility for understanding mediated conversation. Chapter 1—as it addresses the logics foundational to memetic participation—will also outline the imperfect relationship between Dawkins's deterministic perspectives on the "viral" spread of ideas and the more nuanced realities of memetic media. Chapters 2 and 3 will likewise demonstrate that the social dimensions of memetic participation emphasize transformative reappropriation over simple "brain-to-brain" imitation.

Part I is ultimately about those social transformations, and the logics at their heart. In its focus on the logics, grammar, and vernacular that underpin memetic media, the first half of this book connects widening forms of conversation with established cultural theory, complicating our understanding of both. The formal and social analysis of memetic media in part I establishes the strands and threads vital to the shared tapestry of memetic participation. In this way, it's an assessment of a lingua franca produced by the vast constellation of mediated expression.

1 Logics: The Fundamentals of Memetic Participation

The Many Interruptions of Kanye West

On the evening of September 13, 2009, "Imma let you finish" entered the American pop vernacular. It was birthed in a mass media moment, when hip-hop artist Kanye West took the stage at MTV's annual Video Music Awards (VMAs). West may have uttered the phrase, but in the minutes, days, weeks, and years that followed, "Imma let you finish" ceased to be West's alone. The phrase was circulated and transformed by countless cultural participants, in countless contexts through diverse media channels. "Imma let you finish"—and the media moment at its genesis—became a strand of creative play in public conversation. It became a meme.

At the VMAs, West "interrupted" performer Taylor Swift as she received an award for Best Female Video. As Swift began her acceptance speech, West appeared on stage unannounced, telling Swift—and audiences beyond—that the award should have gone to Beyoncé's "Single Ladies (Put a Ring on It)." "Yo Taylor," West interjected, "I'm really happy for you. … Imma let you finish. … But Beyoncé had one of the best videos *of all time*. One of the *best* videos of all time." West's quick exit, MTV's quick cut to a commercial, and Beyoncé winning Video of the Year later that night weren't enough to keep the moment off sites like Twitter and YouTube, as well as traditional media outlets. As it was cemented in the popular imagination, the media moment spawned imitative mass media moments, as when hip-hop artist Jay-Z jokingly interrupted West at the 2012 BET Awards. Or when West—half jokingly—ran on stage after alternative artist Beck beat Beyoncé for Album of the Year at the 2015 Grammys.

But it wasn't just celebrities who entered the conversation. As awareness of the moment spread, "Imma let you finish" began to pepper

Figure 1.1
Kanye West inserted into a photograph of Martin Luther King Jr. during his famous 1963 "I Have a Dream" speech. A caption connects the address with West's interruption of Taylor Swift at the 2009 MTV Video Music Awards. Collected in 2013.

conversations and populate hashtags, as did hyperbolic evaluations about something, anything, being "the *best* of all time. *Of all time.*" And collective play with West's interruption wasn't limited only to words; participants on scores of sites created a flurry of visual "Kanye Interrupts" remixes. West was inserted into the 1963 "I Have a Dream" speech given by civil rights leader Martin Luther King Jr. (figure 1.1), and was used to wreck a multitude of cultural touchstones, disparaging Edward from *Twilight*, Mario from *Super Mario World*, and even the scientific work of Albert Einstein (figure 1.2). I myself applied the moment in an interpersonal context (figure 1.3), crafting an image to congratulate a friend during his presentation about Kanye West at a media studies colloquium (I texted it to him in the middle of his talk). Stitching together multiple strands from a shared premise, each of these images is an intertextual thread in a broader social tapestry. These threads can be vastly public, communally social, or intimately interpersonal. Together, they're the cultural work of public participants who create,

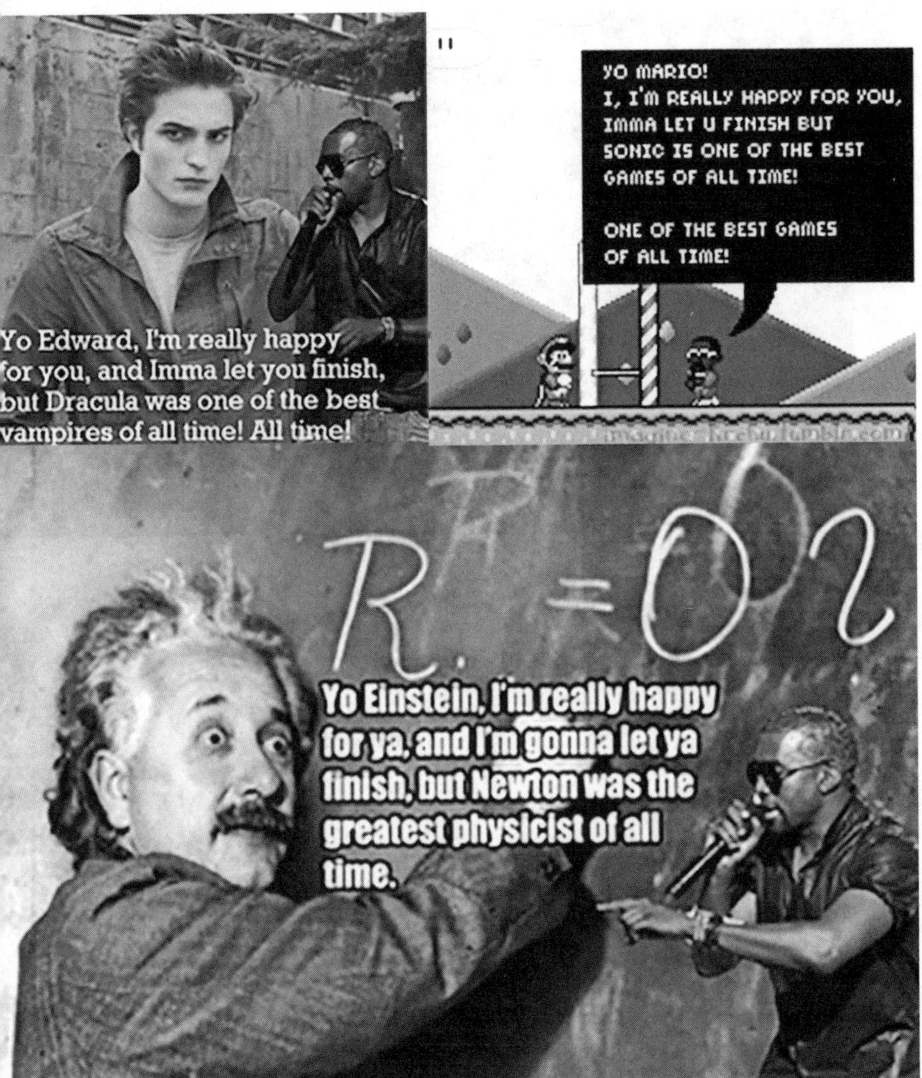

Figure 1.2
Three "Kanye Interrupts" images. Top left: West critiques Edward from the 2008 film *Twilight* about his vampire prowess; top right: West critiques Mario from the 1990 videogame *Super Mario World* on the quality of his game; bottom: West critiques physicist Albert Einstein as he formulates a scientific theory. Collected in 2013.

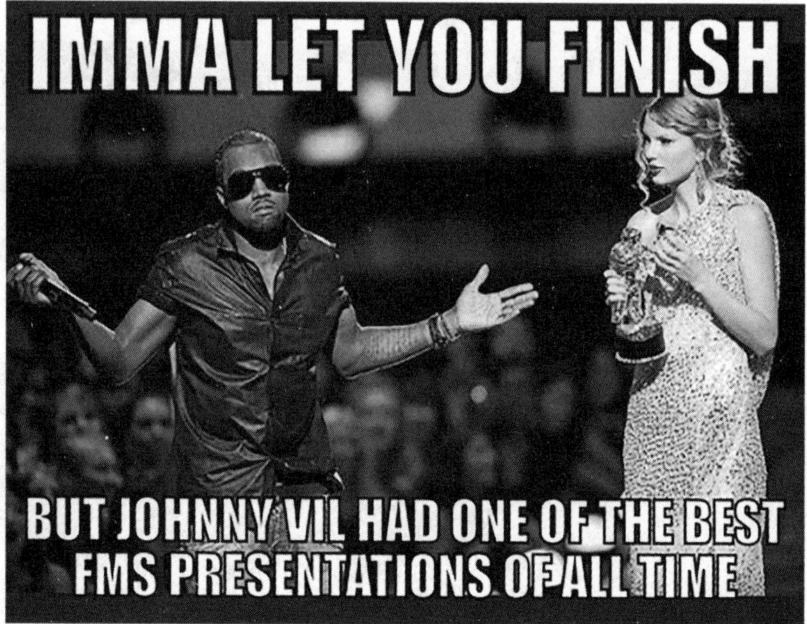

Figure 1.3
An image I created by captioning an Associated Press photo during a colleague's presentation at the 2012 University of Kansas Film and Media Studies Colloquium. John Vilanova ("Johnny Vil") was presenting a paper on the "Kanye Interrupts" moment. Created on January 28, 2012.

circulate, and transform media for their own communicative ends, weaving complex conversations as they go.

Internet memes depend on collective creation, circulation, and transformation. They're multimodal texts that facilitate participation by reappropriation, by balancing a fixed premise with novel expression. In Limor Shifman's definition, internet memes are "(a) a group of digital items sharing common characteristics ... which (b) were created with awareness of each other, and (c) were circulated, imitated, and/or transformed via the Internet by many users" (2014, 41). In their common characteristics, mutual awareness, and transformative circulation, memes are at once universal and particular, familiar and foreign. They're small expressions with big implications.

Internet memes complicate narrow ideas about the singularity of media texts. As the "Kanye Interrupts" meme spread, West and MTV lost ownership of the moment. Instead, participants on sites like Twitter, YouTube, Reddit, 4chan, and Tumblr have made it their own. The texts produced on these sites are the work of vast collectives, even if they're collectives connected only by shared cultural understanding. The images in figures 1.1 and 1.2—like countless memetic texts—circulated without signature or citation. Finding their creator and site of origin is largely impossible, and arguably inconsequential when considering how they resonate. In this case, I gathered the images from the memetic reference site Know Your Meme in mid 2013, but the participants uploading them to that repository could have found them anywhere; there's certainly no guarantee that they were uploading their own creations.[1] But both creation and sharing can be expressive acts. As audiences have mashed West up with Darth Vader, royal weddings, and YouTube's famous "Keyboard Cat"—as they've circulated the creations of others—they've demonstrated what Henry Jenkins, Sam Ford, and Joshua Green (2013) call the "collective" and "connective" work of mediated publics. This public work combines words, images, audio, and video into buzzing, vibrant conversation.

And "Kanye Interrupts" isn't alone. Members of the mediated public consistently punctuate their participation with memetic texts. This vibrant participation is predominant enough that Shifman calls contemporary mediated conversations *hypermemetic*, since "almost every major public event sprouts a stream of memes" (2014, 4). As a memetic moment resonates and spreads, it becomes a new conversational thread in the popular vernacular, one that "permeates many spheres of digital and nondigital expression" (23). In this process, new texts become recognizable strands that are in turn woven into new conversations as participants see fit.

The rest of this chapter will discuss the logics that underlie the hypermemetic media ecology that produces "Kanye Interrupts" and ceaseless other examples. It will first connect memetics as a cultural theory to the media texts that now widely bear its name. *Meme*, from this theoretical lineage, is a term rooted in the work of biologist Richard Dawkins (1976, 1982). In the Dawkinsian sense, *meme* labels units of cultural transmission, but its application to what we call *internet memes* raises critical questions about individual agency in the social spread of information. Having explored this connection, the chapter will then introduce five logics fundamental to memetic participation, building a case for the centrality of multimodality, reappropriation, resonance, collectivism, and spread in participatory media.

(Re)introducing the Meme

Meme is a term coined by Dawkins to describe the flow and flux of culture. Dawkins conceptualized memes as cultural corollaries to genes, deterministic on a social level analogous to genes' biological determinism over individual traits. In *The Selfish Gene,* Dawkins begins with the premise that "most of what is unusual about man can be summed up in one word: 'culture'" (1976, 189). For Dawkins, the unusual power of culture demands a theoretical lens consistent with the transference of genetic traits, provided that the same evolutionary laws govern both biology and culture. To that end, Dawkins introduced the term *meme*:

> We need a name for the new replicator, a noun which conveys the idea of a unit of cultural transmission, or a unit of *imitation*. "Mimeme" comes from a suitable Greek root, but I want a monosyllable that sounds a bit like "gene." I hope my classicist friends will forgive me if I abbreviate mimeme to *meme*. ... Just as genes propagate themselves in the gene pool by leaping from body to body via sperms or eggs, so memes propagate themselves in the meme pool by leaping from brain to brain via a process which, in the broad sense, can be called imitation. (192, original emphasis)

In this articulation, memes are cognitive replicators, passing from person to person through social imitation. To Dawkins, they can be "tunes, ideas, catch-phrases, clothes fashions, ways of making pots or of building arches" (192). Broad cultural concepts like language, art, technology, and religion are composed of "co-adapted meme complexes" (199), or "memeplexes," woven from a series of more micro-level memes.

Dawkins's conception has a fairly long and controversial history within the biological sciences. More recently, the concept and its controversies have made their way to the social sciences and humanities. During this time—and living up to its definitional characteristics—the term *meme* has also evolved within participatory media collectives. And as it has done so, questions about the utility of using memetics to explain cultural practices have persisted. Despite these questions, the term now seems inextricably tied to many mediated conversations. It's a resilient—if problematic—lens, one that has itself spread well. As David Haig says, "the meme of the 'meme' is a tenacious beast, at least for those minds that are vulnerable to its charms" (2006, 64). The rest of this section will outline the associations made between memetics and mediated participation, and will assess the value of that connection.

From Dawkins to Kanye

One early connection between memetic theory and participatory media comes from Mike Godwin, writing for *Wired* in 1994. Godwin expresses frustration with what he calls "the Nazi comparison meme," a phrase he uses to label the tendency of participants on internet forums to compare other forum participants to Nazis during arguments. In his *Wired* piece, Godwin says his memetic framing of the common argumentative tactic met resistance from other forum participants: "Not everyone saw the comparison to Nazis as a 'meme'—most people on the Net, as elsewhere, had never heard of 'memes' or 'memetics.' But now that we're living in an increasingly information-aware culture, it's time for that to change. And it's time for net.dwellers to make a conscious effort to control the kinds of memes they create or circulate." From early connections like Godwin's, the memetic lens gained traction across participatory media and rose to prominence with the popularization of once esoteric online collectives, like 4chan, Reddit, and Tumblr, among others. Participants on these sites have co-opted the term, stripped it of some of its strongly Dawkinsian connotations, and reintroduced it to broader public discourse. These participatory media collectives have applied the term *meme*—if not always memetic cultural theory—to many of the media texts they create, circulate, and transform.

In the contemporary participatory media ecology, internet memes come in a few forms. In this book, I break them down into a few loose subgenres, all meeting Shifman's (2014) criteria of common characteristics, mutual awareness, and transformative circulation. First are *memetic phrases* like "Imma let you finish," introduced into the pop lexicon by the "Kanye Interrupts" media moment. "We are the 99 Percent"—a 2011 slogan used by Occupy Wall Street protestors to affiliate with the bottom "99 percent" of income earners—is another example. The 2010 "Double Rainbow" YouTube video inspired a memetic phrase as well. In the video, the narrator sees two rainbows in the sky above his home, and asks, awestruck, "What does it *mean*?" Countless others have since mimicked his philosophical wonder by applying the catchphrase, with varying degrees of irony.

Second, *memetic videos* were also remixed out of Kanye's interruption, cross-cutting the moment with political speeches, celebrity funerals, and even other memetic videos. One mashup combines "Kanye Interrupts" with the "Hitler Reacts" meme born from humorously subtitling Adolf

Hitler's monologue in the 2004 film *Der Untergang*. Shifman (2011, 2014) has cataloged these memetic videos across her work. She discusses Psy's 2012 music video "Gangnam Style," which inspired prolific remixing when it became a YouTube hit. She also analyzes memetic replies to Chris Crocker's 2007 YouTube video called "Leave Britney Alone," in which Crocker tearfully asks the public to stop harassing pop star Britney Spears.

Third, when Jay-Z interrupted West at the 2012 BET Awards, and when West repeated his interruption at the 2015 Grammys, they were enacting *memetic performances*, referencing, replicating, and escalating an embodied behavior for collective appreciation. Alas, others have not widely joined in, and no "Kanyeing" trend has taken off. But there are more egalitarian memetic performances. The year 2011 brought to participatory media "Planking" (photos of individuals lying flat in unconventional places as if they were planks of wood) and "Tebowing" (photos of individuals on one knee as if they were praying, in ironic homage to devout Christian football player Tim Tebow).

Last are the prolific *memetic images* shared across participatory media collectives (see figure 1.4). These small pictures are pervasive in mediated public conversation. "Kanye Interrupts" inspired the images in figures 1.1–1.3, but the images in figure 1.4 play with multiple source texts and multiple in-jokes.

Memetic phrases, videos, performances, and images are all intertextual, self-aware, and premised on transformation. However, these categories—like any typology—are not objective, intrinsic, or immovable. Their distinctions are my own invention, tied as best I can to the modes of communication that memetic texts inhabit. Overlaps, of course, abound. "Imma let you finish," for instance, is a linguistic phrase taken from a video moment and then applied to countless image files. For this reason, my emphasis here is on the ways participants memetically make their world through their mediated creations, circulations, and transformations, even as typologies, genres, and individual texts flux and flow. The social practices are what persist, as mediated participation moves from Dawkins to Kanye and to the countless memetic texts and collective moments that will inevitably come next.

A Conceptual Troublemaker

As the previous sections attest, internet memes have a conflicted connection to their namesake from biological anthropology. Shifman (2013) calls

Figure 1.4
Six memetic images. They use annotation and manipulation to reappropriate (left to right, top to bottom) a picture of a cat and a turtle; a scene from a 2011 episode of the show *Breaking Bad*; a Reuters photo of American President Barack Obama; a sloth; a print from the Etsy shop of user "sharpwriter"; and a combination of the 1966 television special *How the Grinch Stole Christmas* with a photo of University of California, Davis, police officer John Pike. Collected between 2010 and 2015.

memes "conceptual troublemakers," citing the ambivalent relationship between shared social practices and Dawkins's (1976) theories on cultural imitation. It's true that *meme* is the *in vivo* term cultural participants began using twenty years ago to describe the texts they were creating, circulating, and transforming. But this fact doesn't itself mandate that memetic theory is the best way to understand internet memes. As a tool for explaining cultural processes, memetics is contested both from within and beyond media studies.

The appeal of memetic theory is its power to explain the spread of vast information bit by bit, through micro circulations and transformations. This is how Godwin (1994) frames the utility of memetics in his discussion of the Nazi comparison meme. As the solution to the problematic Nazi meme, he proposes a "counter-meme." To this end, he introduces what he labels "Godwin's Law" as a callout to the Nazi comparison meme. Godwin's Law states: "As an online discussion grows longer, the probability of a comparison involving Nazis or Hitler approaches one." Godwin's point in this branded callout isn't just to bring attention to the negative communicative trend. Instead, Godwin names the law in order to "seed" a countermeme, which he hopes will begin to populate forum threads right alongside Nazi comparisons. His goal is that whenever a forum participant makes a Nazi comparison, another can immediately reference the memorable shorthand that is Godwin's Law. Through collective awareness and use of his maxim, participants can memetically rebuke Nazi comparisons. Twenty years later, Godwin's Law is still occasionally invoked, perhaps demonstrating that Godwin had the right idea. Of course, it's largely invoked when Nazi comparisons are made, which means it survives tangled up with the idea it was meant to counter.

Despite Godwin's aims, the processes that occur when cultural participants conceptualize shorthand "laws"—or when they intertwine Kanye West and Martin Luther King Jr.—may not be as easy as the "leap from brain to brain" that Dawkins (1976) theorized. Perhaps the most prevalent critique of memetic theory is that it favors a biological or cultural determinism instead of valuing the agency of social actors. This perspective has extended to its use in participatory media, especially in conjunction with "viral marketing." As Shifman explains, the meme metaphor "has been used in a problematic way, conceptualizing people as helpless and passive creatures, susceptible to the domination of meaningless media 'snacks' that infect their minds" (2014, 11). This deterministic perspective implies that there's a formula to unlocking the persuasive power of popular "user-generated content."

To Jenkins, Ford, and Green, the connection is dangerous because "simplified versions of these discussions of 'memes' and 'media viruses' have given the media industries a false sense of security at a time when the old attention economy has been in flux. Such terms promise a pseudoscientific model of audience behavior. The way these terms are now used mystify the way material spreads" (2013, 19). The concern is that framing participatory media as memetic diminishes the human agency essential to collective cultural production. Jenkins, Ford, and Green question the utility of a term that implies to advertisers and marketers that there's a top-down method for "infecting" a population with a transmittable unit of culture. They worry about the "false security" that comes with a reliance on a deterministic metaphor.

In Dawkins's (1976) original conception, memes are indeed strongly deterministic, since he conceives of memes as "replicators" acting on passive recipients. When tunes, ideas, catchphrases, and religious systems are passed from one person to another, individual choice is barely worth noting. Instead, Dawkins refers to memes as "self-copying" and "self-perpetuating" as they propagate. This is the lens Godwin (1994) applies to forum participation, even as he admonishes readers to "take control" of the memes they spread. "A meme, of course," Godwin says, "is an idea that functions in a mind the same way a gene or virus functions in the body. And an infectious idea (call it a 'viral meme') may leap from mind to mind, much as viruses leap from body to body." And as recently as 2013, Dawkins doubled down on his determinism when asked by *Wired* how he felt about the application of the term he coined to participatory media. "The meaning is not that far away from the original," Dawkins said. "It's anything that goes viral. In the original introduction to the word *meme* in the last chapter of *The Selfish Gene*, I did actually use the metaphor of a virus. So when any-body talks about something going viral on the Internet, that is exactly what a meme is" (quoted in Solon 2013). Robert Aunger (2000) points out that this sort of "meme as germ" metaphor tends to cast memes as deterministic entities that latch on to hosts and spread without the awareness of those hosts. The agency of individual actors to respond to and influence cultural transmissions is missing from these conceptualizations.

This critique of memetics is well taken. However, *meme*—both as a cultural concept and as a genre of mediated communication—can be applied with enough nuance to still hold theoretical value. Based on the vast creative expression evident in memetic participation, it's an oversimplification to deterministically frame memetics. Rather, memetics can acknowledge the autonomous decisions of social agents while also appreciating how those decisions compound into collective significance through creation, circulation, and transformation. To this point, Shifman sees internet memes as "(post)modern folklore, in which shared norms and values are constructed through artifacts such as Photoshopped images or urban legends" (2014, 15). This framing may be less appealing to marketers and advertisers, but the ambiguity comes with nuance. Memetics doesn't have to end with Dawkins's 1976 conceptualization, or even his 2013 one. An acceptance of parts of the memetic lens doesn't have to mean a wholesale acceptance of determinism. Instead of implying passivity, this understanding acknowledges that every massive internet meme and every singular memetic text is the result of individual decisions intertwining into collective practice.

Through this lens, even the perhaps more problematic concept of *virality* becomes more nuanced. Karine Nahon and Jeff Hemsley (2013) do extensive work in *Going Viral* to shade their titular term. Along with issues of "speed" and "spread," they emphasize the importance of the "human and social" dimensions of viral media. They argue that thinking about virality as a "strategy" is dubious, and instead frame the concept as a lens for understanding the collective flow of information. Virality, to them, is characterized by the social sharing of a media text, its sharp acceleration into popularity, and its subsequent substantial reach in terms of both numbers and social networks.

The memetic metaphor isn't a given for participatory media, and conversations about its utility are worth having. However, the gradual propagation from the individual to the collective, the imitation and transformation during this propagation, and the competition and selection that guide the process are all inherent to memetics, and all a part of how internet memes are shared. And the memetic lens can help us understand that sharing, even as we appreciate the social dimensions inherent to it. Whitney Phillips (2013), mounting a "defense of memes" in an online essay supplement to Jenkins, Ford, and Green's (2013) book, argues that "memes spread—that is, they are actively engaged and/or remixed into existence—because something about a given image or phrase or video or whatever lines up with an already-established set of linguistic and cultural norms." In Phillips's conception, individual expression and collective precedent intertwine; a charge of passivity is an outsider's charge—one advanced by marketers and scholars. To the subcultural collectives Phillips analyzes, memetic spread comes from individual and social decisions. Holding on to the utility of memes as modern, mediated folk texts, while acknowledging the difficulty of unlocking an easy formula for the complex processes at their heart, the next section will address the logics fundamental to memetic media.

Fundamental Logics

In order to disentangle the complex relationship between memetics as cultural theory and memetics as media practice, I posit here that a few

Figure 1.5
An image from KanyeWesAnderson.tumblr.com combining a still of young Margot Tenenbaum in Wes Anderson's 2001 film *The Royal Tenenbaums* with lyrics from Kanye West's 2010 song "Power." Posted on August 26, 2012.

lynchpins of participatory media are also fundamentally memetic. I'll establish five fundamental logics evident in the creation, circulation, and transformation of memetic media: multimodality, reappropriation, resonance, collectivism, and spread. These logics are broader and older than memetic media, but memetic media illuminate their emerging interrelations and implementations. These fundamental logics afford individual innovation and variation within shared criteria. Memetic media—whether playful or serious, interpersonal or public, or all of these at once—exhibit specific tendencies across individual cases and genres. To demonstrate, I'll focus on "Kanye Wes Anderson" (for example, figure 1.5), a series of mashup images curated on the tumblog KanyeWesAnderson.tumblr.com.[2] "Kanye Wes Anderson" images make their joke by overlaying Kanye West lyrics on frames from films directed by American filmmaker Wes Anderson. Using "Kanye Wes Anderson" as an explanatory case study, this section will address each fundamental logic in depth.

Multimodality

Internet memes—just like the media landscape they populate—are fundamentally multimodal. There's a difference, argues Carey Jewitt (2004), between communication *media* and communicative *modes*. Media are "technologies of dissemination," such as newspapers, radio, film, television, or the internet. Modes are "technologies of representation," such as written language, image, audio, video, and hypertext. Gunther Kress and Theo van Leeuwen say different modes of communication carry different "semiotic codes"; a multimodal text is one "whose meanings are realized" through more than one of these codes (2006, 177). Different communication media often afford different communicative modes, and in this way enable unique semiotic codes. The internet as a medium—one premised on the near-universal digitization of information—can carry many modes of communication, blurring word, image, audio, video, and hypertext in its constellation of messages. This blur influences the complex tapestry of mediated conversation; the more semiotic codes participants have to work with, the more versatile their mediated conversations can become.

The "Kanye Wes Anderson" images in figures 1.5 and 1.6 reference and combine multiple modes of communication within individual images. Most evidently, they weave written and visual modes together. Through this sort of intertextual weaving, memetic images can resonate despite the general brevity of each individual text. Audiences do complex work in the fleeting seconds that they glance over an image; they read meanings that are encoded in the text and match those meanings to already-understood contexts. In the case of "Kanye Wes Anderson," that reading employs more than just the visual. Images like figures 1.5 and 1.6 carry complex layers of

Figure 1.6
An image from KanyeWesAnderson.tumblr.com combining a still of Richie Tenenbaum in Wes Anderson's 2001 film *The Royal Tenenbaums* with lyrics from Kanye West and Jay-Z's 2011 song "No Church in the Wild." Posted on August 26, 2012.

meaning, which embed multiple modes of communication: the words in the images are transcriptions from songs, and the visuals in the images are captures from films. For audiences familiar with the Anderson and West source texts, multiple communicative modes intertwine into a single message. Further, hypertext grants the messages on the "Kanye Wes Anderson" tumblog the freedom to spread to other participatory media sites. Both within and beyond the text, a single "Kanye Wes Anderson" image is thus layered with multiple communicative modes.

And other examples on the "Kanye Wes Anderson" tumblog go beyond individual images. For instance, one post on the tumblog is a multimodal minute-long mashup in the form of a video embedded from YouTube. The video's visuals are a scene from Anderson's 2004 film *The Life Aquatic with Steve Zissou*. In the scene, Zissou and his crew are silent in a submarine, awestruck while surveying the deep black ocean in search of an elusive giant fish. Replacing the film's audio, however, is the opening minute of West's 2010 "Run Away." The mysterious ambiance of the scene is punctuated by the slow, distorted, climbing introduction to "Run Away." Film and song collide when West's first lyrics—"look at ya, look at ya"—hit just as Team Zissou's prey comes into full view, careening toward their craft. The mashup moment—and it's only a moment—intertwines multiple communicative modes and multiple layers of understanding to create its expression. Another "Kanye Wes Anderson" text—of Richie Tenenbaum in West's distinct white-rimmed "Kanye Glasses"—is printed on a t-shirt for sale on the site, adding a tactile materiality to "Kanye Wes Anderson." This material extension is significant, even when considering memetic media, which often spill off the computer screen to clothing, jewelry, printed fliers, and even protest signs. Although visuals abound, thinking in terms of the "visual internet" is a limiting paradigm, since more than only text and image exist in multimodal media. Digitization affords engagement through multiple senses, even if it's tempting to focus narrowly on the interplay of words and visuals online. Mediated conversations intertwine language, image, audio, video, hypertext, and more.

In this way, multimodality is a lynchpin logic of memetic media. With digitization, new types of information become easier to create, circulate, and transform. The participatory barriers are lowered, and new forms of communication can be encoded and decoded by a broader group of individuals. While this multimodal potential does produce vast "original content,"[3] it—tellingly—produces perhaps even more memetic content, which further reappropriates multimodal expressions that have come before.

Reappropriation[4]

Reappropriation—which is also older than the internet—is essential to memetic media. Memes spread by weaving novel texts into existing contexts, blurring the old and the new so completely that even Dawkins (1976) acknowledges problems with applying the genetic lens to cultural creation. The "units of culture" he christens as memes are passed on "quite unlike the particulate, all-or-none quality of gene transmission"; instead, Dawkins says, "meme transmission is subject to continuous mutation, and also to blending" (195). This mutation and blending come from reappropriation, from participants applying existing material to new memetic moments.

Reappropriation is a well-established tenet of cultural participation. To Michel de Certeau, navigating popular culture means engaging in the "plurality and creativity" of "use and reuse"; popular participants work within an imposed system, "making use of its scraps" (1984, 28–30). Henry Jenkins applies de Certeau's arguments to mass media fans "who appropriate popular texts and reread them in a fashion that serves different interests" (1992, 23). Memetic media accelerate this "poaching" process, granting public conversations even more richness and complexity. Without reappropriation there would be no memetic media. Digitization allows texts to intertwine with regularity and ease: from mashup to machinima to memes, new creative expression consistently emerges from existing contexts. Memetic media are stitched together by the creative reappropriation of multiple modes of communication.

The images on "Kanye Wes Anderson" exemplify the creative selection and combination of found cultural materials. Most obviously, in their multimodal mashup, these images reappropriate the creative work of Kanye West and Wes Anderson to produce a new hybrid. The image in figure 1.7 wouldn't exist if West hadn't recorded "Robocop" and Anderson hadn't directed *Moonrise Kingdom*. The image depends entirely on those two source texts. In that sense, the image is derivative, but there's creative work in how it intertwines these texts. The image "works" because it captures and connects sentiments from both the film and the song. In *Moonrise Kingdom*, the moment captured here occurs as the film's male protagonist, Sam, first lays

Figure 1.7
An image from KanyeWesAnderson.tumblr.com combining a still of Suzy in Wes Anderson's 2012 film *Moonrise Kingdom* with lyrics from Kanye West's 2008 song "RoboCop." Posted on September 12, 2012.

eyes on its female protagonist, Suzy. Performing in a summer play, Suzy is backstage preparing her makeup. Sam sees Suzy and is immediately taken with her. To Sam, Suzy's troubled past and her strong will combine to make her "bad" in more than one sense.

The lyrics to West's "RoboCop"—about a drama-filled but hard-to-end relationship—match the tenor of Sam and Suzy's romance in *Moonrise Kingdom*. The juxtaposition in the image works because of the creative reappropriation of each source, and how well the tone of each text matches the other. Figure 1.5 does the same work with Margot Tenenbaum, an aspiring playwright who did indeed have her creativity crowded out by adult concerns for much of her life. Likewise, the first verse of West's "Power" centers on the tensions that come from balancing artistry, self-care, responsibility, and success. These reappropriations resonate because they fit together in unexpected ways. Figure 1.6 is a slightly different reappropriation, in that it shifts the mood from its *Royal Tenenbaums* source text. In the moment captured for figure 1.6, Richie Tenenbaum is contemplating suicide (he shaves off his hair to a melancholy Elliot Smith song after this shot), but the West lyrics overlaying the scene in the image are more bravado than remorse, describing a hangover after a hedonistic night. The "sunglasses" connection is enough to create a humorous juxtaposition, one that creatively decontextualizes Anderson's scene to match West's lyrics.

But more than just reappropriating from mass media sources, "Kanye Wes Anderson" also reappropriates an established aesthetic in internet memes. The images in figures 1.5, 1.6, and 1.7 are functionally *image macros*. Image macros are a staple memetic image subgenre, mostly crafting their point by overlaying a quip on a single still image. They take their name from *macroinstructions*, computer science terminology for a pattern or rule that easily connects a predetermined input to a desired output. Many image macros facilitate expression by reappropriating a collectively "predetermined" visual subject. Participants annotate this predetermined subject with a new joke or insight, tying their creative expression to a socially understood premise.

Figure 1.8 is an example of what Shifman (2014) calls a "stock character macro," an image macro used prevalently enough to have a strong personality associated with its subject. Stock character macros are often a single rectangle containing a linguistic setup at the top of the rectangle, a visual anchor character in the middle of the rectangle, and a linguistic punchline at the bottom of the rectangle. The font is generally a sans serif, often Impact, and often white. The stock character in figure 1.8 is known as "Hipster Kitty" and was widely circulated between 2010 and 2012. Each "Hipster Kitty" macro shares a similar image, while making a new joke based on hipster stereotypes. The images in figure 1.8 play on connotations that hipsters, as a social category, are pretentiously and excessively avant-garde and exclusionary. The transmission of "Hipster Kitty" is memetic in that the macro image passes from participant to participant and is reappropriated along the way.

Figure 1.8
Three examples of an image macro called "Hipster Kitty." Collected in 2012.

The bulk of "Kanye Wes Anderson" texts—like countless other images shared through participatory media—reappropriate the established image macro format, even if they're not macros in the "stock character macro" sense we see with "Hipster Kitty." Figures 1.5, 1.6, and 1.7 replicate the specific arrangement of visuals and words prevalent in image macros, reappropriating the established aesthetic for new creative expression. In this way, even the image macro form is in and of itself memetic. For instance, the third image in figure 1.8 pushes its use of this form out to more tactile modes of communication, presenting a capture of a cross-stitched "Hipster Kitty" that reproduces the image macro through its own novel medium.

To use de Certeau's (1984) terms, reappropriation is the "art of making do" within a media ecology of increased participation, even if not of holistic control of the culture industries that own the bulk of media production and distribution. What de Certeau saw decades ago is even more prominent in the digital media ecology. With easier applications to create from and easier platforms to share from, more participants now have more opportunities to use and reuse cultural texts. Now that they can more easily offer their own commentary through creative reappropriation, these participants have more power to craft expression from resonant cultural texts.

Resonance[5]

Media texts become memetic when they connect with enough participants to inspire iteration after iteration from a fixed premise. The nature of that resonance is difficult to articulate definitively or universally, as individual texts resonate with different people for different reasons. Texts carry personal meaning and importance; that meaning and importance motivates the creation, circulation, and transformation essential to memetic media. In this way, memetic media encapsulate a point made by Roland Barthes (1977) about the power of readers over authors. To Barthes, texts are a "multiplicity," and it's the reader who pulls that multiplicity together. Further, Barthes says the reader's connection to a text becomes even more powerful—and even harder to classify—when the text is visual. In his reflections on the resonance of photographic images, Barthes admits that it's hard for him to systematically quantify how he connects with photographs; he writes, "a specific photograph reaches me; it animates me, and I animate it" (1981, 20). Barthes divides the resonance of images between what he calls the *studium* and the *punctum*. The studium is connection with an image at a cultural level; it's a socially coded appreciation. The punctum is connection with an image at a personal level; it's what Barthes describes as a "pierce," a "prick," or a "mark" emanating from some distinct detail of an image that hits the person viewing it.

Each of these dimensions is to Barthes a "co-presence," and both are integral to the memetic texts participants create, circulate, and transform. Participants sharing a common cultural stance are equipped to "get" a "Kanye Wes Anderson" joke; they have the cultural context needed for the images to resonate. But different iterations of the memetic joke will resonate at a punctum level with different participants for different reasons. I myself—from my standpoint as a thirty-something, white, middle-class American—appreciate the "Kanye Wes Anderson" images in figures 1.5–1.7 from that studium resonance. The joke created in the juxtaposition of two unexpected—but culturally familiar—pieces of source material resonates with my social context. But I chose these three specific images out of all the others on the tumblog because I found them exemplary, and that decision is intertwined with their punctum resonance. All three contrast the angst of sullen, broken Anderson characters with the bravado of West's lyrics, and each prick me in that contrast. The creation, circulation, and transformation of memetic texts thus depend on both the studium and the punctum. Whitney Phillips and I (forthcoming) make this argument about the #YesAllWomen hashtag, which circulated on Twitter in the summer of 2014. In the wake of a misogyny-fueled mass shooting, participants used the hashtag to catalog their experiences with gender-based discrimination, violence, and antagonism, demonstrating both cultural appreciation of and personal familiarity with its message.

Due to the importance of studium and punctum resonance, analysis of memetic content or circulation alone can't tell us how texts prick their audience. Merely observing form or flow can't tell us what, specifically, participants get out of the use, reuse, or "misuse" of memetic texts. Still, empirical work has been done analyzing why people share memetic texts and what is evoked by the texts they share. Working from interviews, Kate Miltner (2014) argues that participants who share "LOLCat" images (a venerable macro subgenre consisting of captioned animal photos, often with nonstandard spelling and syntax) do so because they're interested in communal participation on the sites that share memetic texts, interested in the interpersonal communication facilitated by memetic texts, or both. Whatever the impetus, Miltner argues that "emotional resonance" is central to the appeal of the quippy and cute "LOLCat" images. Likewise, Shifman (2014) says we share what's "humorous," "surprising," or "emotionally arousing" (in both positive in negative valences). The whimsy and simplicity of many memetic texts help them connect quickly to diverse and dispersed participants.

In many memetic texts, irony, humor, and play are essential to their resonance. "Kanye Wes Anderson" is prototypical in its memetic play, and its resonance depends on that play. In figure 1.9, West's lyrics match the character's tenor. In Anderson's *Fantastic Mr. Fox*, Ash is a black sheep, living in the shadows of his talented and charming father and cousin. However, he never stops trying to find his place in the family or striving for merit in his own right. The moment captured in figure 1.9 comes as Ash prepares to rescue his cousin. He adorns himself with a bandit mask made out of a sock (his father has not deemed him worthy of a real mask). Ash's underdog resolve fits the story West tells in the third verse of "Gold Digger," which describes a resolute fast food worker: "He got that ambition, baby, look in his eyes; this week he moppin' floors, next week it's the fries."

Figure 1.9
An image from KanyeWesAnderson.tumblr.com combining a still of Ash in Wes Anderson's 2009 film *The Fantastic Mr. Fox* with lyrics from Kanye West's 2005 song "Gold Digger." Posted on September 5, 2012.

Figure 1.9 resonates through a juxtaposition of West's lyrics and Anderson's visuals. A studium appreciation allows participants to connect the disparate media texts, decoding humor from their unlikely fit. The key is what scholarship on humor calls "incongruity." In incongruent humor, "an accepted pattern is violated, or a difference is noted—close enough to the norm to be nonthreatening, but different enough from the norm to be remarkable. It is this difference, neither too shocking nor too mundane, that provides humor" (Meyer 2000, 313). In the case of figure 1.9, the incongruity comes from the surprising relevance of West's lyrics to Ash's character. Audiences familiar with both texts can make a quick—if previously unconsidered—connection between the two. If something in the midst of this studium appreciation "pricks" them on a more punctum level (as Ash's resolute eyes and the heroic wave of his cape do for me in this image), they may be inspired to circulate it themselves (as I have by including it here).

Juxtaposition is predominant in memetic media. Another tumblog, called "Fly Art Productions," remixes hip-hop lyrics with classic high art, playing with a premise very similar to that in "Kanye Wes Anderson." But in "Fly Art Productions," the incongruity stretches even further; the difference in time periods and cultures makes the thematic connection between, say, a Georges Seurat painting and a Childish Gambino lyric all the more surprising (see figure 1.10).

Although humor may be an obvious and prevalent example of memetic resonance, it isn't all that resonates. Noam Gal, Limor Shifman, and Zohar Kampf (2015) focus on the 2010 memetic "It Gets Better" pro-LGBT video campaign, wherein participants followed the lead of activist Dan Savage and posted videos encouraging LGBT youth to remain hopeful. The campaign's argument—that life as an LGBT adult often "gets better" after the pain of being an LGBT teen—resonates for its empowering hope, not its humor. Likewise, Stephanie Vie (2014) examines the memetic spread of the Human Rights Campaign's marriage equality logo. Many Facebook participants made the HRC's red-and-pink equal sign their profile picture in early 2013, displaying support for marriage equality while the U.S. Supreme Court heard two crucial cases on the issue. Vie argues that there was sympathetic power in the resonant appeal of the image.

Whether due to cultural appreciation or personal prick, whether due to distanced, playful humor or invested, political sentiment, memetic texts

Figure 1.10
An image from FlyArtProductions.tumblr.com combining Georges Seurat's 1884 painting *A Sunday Afternoon on the Island of La Grande Jatte* with a lyric from Childish Gambino's 2013 song "II. Shadows." Posted on July 1, 2014.

spread through collectives because they resonate with participants in those collectives. In the process, participants are connected as texts are shared.

Collectivism

In their shared resonance, memetic media are the product of buzzing collectives. Even as this collectivism depends on individual expression, it foregrounds social experience, whether vast or local. Sites like 4chan, Reddit, YouTube, and Tumblr share norms, while they also have norms that are unique to each site—and even have some norms unique to individual groups, pages, and threads. Likewise, relational networks such as Twitter and Facebook afford a unique set of practices for every individual user, even if those practices are still situated within broader social standards. Memetic media are communicatively cohesive in these spiraling environments. As they're applied in vibrant contexts at varying levels of individual and group communication, memetic texts help "the internet"—though it is a multiplicity of texts, sites, perspectives, and experiences—feel more like a "place."

Through memetic media, hashtags populated by millions of users, jokes spawned in a single 4chan thread, and even GIFs shared between friends via text message are woven from and into collective fabric.

This connection is the core of participation in participatory media. Individuals connect to social groups and social identities by and through shared texts and conversations. Because of this, memetic participation is populist and reminiscent of older conceptualizations of oral and folk cultures. Giselinde Kuipers argues that "the 'do it yourself' style of the internet … resonates nicely with traditional oral culture, which includes oral joke cultures. Like the jokes and stories of oral culture, internet jokes have no authors (unless everyone is an author). They are constantly created, adapted and recreated" (2002, 468). The bridge between the individual and the collective is central to both folk culture and memetic media.

"Kanye Wes Anderson" exists as quasi collective, an individual constellation of texts dependent on broader collective aesthetics. These texts are not collectively remixed memes, even if they share image macro aesthetics. By Shifman's definition of *internet meme*, an image like figure 1.11 is certainly a part of a "group of digital items sharing common characteristics" (2014,

Figure 1.11
An image from KanyeWesAnderson.tumblr.com combining a still of Zero and Agatha in Wes Anderson's 2014 film *The Grand Budapest Hotel* with lyrics from Kanye West's 2013 song "I Am a God." Posted on April 8, 2014.

41), both as part of other "Kanye Wes Anderson" images from the site and as part of the broader macro aesthetic. It was also created with an awareness of other images on the site and almost certainly other image macros. However, Shifman's third criterion is harder to apply. By her definition, memes are also "circulated, imitated, and/or transformed via the Internet by many users" (41). "Kanye Wes Anderson"—like many single-topic tumblogs—complicates this collectivist criterion.

"Kanye Wes Anderson" may circulate as much (or maybe as little) as any unique tumblog, like "Fly Art Productions." However, there's not much evidence "Kanye Wes Anderson" has become a meme in a collective sense, through imitation and transformation from many participants. Its collective aspect is at least not as evident as with "Hipster Kitty" or "Kanye Interrupts." According to its contact page, "Kanye Wes Anderson" is explicitly the work of two individuals. A contact email is given, but the blog evidences tight control of its limited texts. Material curated from others is explicitly credited to a creator.

But even "Kanye Wes Anderson" is collectivist, in a broader understanding of the term. Not only does it reappropriate the image macro precedent that came before, but the tumblog also exists within a constellation of other juxtapositional mashup tumblogs. For instance, in addition to being aesthetically similar to "Fly Art Productions" (also credited to a pair of creators), "Kanye Wes Anderson" resembles at least one other mashup tumblog, called "Beyoncé Voters," which mashes up lyrics from Beyoncé songs with images of powerful female politicians. According to *The Daily Dot*—a prominent site for participatory media news—a college senior is the sole creator of "Beyoncé Voters" (Schroeder 2014).[6] Figure 1.12 is in this way an act of individual political commentary embedded within collective aesthetics. It was created on the heels of a landmark Supreme Court decision allowing retailer Hobby Lobby to deny its female employees health insurance coverage for certain types of birth control. Justice Ruth Bader Ginsburg's strong dissent on the decision made headlines, and the macro in figure 1.12 connected Ginsburg's feminist dissent to Beyoncé's lyrics. Ginsburg—like the iconic Beyoncé—is ranked a "10"; her opposition possesses half her prowess and should therefore pay heed.

"Kanye Wes Anderson," "Fly Art Productions," and "Beyoncé Voters" are constellations of individual expression. In this way, single-topic, single-author tumblogs can demonstrate the creation, circulation, and

Figure 1.12
An image from BeyonceVoters.tumblr.com combining a Getty Images photo of American Supreme Court Justice Ruth Bader Ginsburg with lyrics from Beyoncé's 2013 song "Mine." Posted on July 8, 2014.

transformation prevalent in memetic media, even if each individual text they produce isn't itself a meme. These quasi memetic spaces may not meet Shifman's (2014) most explicitly collectivist criterion for internet memes, but they can be memetic in their orientation toward and reappropriation of collective aesthetics.

These ambiguities mean that collectivism does not have to be wholly open. Likewise, collective participation does not entail the erasure of media gatekeepers, despite the wider potential of participants to create, circulate, and transform their own content. An understanding of memetic collectivism must be mindful of gatekeeping influence on this collectivism, whether from the top-down media professionals at sites like *Buzzfeed* or the nebulous boundary-policing in-groups on sites like 4chan. Even if memetic texts resonate enough to be collectively circulated and transformed, we can't mistake an apparent authorlessness for an absence of formal or informal gatekeeping practices. Like the agenda-setting practices hidden behind the "objectivism" of traditional journalism, agenda setting can hide under the "collectivism" of participatory media. This is true even if the system is ideally premised on vibrant conversation. Still, memetic media are dependent on the spread of information by broad collectives, even if gatekeepers are themselves part of that spread.

Spread

The last fundamental logic of memetic media is spread—the pervasive circulation and sharing of resonant media texts. Even with the persistent power of institutional and cultural gatekeepers, the "many-to-many" communication networks possible on digital media produce a more vibrant meme pool. Collective spread is the aspect of internet memes that most closely ties them to Dawkins's (1976, 1982) conceptualization of memetics. If the internet is memetic, it is memetic because participants spread texts when they make them their own.

Spread is so central to Jenkins, Ford, and Green that they build their argument around the term "spreadable media," which "refers to the potential—both technical and cultural—for audiences to share content for their own purposes" (2013, 3). When participants share a YouTube clip of Susan Boyle singing opera, when they create satirical accounts for *Mad Men* characters on Twitter, when they harass other sites from threads on 4chan, they're spreading cultural practices. Sounding very Dawkinsian, Jenkins, Ford, and Green argue that in the participatory media ecology, "if it doesn't spread, it's dead" (1). This participatory spread relies on what Nahon and Hemsley (2013) call "network gatekeeping." Because of the collective participation inherent to memetic media, they explain, "each time we are faced with a decision to forward information into our networks, we are acting as gatekeepers" (9). This spread happens through the proliferation of individual decisions. Ideally, network gatekeeping affords agency and versatility when participants employ media texts.

Here, the distinctions between memes and viral media become more apparent. Nahon and Hemsley (2013) parse out some differences between the two terms from the standpoint of spread. They argue that only one path of textual spread can be sufficiently classified as what they call a "viral event." When a viral event is charted quantitatively—say by search interest or number of page views—it follows a "power-law distribution" which, Nahon and Hemsley explain, "is characterized in a graph by a tall peak on the left that slopes sharply downward and then levels off as the line of the graph goes to the right" (146). Viral spread forms a power-law distribution when a relatively unknown text is shared in a flurry of interest for a short time and then fades from mass interest thereafter.

Google Trends—which measures and graphs the relative popularity of Google searches for a key phrase—shows a power-law distribution for "Kanye Wes Anderson" searches. There's no interest in the term before October 2012 (even though the first post was August 26, 2012), a massive spike in interest during October 2012, and sharp decline in interest after October 2012. In the years that follow, search interest in the term never reaches zero, but its interest is only a shadow of its October 2012 numbers. The long tail of limited interest matches what Nahon and Hemsley call a semi-dormant "afterlife" for viral media. In this afterlife, "virality can be revived and return to the center of attention at any given moment" (129). In the case of Google searches for "Kanye Wes Anderson," the second-highest peak occurred in February 2015, as the long-dormant blog made a post in the wake of West's interruption of Beck at the 2015 Grammys.

Memetic texts need not follow this power-law spread, however, and it may in fact be a more sustained "tail" of popularity that distinguishes memetic reappropriation from viral sharing. *Virality* tends to label a specific type of accelerated information circulation, whereas *memetics* tends to label processes of transformative reappropriation. The media moment of Kanye West interrupting Taylor Swift at the 2009 MTV Video Music Awards may have been a viral event, but hashtagging a tweet "#ImmaLetYouFinish" in 2015 would demonstrate the memetic resonance of the phrase beyond its viral origin. Any individual memetic text may not necessarily garner the attention necessary to be called *viral*, but taken together, these memetic texts demonstrate persistent interest and sharing.

This fact speaks to the importance of understanding spread alongside situated, textual analysis of memetic media. Although collective spread, popularity, page counts, search interest, and other quantifying factors are important, they are not necessarily the whole or even the primary lenses by which we need to assess memetic media. "Big data"-driven questions of spread are worth asking, but there's power in understanding memes as constellations of individual texts, individual expressions situated in collective contexts. A consistently shared, innovatively applied inside joke between two friends could be a *meme*—their meme—even if the spread stops there.

Even if not a vast cultural text, that two-person in-joke could easily adhere to memetic logics. The spread in this case would be to spiraling new contexts, all while anchoring the friends as they share and reshare their joke with each other, reappropriating it further with each new iteration. As Jenkins, Ford, and Green say, "if it doesn't spread, it's dead" (2013, 1). There's just more than one criterion for "spread."

How Memes Matter

Individually, the logics that underpin memetic media aren't new to memetic media, but their unique interrelationship blends the textual and the social in unprecedented ways. Collectivism and spread are situated outside of individual memetic texts in a way that multimodality and reappropriation are not. Resonance blurs the line between text and context, between studium appreciation and punctum prick. Together, working across text and context, these logics underscore the intense multiplicity that makes media memetic. Barthes's (1977) "death of the author" is pushed to its limits when distributed platforms facilitate vast social creation, circulation, and transformation. In this way, the logics presented here redirect the memetic lens away from Dawkins's (1976, 1982) initial determinism. The bridge between Dawkins's conceptualizations and Kanye's interruptions is made up of the *micro* conversational strands woven together by a multitude of cultural participants.

Because of this multiplicity, even singular texts can be bound up in collective practices. For instance, figure 1.13 satirizes a common "mistake" by the subculturally unfamiliar: taking *internet meme* to be the label of a specific genre of texts—or even an individual text—without appreciating the emphasis on collective reappropriation and transformation in the memetic process. The joke in figure 1.13 comes from the idea—one I've forwarded myself—that captioning the top and bottom of a picture with white sans-serif font does not a meme make. Instead, something resonant in that image would need to spread beyond its origin to make the image an image meme. But ironically—and perhaps part of the resonance of the image—the satire of figure 1.13 reproduces the image macro aesthetic, reappropriating it for its own commentary. Like many "Kanye Wes Anderson" images, it's memetic, if maybe not a meme. Just the same, "Kanye Wes Anderson" is no less memetic because of its limited collectivism and spread. It's still

Figure 1.13
An image macro distinguishing the differences between image macros as individual texts and memes as collective creations. Collected in 2014.

multimodal and reappropriational, and can still resonate. It's indicative of the logics of underpinning memetic media, and it's one example of a collective aesthetic that spreads among participants far and wide.

Through their intense sociality, memes are folk media, and—as has always been the case with folklore—these media are premised on collective strands intertwining to create new tapestries of cultural production. Memetic media—phrasal, performative, image, or video—are significant in the same sense that other everyday texts are significant, in the sense that de Certeau (1984) outlined decades ago. They're a participatory means of "making do," of cultural participants poaching from the texts and conversations around them for their own expression. They're significant not just for their undeniable mass popularity; they're significant because their underlying logics—multimodality, reappropriation, resonance, collectivism, and spread—are greater than any individual text or any individual participant. Memetic media are the result of situated political and technological contexts. Drawing from these contexts, they depend on the social processes at the heart of social texts. They are exemplary of a media ecology that blurs vernacular conversation and creative production.

Understanding that ecology helps us understand the situated social actors inhabiting and producing it. This ecology is alive with vibrant conversations, from pirated YouTube footage of celebrity spectacle to captioned pictures of hipster cats to hip-hop lyrics mashed up with high art and establishment politics. These multimodal texts resonate as they spread through mediated collectives, where participants reappropriate them for diverse ends. In this way, micro memetic texts stitch together the macro participatory media ecology. The fundamental logics inherent in individual texts are amplified by the buzzing multitude producing them. Memetic media are made by collective practices more substantial than any individual text; Dawkins's (1976) genes may be selfish, but his memes are social. The rest of this book is about the social implications of memetic media. The logics introduced here will be expanded throughout the book; they are foundational to the grammar and vernacular of memetic participation, which can inspire both antagonism and voice. All of these threads weave together into the vibrant mediated conversations we'll see in the chapters to follow.

2 Grammar: Structures for Making Statements and Making Do

The Death of the Meme

On May 15, 2014, Fernando Alfonso III published a piece for *The Daily Dot* speculating on the bleak future of internet memes. Referring mostly to image macros (such as "Hipster Kitty" from chapter 1), Alfonso (2014) argues that "they've been bled dry of all their novelty, and they're just not funny or relevant anymore." Describing the "dilution" of these once novel texts, he speaks to their rise and resulting "overkill" on Reddit, which he says took steps to broaden its content beyond the visual quips. He speaks to the seep of image memes into "mainstream" sites like Facebook, which had in response adjusted its algorithms to favor articles over images. The mounting evidence suggested a bleak future indeed. For whatever reason, memes—at least as a label for a specific set of niche texts—just weren't cool anymore. Like punk rock and craft beer, memes were dead, crushed under the weight of their own success. In light of these charges, a study of the formal and social structures underscoring memetic media has to reckon with the alleged demise of their cultural resonance.

Like Alfonso's, my moment of reckoning also came in 2014, when I was discussing my Ph.D. dissertation with a student. "I remember memes," the college sophomore said. "They were really big in high school. Junior year." The thought that my two-year-old dissertation was now a historical analysis of a dead communicative genre prompted some angst. And I wasn't alone. Whitney Phillips, expanding her 2012 dissertation into a 2015 book on self-identifying internet trolls, discusses similar shifts and similar angst. Trolling—as the term was employed by Phillips's research informants—emerged from the same media ecology as many esoteric internet memes. They had grown up in the same "cultural soup" on sites like 4chan,

Figure 2.1
A self-referential image macro, ironically pairing the qualifier *dank*—slang for high-quality marijuana—with browsing memes. It reappropriates a character called Gnome Child from the 2001 online game *Runescape*. Collected in 2014.

Something Awful, and others during the early 2000s. Phillips chronicles the increasingly self-referential, intertextual, and esoteric memetic practices of trolls during these years, but also the dilution of these practices toward the end of her study. “By early 2012,” Phillips writes, “it became painfully clear that I was no longer writing a study of emergent subcultural phenomena. I was instead chronicling a subcultural lifecycle” (2015b, 44–45).

By 2012, Phillips (2015b) reports, both the terms *troll* and *meme* were exhibiting simultaneous mass usage and definitional ambiguity. Phillips argues that the rise of the reference database Know Your Meme signaled a major shift in the subcultural dimensions of internet memes, as well as trolling. The database grew from a small 2007 video project affiliated with the site Rocketboom into a popular wiki purchased by the larger Cheezburger Network in 2011. "Know Your Meme was written with the novice in mind," Phillips says, "with detailed, almost clinical explanations of the Internet's most popular participatory content. KYM thus helped democratize a space that had previously been restricted to the initiated" (139). By 2012, Know Your Meme had established itself as the go-to reference guide for internet memes. This was also the year of the last ROFLCon internet culture conference, which founders Tim Hwang and Christina Xu (2014) say became dauntingly commercial. Likewise, in 2012, 4chan's founder Christopher "moot" Poole told *Forbes* that "as online culture has moved offline, pop culture has moved online, they've met in the middle, and become the same thing now" (quoted in Olson 2012). In this intertwine, the subcultural resonance of internet memes had seemingly run its course.

By 2015, it seems we're well past the reign of the pantheon of esoteric stock characters that emerged from sites like 4chan, Reddit, and Tumblr over the last decade. Now the invocation of the very term *meme* on those same sites is more and more ironic. Figure 2.1 is an image macro mocking internet memes and the cultural practices surrounding them. The language in the image reappropriates a memetic sentiment sometimes quoted on participatory media sites. One iteration, posted to Reddit's /r/Atheism subreddit in 2012, posits that "we were born too soon to explore the cosmos, and too late to explore the earth. Our frontier is the human mind. Religion is the ocean we must cross."[1] In figure 2.1, the reference to "dank memes" as the site of exploration in the present compares negatively to the great cultural feats of the past and future. "Dank"—a term of praise for quality marijuana—can be read ironically here, because of its associations with "stoner" slang and its juxtaposition with the high ideals of scientific exploration.[2] Further, the font in the image shifts just as "browsing memes" becomes the subject, indicating a shift in tone, a juxtaposition constituting a punch line. The image—composited from a character in the online game *Runescape* called Gnome Child—resonates in the blank stare of its subject and the dreamlike, glitch art space behind him, which creates a larger, more opaque version of him—almost a psychic projection; the blackness behind the figure birthing asymmetrical neon green, blue, and red lines. All this signals mockery, and uses stoner slang and a preteen-oriented videogame to hone that mockery. Whatever "browsing dank memes" is, exploring the galaxy it is not.

Figure 2.2 also denigrates memes by connecting them to juvenile contexts. This image was posted to /r/TheWalkingDead, a subreddit devoted to the popular *Walking Dead* comic, television, and videogame universe. Part of a playful "photo recap" for season 5, episode 13 of the show, the post shows Carl and his father, Rick—survivors of a zombie apocalypse—at a party in a walled community they have recently entered. Carl is shown socializing with the other teenagers in the town, while Rick socializes with the adults. In the photo caption, Carl tries to bond with his fellow teens by asking them if they remember memes. Rick is not impressed. In the thread accompanying the post, a Reddit participant "didn't get" the meme joke, and asked for an explanation. The answer was that Carl is "a teenager, talking to other teenagers. Who haven't seen the internet in God knows how long. Carl wants to remember memes." The two responses to that answer—coming around the same time—were "dank may mays, if you will" and "dank memes m8." Both responses invoke the faux praise "dank," and both denigrate memes beyond that. The first calls memes "may mays," a common pejorative term (an ironic mispronunciation of the word *meme*), while the second includes the slang "m8" (shorthand for *mate*, or *friend*), another example of slang vernacular invoked ironically. All this, combined with the fact that Carl is not generally a well-regarded character on the subreddit (due to his very teenage awkwardness), contributes to a running joke about texts gone stale.

But the narrative of subcultural corruption is often far too simplistic. The idea of a discrete, bounded subculture that opposes a hegemonic mainstream is fallacious, or at least murkier than an easy binary. Holly Kruse (2003) and Wendy Fonarow (2006) argue that the relationship between "indie" music scenes and "mainstream" music cultures is much more interdependent than the "subcultural authenticity" narrative suggests. The same could be said for the niche practices that have loosely labeled "internet culture" over the last decade. Lamenting that "4chan is too safe now," or that "Reddit is too popular," or that "Tumblr is too commercial" obscures the ways in which those sites, their participants, and the texts they create have always been intertwined with mainstream culture. Even the earliest 4chan memes reappropriated establishment media like pop songs,

Figure 2.2
Two images from a 2015 episode of *The Walking Dead*, captioned by a Reddit participant for an /r/TheWalkingDead "photo recap" thread. It annotates a scene featuring Carl and his father, Rick. Posted on March 10, 2015.

television characters, and videogames. The line between internet culture and popular culture has long been a blurry one.

Memetic media didn't start with 4chan, just as they didn't end with the final ROFLCon. Memetic practices persist, even if the specific resonant texts shift over time. If we're tired of stock character macros in 2015, it doesn't mean that "memes are dead"; it indicates that those memes don't hold the specific cultural capital they did in 2010, or even that they hold cultural capital for people other than us. The relationship between niche collectives and broader cultural practices is always porous. The relationship between subcultural internet memes and broader memetic participation is porous as well.

Memetic logics are alive and well, more vibrant than ever, even if the corpus of texts in 2015 is wider and more widely distributed than the collection of characters and tropes that emerged out of esoteric forums a decade ago. The same memetic logics help craft both "stale" stock character macros and the collective vocal scorn for those stale texts. Despite their denigration of memes as subcultural texts, figures 2.1 and 2.2 still depend on these memetic logics. They're obviously both multimodal, reproducing an aesthetic used over and over in memetic media. They're both premised on reappropriation: figure 2.1 in its single panel combines an aphorism, a videogame character, and slang for marijuana, while figure 2.2 collects two photos from a set of about 150 captioned images, all taken from one episode of one TV show. Both were produced for collectivist participatory media sites. Both figure 2.1 and the conversation about figure 2.2 demonstrate the resonance of the mocking phrase *dank meme*, which spread in late 2014 across multiple participatory media sites. The insult is every bit as memetic as the targets it's applied to. "Memes are dead" is thus a well-worn meme itself, one driven by memetic logics. These logics still underscore the creation, circulation, and transformation of collective ideas, and the memetic lens is apt in understanding a vast array of populist practices, both esoteric and widespread.

To be sure, there is a lot to learn from the "good old days" of memetic participation on sites like 4chan and Reddit, and the rest of this book will draw from this lineage. Even in 2015, more insular or bounded online collectives still have their fair share of inside jokes and esoteric references, and there is value in understanding how memetic logics and texts are used to facilitate both the ingroup affiliations and the outgroup antagonisms we'll see in chapters 3 and 4. Even in a cultural studies moment "after subculture" (see Bennett and Kahn-Harris 2004), the concept of a "social imaginary" is significant. Arjun Appadurai (1996) argues that mass media help to create these imaginaries, collectives that feel a sense of communal identification even if they don't demonstrate the interdependence of a traditional community. Although *subculture* has a different meaning today than it had when Dick Hebdige (1979) penned his study of British punks in the 1970s, it can still describe how members of a collective discursively cast themselves as antithetical to, apart from, or in opposition to a nebulous discursive "mainstream." This analysis would be incomplete if it assessed memetic media without exploring the niche collectives that have become tied to the term. There is utility in understanding both the esoteric imaginaries and the mass participants producing memetic media.

In evidence of that utility, the rest of this chapter—pairing with next chapter's discussion of vernacular—will build a case for the persistent power of memetic logics by examining their communicative characteristics, their social dynamics, and, ultimately, their role as a lingua franca in diverse mediated conversations. The sections to follow will assess the grammar surrounding the memetic logics introduced in chapter 1 and will tie memes to a lineage of reappropriation by bricolage and multimodal poaching. Even if memetic participation has gone "mainstream," even if it's more dispersed now than it was in 2005 or 2008 or 2011, even if Alfonso (2014) and *The Daily Dot* cite legitimate shifts, memes still matter. Whether or not the subculture has lost its edge, memetic logics are as pervasive as ever.

Toward a Multimodal Grammar

Gunther Kress and Theo van Leeuwen (2006) begin their book *Reading Images: The Grammar of Visual Design* by connecting their titular term *grammar* with visual communication. They argue that when analyzing images, it's not enough to assess them at the level of "lexis" (elements of the individual image). Instead, to understand a "visual statement," readers need to understand how both its individual elements and its social contexts "are combined into meaningful wholes" (1). This use of *grammar* refers not to a prescriptive set of rules, but rather to a descriptive account of how systems of culturally specific meaning are constructed and reconstructed through social use.[3] Even if readers don't decode images as explicitly as they do written language, they perform interpretive work when they engage those images. Understanding images depends on understanding the socially situated grammar foundational to them.

Here I'll argue that—far from being dead subcultural texts—internet memes tie into a long line of multimodal communication that has only become more prolific with the rise of memetic media. The grammar underlying these media is largely visual, but not solely visual; it is woven from multiple modes of communication. The next subsections will address the complex social reading and writing granted by this multimodal grammar. Memetic conversations—whether massive or esoteric—depend on these encoding and decoding processes, so assessing those conversations requires assessing the grammar at their heart.

Reading Images

Kress and van Leeuwen (2006) argue that humans, thanks to millennia of encoding and decoding visual messages, have developed the ability to quickly and implicitly read visual grammar. They argue that "visual communication is always coded. It seems transparent only because we know the code already, at least implicitly—but without knowing what it is we know, without having the means for talking about what it is we do when we read an image" (32–33). This is true whether we are subtly judging facial cues, assessing a room's mood by its color scheme, or inferring emotion from the depth of field in a photo.

Images have long been employed for public commentary and public conversation. Caricature was used to ridicule Egyptian pharaohs in the 1300s BCE. Sexually explicit graffiti was found in the first-century ruins of Pompeii. Roman barracks in the third century contained visual mockery of early Christians. Martin Kemp observes that "like us, the later Romans appear to have been image junkies. Temples, public buildings, homes, and brothels all purveyed fine-tuned messages in the pictorial mode" (2011, 384). The European Middle Ages saw illuminated manuscripts, "bibles for the unlettered," and coats of arms with memetic symbolism that spread within and between families. Juliet Fleming (2001) recounts the popularity in Elizabethan and Jacobean England of "posies"—phrasal and visual graffiti (though "graffiti" absent the term's contemporary deviant connotations) that covered the walls of homes and churches, was inscribed onto jewelry and pots, was pinned to curtains, wrapped around gifts, and even tattooed onto the skin. These "portable epigrammes" conveyed commentary, prayers, lewdness, riddles, and solutions to those riddles. In these memetic snippets that spread across England, Fleming says there was "no difference between painting and writing; no difference, again, between writing on paper, a wall, copper, wood, a body, or an axe; and no difference, finally, between writing and other visual patterns" (25).

During the Renaissance, Kemp (2011) writes, "systematic naturalism" and mechanical printing technology inspired a representational revolution. From the sixteenth century, famous artists made black-and-white reprints of their work available, increasing their fame and the fame of their commissioner. Since the Enlightenment, visual storytelling and commentary has been a central component of the press. Reading images has historically been integral to reading the news, from the ambivalent racial portrayals in nineteenth-century publications like *Punch* and *Puck*, to the "Yellow Kid" comics that ran in both the *New York Journal* and *New York World* and subsequently gave "yellow journalism" its name, to the editorial cartoons of the twentieth century. Visual commentary has long been essential to public life, and—as we see with visual texts shared through memetic media—that commentary has long been a mix of powerful argument, silly satire, and combinations of the two.

For instance, figure 2.3 is a 1798 political cartoon by British cartoonist Richard Newton called "Treason!!!" (a title complete with a very familiar and very vernacular use of multiple exclamation points). In the image, John Bull (the national personification of Britain) apparently farts in the face of King George III. From mostly out of frame, Prime Minister William Pitt scolds John Bull. The crude visual gesture works as satire precisely because of its vulgarity. Chris Lamb, in his study of editorial cartoons, comments that "the basic technique of satirists is reduction: degrading or devaluating the targets of their satire by reducing their stature and dignity" (2004, 39). The message in this cartoon is resonant enough in its visual satire that readers more than two hundred years after its creation can still read its critique without much specific context. That I came across this image circulating on Tumblr in 2015—surrounded by GIFs from primetime comedy TV and screenshots from Snapchat—is a testament to its visual resonance.

Images resonate because of culturally encoded ways of seeing, and so the grammar of reading an image must always be understood within those cultural codes. Just as written or spoken grammar doesn't exist outside of the cultural systems that form and are formed by language, images are bound by the same ways of seeing. Roland Barthes's (1981) studium resonance speaks to this bounded perception. Some elements of the 1798 political cartoon (figure 2.3) might resonate with many people today in the same way they resonated with the image's intended audience in 1798. The

Figure 2.3

"Treason!!!," a political cartoon by British cartoonist Richard Newton. The subjects of the image are (from left to right): British Prime Minister William Pitt, John Bull (a personification of Britain), and King George III. Published in 1798.

vulgarity of John Bull's act, his more "common" dress compared to the more "noble" attire of the king, the juxtaposition of the trivial bodily function and the serious (and fully capitalized) charge of treason—all of these scan for me at the studium level. I can read them because they all still carry weight in my cultural context. Other individuals in other cultural contexts may not read those components of the image as I do, however, and there are contextual dimensions to the cartoon I can't understand without an awareness of the cultural and political climate of late eighteenth-century Britain. Perhaps part of the reason this image spread among participants on Tumblr in 2015 was the humor inspired by its seeming anachronism. At least that was the punctum prick I felt when looking at John Bull's elated face during his seemingly out-of-place defiance. To audiences unaware of Enlightenment satire, a political fart joke from 1798 may be a striking surprise, notable enough to spread.[4]

Even with the importance of cultural context in mind, there are formal components we can assess as we read an image. Several sources outline how analysts and audiences can interpret meaning, emotion, and even argument in images (see Kress and van Leeuwen 2006, Lester 1995, Rose 2012). Compositional elements—including color, space, perspective, distance, focus, movement, and detail—can be deconstructed during image analysis. Memetic media add collective elements to this compositional analysis, and are unique for their extensive intertextuality, even within a single image. Limor Shifman (2013) provides vocabulary for assessing the mixture of text and context in memetic images. She argues that memetic texts can be analyzed by examining their "content" (what they say), "form" (how they look), and "stance" ("information [that] memes convey about their own communication," 367). While content and form are largely contained within a single image, assessing how a text stands in relation to broader contexts requires more awareness of those contexts. Stance is revealed in a text's "participation structures" (which voices are included and which are silenced), "keying" (the tone and style it adopts), or its "communicative function" (emotive, phatic, poetic, etc., 367).

The compositional elements of content and form combine with the contextual element of stance to help us decode what might resonate in an image. Resonance—at the studium or punctum level—is essential in fostering the inspiration to create, circulate, and transform memetic iterations of visual texts. If something in an image or its context doesn't resonate enough to spread, it won't spread. And the collective dimensions of this resonance can produce unexpected results; multimodal grammar can be applied in surprising ways.

One such surprise—to Warner Bros. Studios at least—came with a 2014 meme called "Sad Batman." "Sad Batman" began with a promotional photo for the upcoming 2016 film *Batman vs. Superman: Dawn of Justice* tweeted by the film's director, Zack Snyder, on May 13, 2014 (figure 2.4). Snyder posted the photo along with a caption that read, "I shot this with my @Leica_Camera M Monochrom. #Batman #Batmobile #Gotham"—demonstrating either fanlike devotion to or intentional cross-promotion of Leica cameras. To borrow Stuart Hall's ([1973] 1993) term, the "dominant" read on the content and form of the image might tie into the dark and hypermasculine connotations that come with Batman as a pop cultural icon. The image is grayscale, befitting the somber tone that has come to be associated with the caped crusader. Batman and his iconic Batmobile—always the subject of fan discussion when a new Batman film is on the horizon—emerge into focus out of haze to the left of the frame, drawing the

Figure 2.4
A promotional photo for the 2016 film *Batman vs. Superman: Dawn of Justice*, shared on Twitter by the film's director, Zack Snyder ("@ZackSnyder"). Posted on May 13, 2014.

eye of the viewer to the right. From there, we follow the gaze and posture of Batman (a gaze mirrored by the positioning of the Batmobile) to the ground. The high angle in the shot gives us the perspective of looking down at a tortured, stoic, masculine hero. Batman broods, and this is a brooding image.

Or at least it was *meant* to be a brooding image. Neither the camera cross-promotion nor the dominant read is what resonated with many in the image's audience, many of whom were already skeptical of the upcoming film. The man under the batsuit in *Batman vs. Superman: Dawn of Justice* is actor Ben Affleck, a casting decision that had been loudly critiqued as out of step with Batman's character. With reservations about "Batfleck" already resonant, Snyder's photo was an apt target for a flurry of memetic reappropriation. This flurry produced what Hall calls "negotiated" reads on the apparent melancholy mood of the dark knight, which keyed a satirical stance toward Snyder's Batman image. In the days after the photo was posted, "Sad Batman" became its memetic iteration. Sites like *The Verge* and *Buzzfeed* cataloged humorous Photoshops of the image (Malone 2014; Sottek 2014). A tumblog—WhySoSadBatman.tumblr.com—was created on May 13, 2014, and was active for a month. "Sad Batman" remixes crafted new meanings by playing with Batman's archetypical hypermasculine brooding, arguably reinforcing charges that Affleck lacked the gravitas needed to carry the role.

The top image in figure 2.5 inserts the familiar trope of the police officer issuing a speeding ticket as an explanation for Batman's mood. The context emasculates the masked vigilante, who is known to have a tense relationship with the law. The bottom image in figure 2.5 reduces Batman—a figure known to strike fear in the heart of evil—to the passive victim of bullying. The two rings littered in the scene imply at least one person is off camera playing ringtoss with Batman's bat-eared costume. By inserting new elements into the original photo, both images change our reading of Batman's stoic silence in Snyder's original photo. They make explicit a resigned defeat hidden in the image, one that shifts Batman from powerful masculine hero to passive victim.

The images in figure 2.6 do similar work by removing Batman from his original context, exaggerating the loneliness of Batman in the process. In figure 2.6's top image, Batman's defeat comes not from the villains Joker or Bane, but from a spilled glass of milk. If we follow his eyes, he's staring

Figure 2.5
Two "Sad Batman" memetic reappropriations of figure 2.4, each giving the original image a new context to create a humorous juxtaposition. Collected in 2014.

directly at the mishap, consumed; the masculine hero has succumbed to a domestic tragedy. The bottom image in figure 2.6 places Batman in a setting that should be happy, a log ride at an amusement park. Instead, he's got no one to share it with, and reverts to his forlorn gaze as the ride—hardly a Batmobile—carries him toward the edge of the frame, a sad moment for the orphan hero. Both images use space to create their humorous juxtaposition. These images keep Batman relatively small in bigger, open settings, and they keep him alone in typically social spaces. In doing so, they turn cultural understandings of Batman on their head to make a joke at the hero's expense. The memetic process that birthed "Sad Batman" depends on cultural participants' ability to read images and then to write their own iterations, playing with a socially situated, visual grammar.

The easy creation, circulation, and transformation of "Sad Batman" images—along with the countless other image memes that pepper mediated cultural participation—support Kress and van Leeuwen's contention that "visual communication is coming to be less and less the domain of specialists, and more and more crucial in the domains of public communication" (2006, 3). Even if the esoteric pantheon of characters that rose to prominence between 2002 and 2012 are fading, memetic texts spread now more than ever. As tools of media production and distribution become increasingly inexpensive and accessible, participants can increasingly create, circulate, and transform visual commentary of their own.

Multimodal Texts

But despite the prevalence of memetic images, participatory media allow for the inclusion of more than just stationary visuals. Words, sounds, videos, and hypertext all abound through memetic media, and memetic participation is punctuated with multimodal communication in a way that a static book on memes can't fully capture. Any grammar of memetic texts can't be merely linguistic, or even merely visual. The texts we read are multimodal, and multiple modes of communication can be employed for the purposes of expression, commentary, and conversation.

Multimodality is central to the grammar of memetic conversations, whether they're massive, niche, or interpersonal, and multiple modes of communication can have memetic dimensions. Hashtagging an old photo of yourself with "#TBT" for "throwback Thursday"—common in 2014 on sites like Twitter, Instagram, and Facebook—employs memetic grammar.

Figure 2.6
Two "Sad Batman" memetic reappropriations of figure 2.4, each pulling Batman from his original context to create a humorous juxtaposition. Collected in 2014.

Auto-Tuning a presidential address to sound like a song does too. The classic "Rickroll" bait-and-switch—a meme in which participants promise to hyperlink to something relevant to the conversation and instead hyperlink to the music video for Rick Astley's 1987 hit "Never Gonna Give You Up"—is premised on similar structures. Likewise structured on memetic grammar is the "Ice Bucket Challenge" that spread across sites like Facebook and YouTube in 2014 and 2015. For the challenge, participants dumped cold water on their head, posted the act to social media, and asked specific people either to do the same or to donate to ALS research. Across these multiple communicative modes and multiple social contexts, participants make statements through memetic logics.

In these examples, word, image, audio, video, hypertext, and even physical performance intertwine. #TBT is a phrasal acronym, but the hashtag makes it hypertext on many sites, and its predominant use is to label an image. Auto-Tuning often depends on the memetic manipulation of a video recording along with its source audio. The hypertext "Rickroll" joke connects its targets to a music video. The "Ice Bucket Challenge" is a physical performance, but it becomes an internet meme when people capture its iterations on camera and share them online. The visual dimensions of memetic media are vibrant, but their multimodal dimensions shine just as brightly.

For instance, a unique multimodal hybrid has become prevalent in the participatory media ecology. Not quite image, not quite video, animated GIF files are staples on sites like Tumblr, Reddit, and Imgur, among many others. Typically, GIFs are small, looping video files (made from the quick, successive display of individual images) that are absent audio or playback controls.[5] GIFs may seem too small and limited for the high-definition digital age. However, their versatility and spreadability have made them a resonant genre of memetic media. They pepper comment sections and punctuate text-message conversations. Jason Eppink (2014) argues that GIFs have their own "ethos," "utility," and "aesthetics," which have facilitated their pervasiveness. Eppink says the small files "are promiscuous and frictionless, with low barriers for viewing, processing, and sharing. It is largely *because* of its limitations that the GIF thrives" (303, original emphasis).

Figure 2.7 presents six individual frames from a "Sad Batman" GIF file. The whole file contains fifteen frames, producing less than a second of

Figure 2.7
Six selected frames from a "Sad Batman" GIF file, which reappropriates figure 2.4. The images loop to create the illusion that Batman is pushing an empty swing in the rain. Collected in 2014.

looped image (not too far off from the twenty-four frames per second that is standard in film). The fifteen images come together to tell the story of Batman pushing a vacant swing in the driving rain. The "perfect loop" of the GIF causes the swing to ceaselessly glide back and forth, as Batman gazes at its emptiness. Through the GIF format, the image uses motion to further the "Sad Batman" aesthetic, while the file remains small and static enough to sit seamlessly alongside still images. This multimodal liminality provides GIFs resonance as memetic texts.

The multimodal grammar essential to memetic participation can be applied to contexts large or small, subcultural or mainstream, public or private. Just as linguistic grammar facilitates the shared understanding of spoken and written language, multimodal grammar facilitates the shared creation, circulation, and transformation of memetic media. And while creation, circulation, and transformation are each vital, the transformational nature of memetic media carries unique significance. Participants make statements through multimodal grammar; they make do by weaving those statements from what has come before. Reappropriation is therefore as essential to memetic grammar as multimodality. The next section will discuss the centrality of that reappropriation. From the depths of 4chan in-jokes to the prominence of Facebook charity videos, novelty is woven from existing threads.

Bricolage, Poaching, and Reappropriation

The multimodal reappropriation inherent to memes ensures that they're layered texts. The same tools that facilitate multimodality facilitate the remix of found materials. In an environment of prevalent reappropriation, memetic grammar isn't just about reading and writing images, or even reading and writing multimodal texts. It's about doing that work by borrowing from the contributions of others, and transforming those contributions into something unique. In this way, a grammar premised on memetic logics depends on bricolage and poaching. Here, I'll discuss the lineage of reappropriation in creative production, and tie memetic media to that lineage.

Memetic Media and Bricolage

Creative production has long been theorized in terms of reappropriation. Claude Lévi-Strauss ([1962] 1966)—himself reappropriating the verb for "extraneous movement"—speaks of the centrality of "bricolage" in folk cultures. The "bricoleur," he argues, is a cultural participant who produces differently than the "craftsperson." The craftsperson has the resources and support needed to produce within the sanctions of cultural systems; the bricoleur, conversely, is "someone who works with his hands and uses devious means" (16–17). When bricoleurs contribute to culture, they do so by "making do" with "whatever's at hand." Bricoleurs' tools are "finite" and "heterogeneous," since they don't own the means of production or have the resources to work with sanctioned materials. Bricoleurs' contributions to culture come from reappropriating what others have already created. Michel de Certeau (1984) makes similar claims about cultural participants who poach from cultural systems that don't belong to them. Both the bricoleur and the poacher produce from within ecologies they do not control, using materials they do not own.

And these creations are foundational to memetic participation; memetic media are ripe with bricolage. Indeed, if *grammar* labels socially constructed systems of understanding, then memetic grammar depends on bricolage.

It's the heart of the memetic social system. The examples of bricolage in memetic texts are countless; intertextual references layer one after another as content spreads. No media text is safe from memetic reappropriation. So far—only a chapter and a half into this book—we've seen references to the 2009 Video Music Awards, Martin Luther King's "I Have a Dream" speech, *Twilight*, Mario, *How the Grinch Stole Christmas*, *Breaking Bad*, American President Barack Obama, several Wes Anderson films, several Kanye West lyrics, impressionist art, *Runescape*, *The Walking Dead*, a British satirical cartoon from the eighteenth century, and Batman. All of these texts have been the subject of memetic circulation and transformation.

To say that such bricolage is grammatical is to say that it provides an implicit and flexible guide for social participation, just like written grammar's foundational role in language. Understanding reappropriation—just like understanding the multimodal dimensions of memetic grammar—allows participants to read other people's contributions to a conversation and to write their own. For instance, figure 2.8 samples a 2012 collection of annotated "monster" images which were created for a thread on 4chan's /co/ ("Comics and Cartoons") board[6] and were cataloged and shared on Imgur and Reddit thereafter. "Created" here, though, really means *poached* from another source and annotated by participants. The images that inspired those in figure 2.8 come from a blog dating back to 2009 by artist John Kenn Mortensen (known as Donn Kenn). On the blog, "Donn Kenn Gallery," the artist describes himself this way: "Born in Denmark 1978. I write and direct television shows for kids. I have a set of twins and not much time for anything. But when I have time I draw monster drawings on Post-It notes. ... It is a little window into a different world, made on office supplies." Kenn's work—in an unannotated form—has garnered attention of its own through participatory media: his blog gets regular comments, has a shop, has been linked to from Reddit, and has been the inspiration for a pair of books.

But for all of Kenn's production, his Post-It note scenes were the start, not the end, of the creative expression on the /co/ thread that produced the images in figure 2.8. The annotative work in the images is simple, the result of basic text placement in some kind of photo-editing software. However, meanings can shift in those small annotations; implicit dimensions of the images—ones that resonated with their annotators—become explicit through their annotation. The top image in figure 2.8 interprets a specific

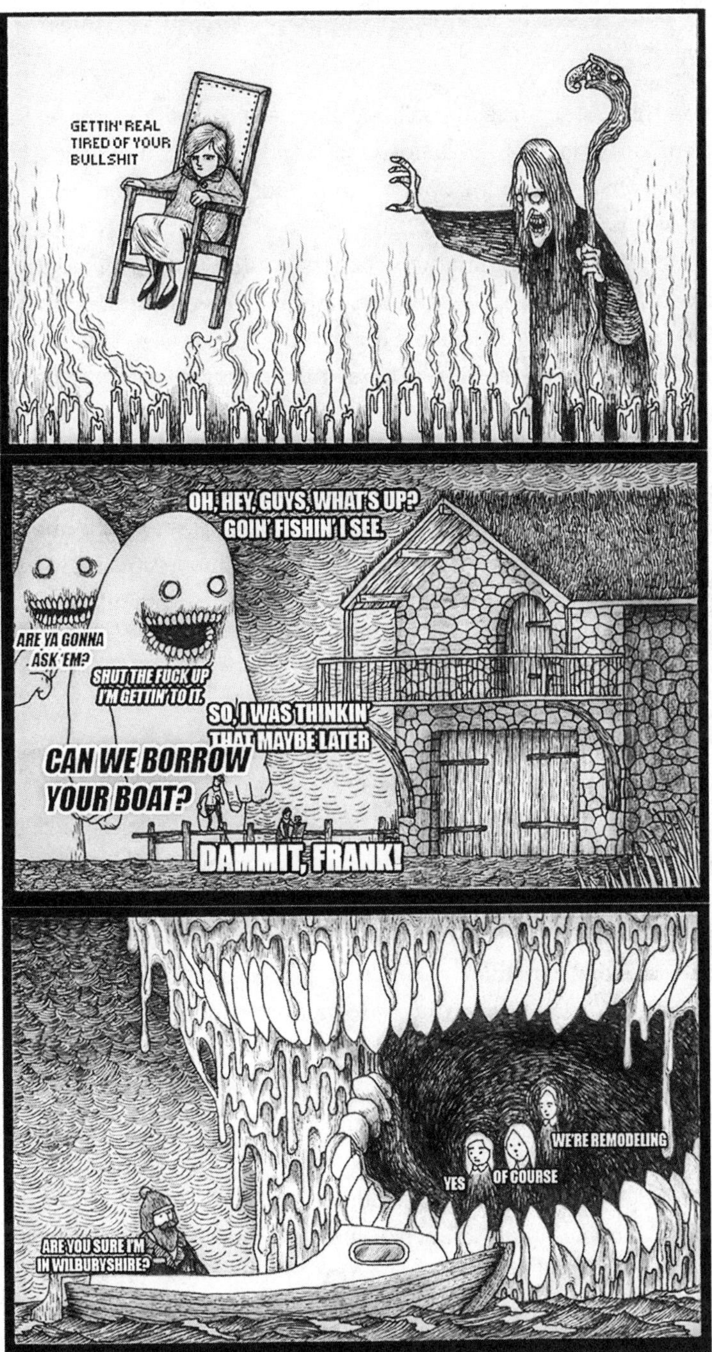

Figure 2.8

Three of Donn Kenn's "monster drawings" from JohnKenn.blogspot.com, captioned by participants on 4chan, and shared to Reddit and Imgur. Collected in 2012.

emotion on the abstract face of its child subject. In the middle image, the arrangement and format of the dialogue signals the flow and tone of a fictionalized conversation, telling one of a multitude of possible stories. The bottom image juxtaposes its banal dialogue with its conspicuously outlandish visuals. All these reappropriations craft their humor by using words to emphasize specific emotions their creators saw in Kenn's drawings. Through their small creative acts, participants on the /co/ thread were able to add their voice to Kenn's expression. Those images became conversational through bricolage, and resonated in their reappropriation.

In all, memetic media, like many popular media forms before them, are premised on bricolage and poaching, taking elements from established contexts and weaving them into a new expression. The ease of multimodal creation, the collectivist dimensions of this creative process, and the participatory spread of memetic texts add even more to the significance of bricolage and poaching in popular culture.

Imitation, Reappropriation, and Creation

The centrality of bricolage and poaching to media participation complicates its ties to memetic theory, and pushes the theory further away from the deterministic perspectives critiqued in chapter 1. Richard Dawkins (1976) originally introduced the same criteria for memetic success that he established for genes: longevity (how long a meme lasts), fecundity (how far a meme spreads), and fidelity (how true a meme stays to its origin). But transformative reappropriation means that those genetic criteria are an imperfect match for internet memes. At the least, "success" might mean something different for internet memes than for genes. Longevity can be defined in many ways and measured by many metrics. The "Binders Full of Women" meme born out of former Governor Mitt Romney's gaffe during a 2012 American presidential debate—he claimed that when he searched for qualified female officials during his tenure as Massachusetts governor, he was brought "binders full of women"—may not have lasted long, but it spread widely in its brief period of resonance. "LOLCats"—around since at least 2008—are older memes by the standards of internet culture, but less so beyond that framing. Fecundity may matter when discussing how viral a text or an idea is, but a text can be memetic even between only a few friends, provided they're imitating and transforming from a shared ingroup premise. Both these criteria are complicated by the flexibility of participatory media. A grammar premised on reappropriation and transformation produces conversational mutations that influence the duration and flow of memetic media.

But reappropriation and transformation make fidelity, in particular, an ill fit for memetic media. This mismatch underlies the common critique that memetic theory overemphasizes strict imitation in its understanding of the social spread of ideas. As David Haig argues, memetic replication is "nothing like the elegant simplicity of the double helix" (2006, 61). Instead, the spread of culture makes tangled knots. Fidelity may be an asset to genes, but memes may be stronger when transformative practices allow individual variations on collective premises, even at the cost of fidelity. In the most biological conceptions of memetics, the fact that culture changes as it is transmitted is a hindrance to the utility of the metaphor because genes, by contrast, are copied with high fidelity. Dawkins (1982) admits to this complication, commenting that in cultural practices, "the copying process is probably much less precise than in the case of genes: there may be a certain 'mutational' element in every copying event. … Memes may partially blend with each other in a way that genes do not" (112). To Dawkins, "these differences may prove sufficient to render the analogy with genetic natural selection worthless or even positively misleading" (112).

Fidelity is a helpful idea to a point, at least in some cases. Imitation of others' language may facilitate the spread of memetic hashtags like #TBT or phrases like "dank memes." Imitative spread brought Donn Kenn's Post-It-note monster images—unaltered—to a popular thread on Reddit's /r/WTF, which in its top comment linked to his blog and his books. On Tumblr in particular, GIFs often transcribe scenes from film and television verbatim. These GIFs recreate moments from shows like *Supernatural, Power Rangers,* and *Parks and Recreation,* or from movies like *Anchorman: The Legend of Ron Burgundy, Lilo and Stich,* and *The Dark Knight.*

But the imitation and transmission of media texts is only part of memetic participation. Bricolage and poaching—the social processes that guide these multimodal texts—demonstrate the inadequacy of an emphasis on imitation in memetics. At the least, they force us to acknowledge that imitation is only the beginning of reappropriation. #TBT resonates because participants can add their own "throwback" to the shared understanding. This addition can be a typical "throwback" photo (something from an expected range of "earlier" in the creator's life, like a childhood photo) or it can ironically deviate from the norm (something outside of that range, like a photo from the day before or a sonogram picture of a fetus *in utero*). The typical use skews more toward imitation of the hashtag, and the ironic use more toward humorous reappropriation. Both, however, depend on creative participation in a social process. The "imitation" is willful and hardly mindless; it's based on socially situated expression.

Even the unaltered translation of films and television shows into image and GIF files is reappropriational. These scenes are central to the "reaction shot," "MFW" ("my face/feeling when"), and "MRW" ("my reaction when") images shared on sites like 4chan, Reddit, Tumblr, Twitter, and *Buzzfeed*. These reaction shots reappropriate popular media to provide social cues in mediated conversation, even as they leave the source text unaltered. The images in figure 2.9 are all frames from GIFs on Reddit's popular /r/ReactionGIFs subreddit, which explains in its description that "a reaction GIF is a physical or emotional response that is captured in a GIF, which you can link in response to someone or something on the Internet." More than simply transcribing media texts, participants on /r/ReactionGIFs poach them for new uses.

The images in figure 2.9—like the comics in figure 2.8 and the *Walking Dead* stills in figure 2.2—become something new when applied to new contexts. The first image in figure 2.9 is of an excited Andy from the show *Parks and Recreation*. This excitement gets new context when accompanied by the image's title on /r/ReactionGIFs: "MRW my parents found a pack of cigarettes in my 13 year old brother's backpack, and he responds with

Figure 2.9
Three frames from "reaction GIFs" posted to /r/ReactionGIFs, reappropriating popular mass media. Left to right: a surprised Andy Dwyer from a 2013 episode of *Parks and Recreation*; a pair of grimacing Power Rangers from a 2013 episode of the show *Unofficial Sentai Akibaranger*; the excited news team from the 2004 film *Anchorman: The Legend of Ron Burgundy*. Posted respectively on March 27, 2014; December 19, 2014; and March 24, 2015.

'But I only smoke when I'm drunk!'" The second image shows the Power Rangers in anguish; their pain is used to convey "my reaction when I opened the oven to get my lasagna, just to discover I had never turned on the oven." The news team from *Anchorman* jumping for joy in the third image is "CNN's reaction upon hearing about ANOTHER plane crash." On /r/ReactionGIFs, a post will often spawn a chain of accompanying GIFs reappropriated from other pop media; these GIFs respond to each other in the comments, creating a multiturn, multiparticipant conversation around a single reaction shot. Reaction shots are the result of not the mere imitation or transmission of a media text, but the reappropriation of that text for conversation.

The transformation of pop media is essential to memetic participation. For instance, the "Sad Batman" meme wasn't the first time the caped crusader resonated on participatory media. Quotations from the 2008 Batman film *The Dark Knight* have been employed on collectives like 4chan, Tumblr, and Reddit in the years since its release. The claim from the film that Batman is "the hero Gotham deserves" is translated into "the hero Reddit/Tumblr/4chan/this thread/this board/the internet deserves" in various contexts. When the Joker, Batman's archenemy, burns a giant pyramid of cash in the film, he insists that "it's not about the money; it's about sending a message." The phrase has become a popular retort when one participant asks another about the cost of something.

Another Joker line from *The Dark Knight* inspired massive memetic reappropriation. The villain, costumed as a nurse and explaining his motivations to Gotham District Attorney Harvey Dent, exclaims, "If tomorrow I tell the press that, like, a gang banger will get shot, or a truckload of soldiers will be blown up, nobody panics, because it's all 'part of the plan.' But when I say that one little old mayor will die, well then everyone loses their minds." The Joker's "everyone loses their minds" response to a perceived logical inconsistency became the inspiration for a stock character macro in 2013. The images in figure 2.10 apply the Joker's rant to topics like technological innovation, gender identity, gaming, and personal hygiene. The images demonstrate fidelity to their source text in that each caption comments with bewilderment on a societal inconsistency, and in this way the texts spread the central idea of the original scene (as well as awareness of the film and franchise itself). Shared understandings of the Joker's

Figure 2.10
Four memetic variations of the "Everyone Loses Their Minds" Joker stock character macro, reappropriating a scene from the 2008 film *The Dark Knight*. Collected in 2015.

monologue in *The Dark Knight*—or at least an awareness of the Joker character in general—premise the contributions here.

In their form, the images in figure 2.10 demonstrate fidelity to the prototypical image macro aesthetic as well. In image macros, the top-line setup flows into the bottom-line punch line through the visual subject in the center of the frame. This structure produces what Kress and van Leeuwen (2006) call a "vector": a sort of visual "action verb" that indicates process by moving the eye through the image. In the case of standard image macros, the top-to-bottom vector creates a sort of ellipses, where the visual subject of the image stands between the written setup and the punch line, prompting the reader to pause to take in the subject (in figure 2.10, the Joker) before finishing the joke. Further, even the prevalent use of the Impact font in image macros is a formal imitation that facilitates transformative reappropriation. Kate Brideau and Charles Berret (2014) argue that Impact resonates as a typeface due to its strength, clarity, and rhythm, making it ideal for statements conveyed in short bursts. Because of the predominant use of Impact in image macros, the font has become a signal for memetic expression.

But even with these imitative dimensions, the fidelity of the images in figure 2.10 to *The Dark Knight*'s content and to the prototypical image macro form exists only to provide a recognizable premise for transformation. In the case of these four images, the Joker's more dubious logic about murder, as expressed in the movie, is boiled down to more agreeable social arguments. The Joker's exact phrasing mutates with each reappropriation as well. For instance, the Joker's original "nobody panics" becomes "no one bats an eye" and "no one cares" in the bottom two images. In the top two images, the sentiment is even less explicit; it's merely implied. Three of the four images also transform the Joker's original use of "everyone" to "everybody," a common shift in the meme. Each new iteration of the "Everyone Loses Their Minds" macro is unique, and that macro can carry innovations as limitless as the participants creating them.

Within a grammar premised on memetic logics, fidelity only resonates to a point. Too much fidelity to an original idea or text—what Shifman (2014) calls a "founder meme"—may actually undermine the longevity and fecundity of a memetic idea. Noam Gal, Limor Shifman, and Zohar Kampf (2015) make a similar argument about the "It Gets Better" LGBT-empowerment YouTube video series. Memetic iterations of the founder video—produced by activist Dan Savage—adhered closely to their source, and therefore, counterintuitively, did not open up the conversation to diverse identities and perspectives. Likewise, too much fidelity is what caused Alfonso (2014) to charge that stock character macros have been "bled dry" of their novelty and robbed of their relevance. On the other hand, too little fidelity might make a memetic text too unrecognizable to carry a coherent message. Stephanie Vie (2014) makes this argument about brands that appropriated the Human Rights Campaign's Facebook "Equality Logo" for LGBT rights, twisting the memetic display picture to fit their brand first, and second to send a message of empowerment. When it comes to fidelity, the Goldilocks "just right" value is apparently somewhere between extreme imitation and extreme transformation. And—as we'll see in the next chapter—different participants, forums, boards, sites, and collectives can have different standards for that Goldilocks balance.

This tension between imitation and transformation manifests in the anxiety that memetic conversations reduce participation to pastiche, which to Andrew Murphie and John Potts "is a recycling of the past without the critical edge of satire or the subversive role of parody" (2003, 59). But this anxiety assumes that memetic media have a singularity of purpose, utility, and audience, whereas they are actually made up of innumerable texts that are produced by participants with diverse goals, literacies, motivations, and perspectives. The pastiche charge is leveled when the criterion for successful memetic reappropriation is some sort of social commentary, or some sort of subcultural identification. When, instead, bricolage and poaching are thought of as the multimodal fabric of collective conversation—just as linguistic grammar is the fabric of collective conversation—playful imitation and recycling have a different utility, and can "work" for wider ends.

Some memetic texts may be mere pastiche. Some may be poignant commentary. Some—as we'll see in chapter 5—may flirt with both. Some may be neither, but rather may do their "recycling" for reasons entirely outside of any sort of critical, political edge. Memetic reappropriation may fit the "collective, aphoristic, and inscriptive" logics Fleming (2001) sees in Elizabethan posies better than the "individualist, lyric, and voice-centered" logics that scholars are trained to value in poetic expression today. On collectives like Reddit, 4chan, and Tumblr, the social, conversational, and collective value of memetic reappropriation might trump the temptation to look down on them as imitation, overkill, or pastiche.

Reddit, for instance, has several subreddits devoted to the collective reappropriation of pop media GIFs in the name of social play. /r/ReactionGIFs is only the surface of this reappropriation. On /r/GIFTournament, participants create reaction GIFs that are set in head-to-head competition and voted on by subscribers to the subreddit. On /r/DubbedGIFs, participants make a joke or a point by providing altered subtitles to pop media GIFs. On /r/BehindTheGIFs, participants create images of "backstory" explanation as a setup to a punch line consisting of a familiar GIF. Its top-voted post of all time provides context for a puzzling GIF of a mob kicking a trashcan. "Behind" that GIF, the creator of the post adds a crudely drawn trashcan telling us that "Hitler did nothing wrong" (an oft-quoted memetic phrase in its own right). The trashcan's declaration is what inspired its mob beating.

Another Reddit staple, the /r/PhotoshopBattles subreddit is premised on participants editing an original image in the comments to its thread. The "battle" is won by the contribution that is most upvoted. On the subreddit, photos of North Korean supreme leader Kim Jong-un are frequently used as a source of playful participation. This repeated jabbing at the dictator may be pastiche, pop commentary, or something in between; multimodal grammar may facilitate social participation and public expression simultaneously.

For instance, one 2013 thread asked participants to Photoshop a Korean Central News Agency image of Kim overseeing the construction of a "ski center" (figure 2.11). Responses were playful jabs at Kim, and the playful tone of the subreddit was evident in the commentary around the images. Playful collective conversation "won out" in the thread over "political commentary." However, some remixes of the image could be read as more explicitly "political" than others. For example, figure 2.12 features images that lampoon Kim (having him join the Power Rangers, replacing his body with Ned Flanders of *The Simpsons*), but make no overt political comment

Figure 2.11
A photo by North Korea's Korean Central News Agency of supreme leader Kim Jong-un overseeing a ski center's construction. Released on May 27, 2013.

Figure 2.12
Two memetic reappropriations of figure 2.11, from an /r/PhotoshopBattles thread. Both images connect Kim Jong-un to popular media characters: Kim is posed with the Power Rangers from the show *Mighty Morphin Power Rangers* (top); Kim's body is replaced with that of Ned Flanders from the show *The Simpsons* (bottom). Posted on December 31, 2013.

beyond belittling the dictator. The images in figure 2.13 play with the super-villain dictator trope more explicitly, having Kim oversee the construction of "Jaeger" mech warriors from the film *Pacific Rim*, and having him melt the face of one of his subordinates. Political, social, and playful purposes exist simultaneously in these images. Their very form makes Kim the butt of a memetic joke, like a collective version of World War II Warner Bros. cartoons that used Bugs Bunny to mock Hitler. Pastiche, maybe, but also evidence of the collective conversations inherent to memetic reappropriation.

In all, if memetic cultural theory is going to apply to memetic media, then that theory has to account for the blend of imitation and transformation in social conversation. Cultural participants transform texts as they share them. An emphasis on imitation in memetics misses that point, just as "transmission" models of communication have long missed that same point. Bricolage and poaching are central to the "system of rules" underlying memetic communication in a way that Dawkins's (1976) genetic fidelity doesn't account for or doesn't value. Fidelity, in memetic media, can only be kept to a certain degree. As the next chapter will demonstrate, a shared premise has to remain just recognizable enough to allow for creative innovation within a social vernacular. This social sensitivity reminds us that we need to think about process when considering the memetic dimensions of bricolage and poaching, and reminds us to appreciate the creative and conversational dimensions of reappropriation. Along with multimodality, this reappropriation is central to the grammar of memetic participation.

Memes Are Dead; Long Live Memetics

The grammar of multimodal reappropriation outlined in this chapter is pervasive in participatory media. Because of its prevalence, even mediated texts that might not narrowly be called *memes* are memetic in their creation, circulation, and transformation. Media genres such as mashups, song covers, fan edits, and videogame modifications contain elements that are premised on the logics outlined in chapter 1 and the grammar outlined in this chapter. From this lens, memetic media are thriving.

Despite his skepticism about whether subcultural memes can survive, Alfonso (2014) ultimately argues for the persistence of memetic logics in

Figure 2.13

Two memetic reappropriations of figure 2.11, from an /r/PhotoshopBattles thread. Both images play with "evil dictator" tropes: Kim is posed with "Jaegers," mech suits from the 2013 film *Pacific Rim* (top); Kim is shown vaporizing the head of an advisor (bottom). Posted on December 31, 2013.

participatory media. As burnout occurs, memes "are returning to their roots," he claims, continuing that "Internet communities will never stop creating inside jokes as a form of playful communication, even if they don't cross over into the mainstream." Hwang, speaking of established internet memes as settled territory, speculates that "all the really cool, just-on-the-edge-of-popular-Internet-culture stuff may just be happening somewhere else. ... Maybe the frontier is elsewhere" (Hwang and Xu 2014, 281). And to Phillips (2015b), the cultural sites that housed troll subculture—and the cultural practices that built them—are not collapsing, but expanding. "The subcultural well may not run as deep," Phillips says, "but the water now covers a much wider area" (152).

Memetic logics were never the sole domain of a narrowly bounded subculture, and memetic media don't have to be the product of a narrowly bounded time. These logics apply to #TBT hashtags on Instagram and grainy cartoons on Facebook as much as they do to the depths of 4chan. When participants tag an old photo of themselves or use a picture of a cat to complain about teenagers, they are implementing memetic grammar just as much as when 4chan participants reference "dank may mays." This grammar is built on the multimodal reappropriation of cultural texts, and it therefore facilitates social participation in a wide variety of contexts.

Further, even dated memes are sometimes only a breath away from reemerging into resonance. We saw this in the last chapter, when Kanye West interrupting Beck at the 2015 Grammys propelled "Imma let you finish" back into pop culture relevance. "Rickrolling" provides another example. As Whitney Phillips and I outline (Milner and Phillips 2014), the "Rickrolling" bait-and-switch has inspired a near-decade of intermittent interest since it emerged from 4chan sometime in 2007. Over the years, "Rickrolling" has fallen in and out of use as it's been forgotten and remembered and forgotten, all the while moving farther afield from its subcultural roots. During this time, the meme has had low moments and high moments. Depending on your perspective, Rick Astley popping out of a float during the 2008 Macy's Thanksgiving Day parade in New York could be either. But in the last eight years, the safe, accessible, and silly byproduct of a very nasty social space has inspired new innovations as it's moved to new contexts.

Testifying to its resonance, I was Rickrolled three different times on three different platforms in early 2015, each joke furthering the premise of the meme with increasing complexity. One was a false link on Facebook—complete with the headline, subhead, and photo standard for shared news links on Facebook—which didn't link me to a promised story about Jon Stewart of Comedy Central's *The Daily Show* taking over NBC's *Nightly News*. Instead I got sent to YouTube for a Rickroll. Next, a small, looping Vine video recreated a scene from the 2002 film *Lilo and Stitch*, wherein the alien Stitch puts his claw on a spinning record and Elvis plays from his mouth. In this Vine, though, I got "Never Gonna Give You Up" instead of "Suspicious Minds." Last was a secret supposedly hidden in the 2015 mobile version of the videogame *Legend of Zelda: Majora's Mask*. The purported video footage from the game shows the main character Link idly playing his ocarina, but after about twenty seconds of the video, it's clear that Link is "Rickrolling" audiences, playing his own version of Astley's infamous track. An internet-culture dinosaur, "Rickrolling" has sustained relevance and only become more complex in the years since the first iterations of the joke. The initial memetic reappropriation of Astley's song continues to inspire new reappropriations of its own.

Lévi-Strauss says that to the bricoleur "it is always earlier ends which are called upon to play the part of the means" ([1962] 1966, 21), and this practice is essential to memetic participation. In Dawkins's (1976) terms, multimodal bricolage and poaching are "vehicles" for the transmission of internet memes, just as linguistic grammar is a vehicle for linguistic expression. Ideas and texts replicate and transform as participants add new dimensions to existing contributions. Memetic media are the result of countless expressions, transformed to fit new cultural, social, and individual contexts as they spread.

With this focus on an overarching grammar of memetic participation, the question becomes not "Are memes dead?," but perhaps "What isn't a meme?" If memetic participation is characterized by the creation, circulation, and transformation of collective texts, then how much mediated participation could fall under this purview? Indeed, the transformative spread of ideas is so essential to culture itself that Dan Sperber claims memetics is a "mere rewording of a most common idea: anthropologists have always considered culture as that which is transmitted in a human group by non-genetic means" (2000, 163). Is the idea of memetics so big that it's of no utility when talking about how people use participatory media to have public conversations? In this chapter I've argued that memes are multimodal media, but so is essentially everything shared online. I've argued that memes are premised on reappropriation, on bricolage and poaching, but, then again, so is a vast amount of cultural creation. If these are the criteria, then haven't cultural participants long been making their social worlds through memes?

The critique is well taken; the temptation to inflate memetics to inevitable meaninglessness should be understood and avoided. That said, the fundamental logics provided in chapter 1—including the multimodality and reappropriation essential to the grammar articulated here—already help limit the conversation. *Meme* will always be a nebulous label. Even putting aside the baggage that comes with memetics as a social theory, *internet meme* can be employed to describe an individual image, a subcultural in-joke, or a massive thread of collective commentary. Embracing this admitted ambiguity comes with the benefit of sidestepping the need to prescriptively arbitrate what is or is not a meme, and opens up our focus to the logics that underscore mediated participation. The memetic lens is helpful in assessing a discrete enough set of mediated practices—practices that facilitate mediated expression by the grammar of multimodality and reappropriation.

Assessing the collectivism essential to this grammar, chapter 3 will argue that memetic media are bound by a balance of what Deborah Tannen ([1989] 2007) calls "fixity" and "novelty." It will then delve into the social applications of the memetic grammar introduced here. Just as linguistic grammar has a reciprocal relationship with social vernacular, the multimodal grammar of memetic media exists in a reciprocal relationship with social vernacular. Reappropriation requires a constant balance between fixity and novelty in memes. This reappropriation—situated within collective conversations—facilitates creative expression, but creative expression that is socially managed. Despite the objections of *The Daily Dot* and all those rolling their eyes at "dank may mays," this memetic vernacular is alive and well. To modify that well-worn refrain, if memes are dead, then long live memetics.

3 Vernacular: Everyday Expression in the Memetic Lingua Franca

The Year of the Doge

In 2013, a new memetic trend arose when "interior monologue captioning" (see figure 3.1) emerged from sites like 4chan, Reddit, and Tumblr. According to its entry on Know Your Meme, interior monologue captioning "involves placing randomly dispersed text on top of an image to represent what the subject is thinking or feeling" ("Interior Monologue Captioning" undated). The genre had been around for years, but in 2013 it saw its most notable iteration to date: a macro known as "Doge." The term—generally understood as a corruption of *dog*—labels a particular family of interior monologue captions. "Doge" images are typically pictures of Shiba Inu dogs, overlaid with fractured commentary written in colorful Comic Sans font (see figure 3.2). Throughout 2013, participants created and circulated their own iterations of "Doge," adapting its aesthetics to new contexts as they did. The resonance of "Doge" in 2013 was codified in year-end "best meme" lists on Know Your Meme ("Best Memes of 2013" 2013), *Time* (Carbone 2013), and *Wired* (Watercutter 2013). Wrapped up in the story of "Doge" is the story of memetic logics and grammar facilitating a rich and complex social vernacular. To the collectives conversing through it, this vernacular functions as a lingua franca that facilitates expression and conversation spanning vast geographic and social contexts.

"Doge," like all interior monologue captions, exists within this memetic lingua franca. Being a memetic subgenre, "Doge" is a unique reappropriation of jokes, tropes, archetypes, and references that have come before. "Doge" images are similar to the stock character macros that have been staples of memetic participation for years, even though the white Impact font and setup/punch-line format common in stock character macros are

Figure 3.1
An "interior monologue captioning" of a preindustrial peasant mocking a nobleman's crop-handling abilities. Collected in 2013.

absent in "Doge" images. Impact is traded for Comic Sans, the white for a rainbow of colors, and the rigidity of a setup/punch-line format for fragmented stream-of-consciousness. But even with these shifts, "Doge" is a stock character connected to collective precedent. In particular, "Doge" is linguistically and visually similar to the iconic "LOLCat" image macro subgenre, which emerged from 4chan at least a half-decade earlier. Like "Doge," "LOLCats" are premised on pictures of cute animals and are captioned with fragmented monologue in nonstandard English. Annalee Newitz, writing for *io9* in 2013, points out that "Doge" and "LOLCats" are so linguistically and generically linked that "we who spoke LOLCat now speak Doge." 2013 may have been the Year of the Doge, but it might not have been if 2008 hadn't been the year of the LOLCat.

Figure 3.2
Archetypical "Doge" images, in which the "Doge" aesthetic is connected to online interaction, Canadian travel, and the hipster subcultural identity. Collected in 2013.

Even the elements of "Doge" that are different from "LOLCats" are not wholly unique to "Doge." Just as "LOLCats" tend to follow the white Impact, setup/punch-line format that emerged in other macro genres, the Comic Sans interior monologue captioning of "Doge" has its own predecessors. Know Your Meme traces the images back to a tumblog in 2011 with photos of actor Elijah Wood (see figure 3.3) overlaid with prototypical interior monologue captions ("Interior Monologue Captioning" undated). At least two years before *Time* or *Wired* crowned "Doge" top meme, Comic Sans was being used to map humorous, fragmented stream-of-consciousness onto resonant images.

The two captioned Elijah Wood photos in figure 3.3 are annotated in a way that draws out an awkward energy from the photos. As with "Doge," the small clauses that flood the images wash readers through the entire frame, moving them without linearity, accentuating the stream of consciousness of the text. Changes in capitalization and text size are analogs for changes in volume and tone. In figure 3.3's right-hand image, the two smallest clauses, "am i dreaming" and "am i dead???," are humorous for their haunting existentialism, as stressed by the whisper implied by their

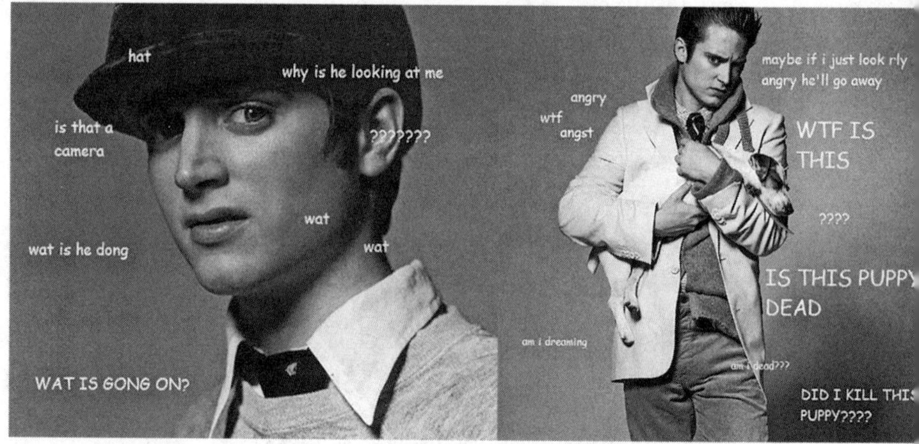

Figure 3.3
Two interior monologue captions annotating photos of actor Elijah Wood. Collected in 2015.

small font. They appear to be dreadful, fearful doubts creeping into the more vocalized anger communicated by the rest of the clauses. The two largest clauses, "WTF IS THIS" and "IS THIS PUPPY DEAD," are both fully capitalized, conveying a screaming outrage. The choice of Comic Sans—a font maligned by designers for its childlike and cartoony connotations—is ironic punctuation itself. It fits what Nick Douglas (2014) calls the "internet ugly" aesthetic; to Douglas, a large swath of everyday memetic media content is "supposed to look like shit" because it's more about quick and easy conversational play than formal expression. All of these tropes exist in "Doge" images. 2013's most resonant stock character thus reappropriated collective practices that had been used two years before.

Though "Doge" resonated widely, interior monologue captioning manifests in other images shared more esoterically, on more bounded online collectives like 4chan and Reddit. The similarities between these contexts speaks to the blur between "subcultural" and "mainstream" practices proposed in the last chapter, but—at the same time—their distinctions speak to the specific influence of situated social imaginaries woven together through shared conversational practices. For instance, figure 3.1 is from a 2013 4chan /v/ ("Video Games") thread, comparing the "master race" of gamers who play on highly customizable personal computers to the "filthy peasants" who play on stock videogame consoles like the Xbox,

PlayStation, and Wii. Interior monologue captioning is used in this image to glamorize the peasant underclass of console players. It maps a stream-of-consciousness text around a smug, strutting agrarian. The image is ironic in its arrogance, given its oppressed subject. Even if the "Doge" trend largely missed 4chan, the memetic practices foundational to "Doge" existed and still exist on the more esoteric site. At the same time, references shared by participants on 4chan shaded and texturized those memetic practices in unique ways. The lingua franca worked in contexts big and small.

In all, "Doge" resonated broadly in 2013 because it was a novel take on established forms and recurring tropes prevalent in internet memes, one that spread and shared well. Like "Rickrolling," "Doge" strikes a balance between subcultural esotery and mass enjoyment, thus fueling engagement from multiple audiences. Accessible and cuddly, "Doge" maps well onto the non sequitur visual humor predominant in memetic media. The most popular meme of 2013—like that of any year—was woven together from threads already established, woven from the vernacular that preceded it.

"Doge"—like memetic media more broadly—exemplifies what Jean Burgess calls "vernacular creativity," which "in being ordinary, is not elite or institutionalized; nor is it extraordinary or specular, but rather is identified on the basis of its *commonness*" (2007, 32, original emphasis). This contextually specific creativity is the domain of "the everyday, the mundane, and the in-between" (29). This liminality is key to the etymology of the word *vernacular*, which has long labeled practices outside narrow and elite dimensions of expression. Going back to its Latin origins, Burgess says *vernacular* denoted practices that were "not Latin," which coded to "not learned." Therefore, vernacular "was the language of folk, magical, or superstitious knowledges, rather than the language of literacy" (30). Through this connotation, the vernacular came to be associated with the "ordinary."

Understanding internet memes as everyday vernacular illuminates the tensions we've seen already between the subcultural and mass connotations of the term. Push and pull between those connotations is embedded within the very idea of *vernacular*. Like Burgess, Robert Glenn Howard (2008) traces the root of the word to the Latin *verna*, which labels a "home-born slave," who is not entirely "other" but not entirely "us." Howard carries this etymology through to our definition of *vernacular* today, which will often refer either to the "subaltern" or to the "common," and often both.

The same term refers to both the speech of denigrated and marginalized populations and the speech of the everyday and banal. "Based on this dual meaning," Howard argues, "the vernacular came to refer to discourse that coexists with dominant culture but is held separate from it" (493), and therefore mediates between the marginalized, the popular, and the institutional. When internet memes move from "novel creative expression" to "overdone to death," they are moving from *vernacular* as subaltern to *vernacular* as common, evidencing the porous relationship between the two. The popularity of "Doge" charted along this path. Like many internet memes, it burned bright and faded quickly, peaking in late 2013 when it was appearing on multiple "top meme" lists. Since then it has taken its place as one thread among many in the memetic tapestry. In the years since, new memetic texts have bubbled up from esoteric origins to mass proliferation, emerging out of vibrant collective conversations.

As often as this process repeats, micro expressive strands weave into meso social threads and eventually into macro collective tapestries. Understanding the social dimensions of memetic participation is essential to charting its public potential. The grammar developed in the last chapter—premised in particular on the logics of multimodality and reappropriation—is applied in this chapter to collective vernacular. Though mediated cultural participants can and do hail from diverse locations, they can innovate from accepted practices during their mediated interaction. They bridge the distance by crafting a metaphorical space in the midst of very real social practices. In this way, memetic logics and grammar underscore a lingua franca—a shared social vernacular prevalent within and across participatory media collectives.

The rest of this chapter will assess the collective and social dimensions underscoring memetic participation. First, I'll argue that memes—echoing what discourse analyst Deborah Tannen ([1989] 2007) says about conversation more generally—balance "fixity" and "novelty" in their creation, circulation, and transformation. Next, I'll tie this fixity and novelty to Burgess's (2007) vernacular creativity, which simultaneously is influenced by and influences collective conversations. Because of this reciprocity, vernacular creativity is susceptible to the jargons, marginalizations, and antagonisms inherent to all collective conversations. These conversations are vibrant, even if imperfect. From "LOLCats" to "Doge" to the collective texts that have come since and will come next, memetic media are a lingua franca formed by intertwining strands of vernacular creativity. Unpacking that vernacular requires an attention to both the most niche corners of online participation and to the most popular sites on the web. The sections to follow will delve into both in order to assess how social processes make media memetic.

Fixity and Novelty

In his discussion of bricolage, Claude Lévi-Strauss writes that when the bricoleur reappropriates, "the possibilities always remain limited" because the bricoleur is "pre-constrained" to collecting and using existent cultural materials ([1962] 1969, 19). Memetic reappropriation is constrained by the cultural systems that simultaneously facilitate it. The collective dimensions of memes, like the reappropriations of the bricoleur, "already possess a sense which sets a limit to their freedom to maneuver" (19). The memetic grammar introduced in chapter 2 is therefore always situated within a collective vernacular. Even in a media ecology with seemingly endless cultural material to reappropriate, social precedent shades and texturizes memetic participation. Just as "LOLCats" and interior monologue captioning shaped "Doge," standards shape memetic vernacular. In discourse analysis, Tannen ([1989] 2007) calls this blend of fixed premise and novel contribution during everyday conversation *prepatterning*.

According to Tannen, prepatterning is essential to every conversation we have. In her analysis of intertextuality and repetition in dialogue, Tannen argues that it's "the play between fixity and novelty that makes possible the creation of meaning" (49). Our conversations are a fluid blend of existing templates—tropes, colloquialisms, conversational sequences, etc.—and individual expressions appropriating those templates. In this way, "speakers weave the words of others into the fabric of their own, the thread of which is, in turn, picked up and rewoven into the pattern. Repetitions and variations make individual utterances into a unified discourse" (67). Repetition and variation—novel iterations of established premises—are essential to collective memetic participation.

In this section, I'll argue that prepatterning in memetic participation is analogous to prepatterning in linguistic conversation; I'll then assess its collective dimensions. Tied to memetic reappropriation, prepatterning places restrictions on participation, as participants converse within accepted frameworks. However, it also affords depth and expression, since these same participants can innovate within the accepted vernacular. To use Tannen's lens, memes balance "fixity" and "novelty"; innovation occurs within prepatterned vernacular.

Prepatterning and Memetics

Chapter 2 established how essential reappropriation is to memetic grammar. Whether Photoshopping Batman or sharing an eighteenth-century political cartoon or hashtagging "#TBT" on an Instagram photo, participants' individual expressions are memetic when they transform an existing premise. This multimodal blend of fixity and novelty is evident in "Doge" and the other interior monologue captions that introduced this chapter. The fixed tropes of interior monologue captions—stream of consciousness, scattered text placement, and variations in text size, capitalization, grammar, and spelling—all define the genre. Likewise, classic image meme genres—ones that interior monologue captioning itself reappropriates—evidence their own fixity and novelty. Image macro subgenres like stock character macros and "LOLCats" balance fixed premise and novel expression in each new entry.

For instance, the image macros in figure 3.4 create their satire by combining the fixed aesthetic clue of thick-rimmed black glasses with stereotypical "hipster" values. In the images, fixed hipster stereotypes—namely, the arrogant celebration of the obscure and the rejection of the mainstream—intertwine with the fixed characteristics of the images' subjects to craft a novel joke. In the film *The Little Mermaid*, the mermaid Ariel is implored by her crab advisor Sebastian to stay safe "under the sea"; here the obscurity of Ariel's geographic location comes with hipster subcultural cred. In the television series *Seinfeld*, George Costanza is forced by his domineering father to celebrate the faux holiday Festivus; here it's the marker of avant-garde taste. In a famous piece of historical legend, painter Vincent van Gogh supposedly removed one of his own ears in a moment of self-harm; here it's presented as a statement against "mainstream" sensibilities. Understanding hipster stereotypes—and registering thick-rimmed black glasses as a visual cue for these stereotypes—is essential to understanding each joke in figure 3.4. So is understanding the biography of each figure tied to the stereotype. Intertwining these two sets of fixed understanding produces novel parody. As Barre Toelken argues, "in parodies, the whole

Figure 3.4

Image macros satirizing archetypical hipsters by connecting hipster tropes to (left to right) Ariel from the 1989 film *The Little Mermaid*, George Costanza from the 1990s show *Seinfeld*, and postimpressionist painter Vincent van Gogh's 1889 *Self-Portrait*. Collected between 2011 and 2012.

point is to juxtapose one level of understanding with another in such an appropriately congruous way … that the result is a larger burst of meaning than the listener could get from either level by itself" (1996, 258). In this way, the images in figure 3.4 are prototypical parody. They're also prototypical image macros, meaning that their form demonstrates the same mix of fixity and novelty as their content.

Phrasal, video, and performance memes exhibit fixity and novelty as well. Figure 3.5 collects novel iterations of the fixed phrase "Haters gonna hate," which connotes a disregard for doubters and naysayers. The phrase is emphasized in figure 3.5 by images of figures nonchalantly defying contextual expectations, exemplifying the expression's dismissive confidence. In video iterations of the "Hitler Reacts" meme, novel subtitles are written into a fixed clip from the film *Der Untergang*. "Rickrolling" is a fixed text made novel by the way the source video is invoked; the more novel its invocation, the "better" the Rickroll. The same could be said for "Planking," "Tebowing," or the "Ice Bucket Challenge," which are fixed performances made resonant by novel implementation.

In all, memetic texts weave established tenets, characters, and themes into new iterations. This ensures that participants are able to add their own transformative voice to a text, while still giving audiences a recognizable premise by which to read that text. This process depends on reappropriational grammar, allowing a broadly understood—but contextually versatile—vernacular to emerge. Just as several jokes begin with "Knock,

Figure 3.5
Multimodal iterations of the phrase "Haters gonna hate." From left to right, the phrase captions a candid shot of Leonardo DiCaprio on the set of the 2010 film *Inception*; a Photoshopped image of Albert Einstein riding a bicycle in the shadow of an atomic blast; and a photo of late Libyan President Muammar Gaddafi. Collected between 2011 and 2013.

knock" or "A guy walks into a bar," memetic media share stable elements that collective participants can innovate on. The texts already prevalent in the shared social corpus set the precedent for participation. However, this shared corpus still inspires novel expression: "Doge" was a new meme, but a new meme dependent on "LOLCats" and interior monologue captioning. Prepatterning, in sum, depends on social practice, as reappropriational grammar intertwines with collective vernacular. What gets reappropriated, what resonates, and what spreads—from the whole world of source texts available—is decided through interaction.

Fixity, Novelty, and Collectivism

Not only do fixity and novelty underscore memetic texts, this same prepatterning also underscores shared communal and collective experience. Fixed premises allow participants to understand the novel conversational contributions of others, even those who are globally dispersed. Shared understanding can develop despite the relative anonymity and ephemerality of mediated public participation. When individuals converse on a subreddit, a 4chan thread, or a Twitter hashtag, when they contribute to YouTube or Tumblr or Imgur, the fixity and novelty of memetic participation ensures that they can begin with some degree of common understanding. They can converse within a loosely bound mediated imaginary. In many ways, speech acts themselves create the collective; the speech community is defined by the shared communicative practices evidenced in the memetic blend of fixed premise and novel expression.

Of course—and again—these practices are not new to participatory media, even if their scale and vibrancy seem unprecedented. Tannen's ([1989] 2007) whole argument comes from an analysis of spoken conversation, and participation by identification is central to predigital memetic practices as well. For instance, Limor Shifman (2014) cites the memetic emergence of the phrase "Kilroy was here" in the mid twentieth century. The meme has been globally peppering graffiti since at least World War II, when American soldiers took up the practice. Often accompanied by a simple doodle of a bald head with an exaggerated nose peeking out from behind a wall, the phrase was scrawled all over the world by American soldiers in the 1940s. It was a memetic message that could be recognized and then furthered by the allies who came across it. "Kilroy was here," from this read, is part of a long line of memetic practices—from 1960s protest songs to oral folk tales to Elizabethan posies—that help dispersed cultural participants connect to and innovate on what has come before.

Participatory media make the memetic dimensions of collective conversation all the more apparent, as established texts and novel iterations intertwine over and over again on vibrant platforms. Social and cultural identification thus inspires memetic participation. The collectivist dimensions of this identification are enhanced by reappropriation, since new contributors can weave their strands into a conversation already rich with others' unique expressions. Whitney Phillips (2015b) notes that layers upon layers of subcultural understanding were required to untangle the rat's nest of intertextuality that constituted participation in trolling subcultures. Conversations knotted with memetic reference allowed the trolls Phillips studied "to speak clearly and coherently to other members of the collective while baffling those outside the affinity network" (22). Referencing and reappropriating established memes was essential to creating collective identity in predominantly pseudonymous and even anonymous subcultures.

But the interplay of fixity and novelty in memetic media isn't useful only for subcultural cohesion. Connection via memetic texts can occur on a massive popular scale. Tama Leaver (2013), speaking of memetic participation surrounding the 2012 Summer Olympics, writes that the global audience for the events enabled Olympic moments to be circulated and transformed on a worldwide stage. Compared to the esotery of more explicitly subcultural memetic practices, participation in conversations surrounding the 2012 Olympics had a low barrier of entry, allowing an easier translation of memetic moments to traditional broadcast media outlets. Memetic participation can facilitate intimate interpersonal connections as well. Kate Miltner (2014), in her study of "LOLCats," finds that memetic texts can punctuate interpersonal relationships as much as they can facilitate connections between public collectives. Just as conversational prepatterning is versatile enough to facilitate interpersonal connection and public conversation, so too is memetic participation. Whether massively public, esoterically subcultural, or intimately interpersonal, memetic media afford collective connection by intertwining individual expression with social precedent. Memetic tools can facilitate conversations both large and small, as shared practices facilitate a whole continuum of participation.

Prepatterned tropes can be employed in diverse contexts, and collective precedent can produce diverse ends. As we saw, the interior monologue captioning that opened this chapter became massively popular through "Doge," but other iterations are more constrained to subcultural imaginaries on sites like 4chan, Reddit, and Tumblr. And the linguistic features that shape the expression in "Doge" and "LOLCats"—fragmented vernacular presented with nonstandard spelling and grammar—can produce texts with a darker edge. Figure 3.6 features a 4chan-famous comic parody of Donald Duck called "Dolan." In figure 3.6—one of the tamer "Dolan" entries—Dolan invites Goofy over to eat some steak, apparently made from Goofy's romantic partner. Other iterations often center on sexual assault, murder, and various violent acts. "Dolan" comics—despite their vernacular similarity to "Doge" and "LOLCats"—haven't garnered the crossover attention of their more famous counterparts. And few on 4chan might protest that relative obscurity. When "Dolan" started spreading on Tumblr in mid 2014, some 4chan participants—as 4chan participants long have—lamented the softening of yet another iconoclastic collective icon.

The interior monologue in "Doge" and the fractured dialogue of "Dolan" also bear similarities to another memetic subgenre, this one gaining popularity on Reddit in late 2013. /r/YouDontSurf was born out of the image in figure 3.7, a caption on a stock photo of an older man and a young boy, an

Figure 3.6
A "Dolan" comic, which crafts its dark humor by reappropriating the Disney characters Donald Duck and Goofy. Collected in 2013.

apparent representation of a grandfather and grandson. The static image, drawing attention to the toddler's shirt (which reads "Surf"), becomes a story in motion with the addition of a second panel cropped from the same image. The second panel's zoom into the grandfather's face focuses readers on his reaction to his grandson's shirt. Across both panels, the juxtaposition of the wholesome implications of the grandparent/grandchild relationship and the antagonism of the added text create incongruous humor. This dark humor resonated enough to launch a subreddit devoted to the humorous captioning of (often notoriously vague and nonsensical) stock photos. In these images, fixed practices inspire novel collective expression.

Figure 3.7
A vertical comic posted to /r/YouDontSurf, created by reappropriating a stock photo. Posted on October 30, 2014.

Although /r/YouDontSurf remixes (such as figure 3.8) are often vertical comics, they share quite a bit with the aesthetics and practices that define the interior monologue captions that opened this chapter. Both reappropriate stock photos through juxtapositional captioning, and feature fractured monologue. Both use brightly colored Comic Sans for their text, in keeping with the ironic "internet ugly" aesthetic that Douglas (2014) describes. In fact, the centrality of "internet ugly" to /r/YouDontSurf images is pronounced enough that figure 3.7—posted as a "high-definition remake" of the original "You Don't Surf" image—was met with expressions of sadness by participants on the subreddit. The low-definition "bad" design choices

Figure 3.8
Three vertical comics posted to /r/YouDontSurf, created by reappropriating stock photos. Posted respectively on August 31, 2014; March 7, 2015; and December 31, 2014.

and the inclusion of the watermark from the stock photo site where the image was found (implying it was taken for free) all were seen as essential to the subreddit's aesthetic.

From "LOLCats" to "Doge" to monologue captions to /r/YouDontSurf, a set of relatively fixed aesthetic practices have inspired a whole branching family tree of intertwined memetic texts. Diverse participants can use collective precedent and understanding to communicate across a wide variety of contexts. Lee Knutilla (2011) makes this point about reaction shots on 4chan, which he says allow a "connection to otherness" through a "communal pool" of versatile texts. Likewise, the reaction GIFs discussed in the last chapter filter social cues into mediated conversations. Through acts of bricolage and poaching, participants can express a desired mood,

Figure 3.9
Three reaction shots with captions. From left to right: Willy Wonka from the 1971 film *Willy Wonka and the Chocolate Factory*; Han Solo and Lando Calrissian from the 1980 film *Star Wars: The Empire Strikes Back*; an image from the 2009 Marvel comic *Incredible Hercules*, issue 122. Collected in 2011.

assessment, or response by reappropriating a facial expression, gesture, phrase, or any combination of these from a pop media text.

The reappropriational grammar assessed in reaction shots in chapter 2 facilitates the collective vernacular assessed here, as evidenced by the 4chan reaction shots compiled in figure 3.9. Because of the format of 4chan's threads, images like these sit right beside the written text posted by participants. The shorthand for emotional expression conveyed in the images accentuates the more nuanced point articulated in the written text. Further, this shorthand ties into established sentiments on the site's different boards, as evidenced in figure 3.9. "You must be new here" is used to rebuke someone for not acting appropriately according to collective norms on the site. "He mad" is used to mock the perceived seriousness of another participant's protest or critique. "Cool story, bro" is used ironically, implying a dismissal of another's post. Through their easy recognition and diverse application, reaction shots like these—and the GIFs we saw in figure 2.9—help add coherence to overlapping speech communities across sites, forums, and boards. As Jason Eppink argues of GIF files, "a successful GIF is one that is shared, eclipsing its creator to become an essential part of a cultural conversation. The result is a digital slang, a visual vocabulary unencumbered by authorship. … Even though individuals process the pixels, communities make the GIFs" (2014, 301).

And these collectives are prolific. The sheer number of images and GIFs circulating on sites like 4chan, Reddit, and Tumblr seems impossible to quantify. Participants ceaselessly reappropriate media moments for their own uses. For instance, between 2012 and 2014, an Imgur participant compiled a "reaction GIFs archive" at ReactionGIFsArchive.imgur.com, which contains 47 albums categorizing GIFs by feeling (such as "disgust," "sad/upset/angry," or "mind blown"), action ("clapping," "laughing," or "dancing"), and source media (such as the television shows *SpongeBob SquarePants*, *Community*, or *Adventure Time*). The creator of the page curated over 3,200 images in two years of operation, eventually relenting to the impossibility of keeping up with the collective production of reaction GIFs. "Previously I acted as if this library could be 'completed.' I understand now that won't be the case," the sidebar on the page reads in 2015. The participant instead urges others to "think of this as a tribute" to GIFs that resonated between 2012 and 2014.

Just as fixity and novelty are essential to spoken conversation, they're essential to mediated conversations. The grammar of multimodal reappropriation we saw in the last chapter is employed toward collective vernacular across different sites and contexts. The next section will tie this prepatterning to vernacular creativity.

Vernacular Creativity

Tannen writes that it's "the eternal tension between fixity and novelty that constitutes creativity" ([1989] 2007, 29). As fixed premise and novel expression intertwine, unique expressions are born from prepatterned tropes. Far from being mere formula, the memetic balance of imitation and transformation is evidence of both social utility and creative adaptation. Understanding patterns and precedents well enough to imitate them, reappropriate them—and even contrast or violate them—is the basis of wit, irony, humor, and social commentary. In the case of memetic media, *vernacular* becomes *vernacular creativity* when collective conversations intertwine with multimodal expression. The memetic lingua franca is conversational, but it's not merely conversational; it's also a language threaded together by individual acts of creative expression. These creative acts can be *vernacular* both in the mass and the subaltern senses that Howard (2008) suggests. Vernacular creativity is evidenced in both "everyday" popular memetic expressions and more overtly "subcultural" boundary policing.

This section will address the multifaceted dimensions of this creativity, and the ambivalent social practices that emerge alongside it.

Everyday Expression and the Ambivalence of Vernacular

Understood as examples of vernacular creativity, memetic media are significant for their expressive and conversational potential. As we have seen, memetic media are not mindless imitation or artless pastiche; they are instead everyday acts of conversational creativity, tying into a tapestry of texts that came before them. They're situated within common creativity, which—aesthetically good or bad, ethically right or wrong[1]—is essential to popular participation. Burgess (2007) rightly suggests we avoid equating *vernacular* with practices that are more "authentic" or "pure" than the manufactured hegemonic literacies of "high culture." However, vernacular is nonetheless more connected to the folk than the formal, more to the amateur than the professional, and more to the bricoleur than the craftsperson. Vernacular expression carries with it all the vibrancy and ambivalence of everyday conversation, as participants converse in a memetic lingua franca.

The vernacular dimensions of memetic participation shade its reappropriation. The grammatical processes we saw in the last chapter are often applied to "everyday" acts of creativity, which recontextualize media to conversational ends. For instance, figure 3.10, shared on Tumblr in 2015, annotates a scene from the 1939 film *Gone with the Wind*, in which Rhett Butler is leaving his tumultuous love interest Scarlett O'Hara. In this iconic moment, O'Hara expresses her anxiety about a life without Butler: "Where shall I go? What shall I do?" Butler's response is cold: "Frankly, my dear, I don't give a damn." The line—resonant in American popular culture for three-quarters of a century—gets a vernacular update: "Frankly, my dear, I don't give a damn" becomes "tbh bae idgaf," and humorous juxtaposition is born from the translation of the iconic 1939 sentiment into 2015 slang.

Annotating Butler and O'Hara in this Tumblr image is a series of letters that would have read as gibberish seventy-five years ago, and may well read as gibberish in another seventy-five years—if they don't already. However, to the participants who shared the image, they're understandable as "everyday" expression, and their clever memetic implementation is what makes the joke work. To translate: "tbh" is shorthand slang for "to be honest";

Figure 3.10
A scene from the 1939 film *Gone with the Wind,* which replaces Rhett Butler's iconic "Frankly, my dear, I don't give a damn" with the contemporary slang "tbh bae idgaf" (To be honest, bae, I don't give a fuck). Collected in 2015.

"bae"—either a corruption of *babe* or an acronym for "before anyone else"—is a label for a partner in an intimate interpersonal relationship; and "idgaf" abbreviates "I don't give a fuck." This 2015 slang precisely maps onto Butler's 1939 sentiment: "tbh" matches with "frankly," "bae" with "my dear," and "idgaf" with "I don't give a damn."[2] That unexpected aptness combines with the emotion carried by the image to create an expressive act that reappropriates a cultural icon for a novel conversational sentiment. The iconicity of the source text juxtaposes the low-culture connotations of the slang employed. In the process, humor is produced from the recontextualization.

The populist dimensions of vernacular creativity mean diverse use, but also ambivalent ends. Memetic media possess the same tensions common across vernacular communication. The reappropriations essential to memetic participation can also be *appropriations* of more marginalized subaltern practices. These appropriations can be employed to create further hegemonic stereotypes, as illustrated by screenshots from the "Medieval Reactions" Twitter account, which annotates European imagery from the

Middle Ages and Renaissance with contemporary vernacular (figure 3.11). On the surface, this recontextualization seems no different from many of the humorous juxtapositions we've seen so far, in which contemporary slang has been mapped onto the likes of Rhett Butler, agrarian peasants, and Donald Duck. "Medieval Reactions" certainly exists within this lineage, connecting contemporary vernacular to both iconic and surprising images from past centuries. However, the reappropriations on "Medieval Reactions" at times decontextualize and therefore stereotypically pantomime African American vernacular, normalizing narrow perspectives about the content and tone of that subaltern vernacular in the process.

Figure 3.11
Three captures from the "Medieval Reactions" Twitter account ("@MedievalReacts"). Left: a contemporary caption is added to Guido Reni's painting *Drinking Bacchus* (c. 1623); top right: a scene from an illuminated French translation of Augustine's *City of God* (c. 1475) with a contemporary caption; bottom right: Guercino's painting *Christ with the Woman Taken in Adultery* (1621) with a contemporary caption. Posted respectively on March 16, 2015; March 19, 2015; and March 16, 2015.

Many memetic practices carry this ambivalent appropriation. The "Kanye Wes Anderson" and "Fly Art Productions" tumblogs seen in chapter 1 juxtapose a film school icon and high art with the African American vernacular often found in hip hop; the joke hinges on audiences reading the combination as an inconsistency. Similarly, Imgur participants share screenshots from a social imaginary known as "Black Twitter"—which André Brock calls "Twitter's mediation of Black cultural discourse" (2012, 530)—in order to appropriate and decontextually display situated cultural conversations among Black Twitter participants. Reddit's /r/BlackPeopleGIFs reminds participants in its subreddit rules that "we're all black here. Be cool." Participants on the subreddit then reproduce both positive and negative stereotypes about African Americans in the GIFs they share. 4chan participants have long appropriated stereotypical African American vernacular in their conversations, from the "he mad" and "haters gonna hate" we've seen already, to the more explicitly racist appropriations we'll see in the next chapter. This representational ambivalence isn't restricted to text or images. "The Harlem Shake" is a performance meme shared heavily on YouTube in 2013, in which participants film themselves doing a mundane dance to Baauer's 2012 song "The Harlem Shake" before quickly cutting to a more ridiculous version of the dance as the song changes tempo. Catherine Knight Steele (2013) critiques "Harlem Shake" remixes for decontextualizing the song and accompanying dance from its namesake, the predominantly minority Harlem, New York, community. When mostly white high school sports teams, colleges, and workplaces make their own versions of the meme, Steele says that they "further marginalize rather than liberate."

Similar charges could be leveled at conversations surrounding the "internet famous" African American figures Antoine Dodson and Sweet Brown, who gained attention in 2010 and 2013 for resonant local news interviews. Antoine Dodson responded to a home invasion by imploring the community to "hide yo' kids; hide yo' wife." Sweet Brown responded to a building fire by exclaiming that "ain't nobody got time for that." In both cases, the memetic resonance of the moments and the vernacular of their subjects inspired creative play, but that play raises questions about mass appropriation, stereotypes, and the humorous whitewashing of very real concerns to minority communities. In these examples, the situated "signifyin" conversational practices that Brock (2012) argues help craft a "cultural commonplace" in environments like Black Twitter are disassociated from their subaltern ingroup. On Black Twitter, a cultural commonplace is created by participants' identities, who they follow, who follows them, and how they "command the form" of mediated vernacular expression. Decontextualized from these roots, the stance in the examples above shifts the register to dominant appropriation. As we'll see in chapter 4's discussion of racial antagonisms, creativity serves ambivalent ends when the lingua franca appropriates and absorbs marginalized perspectives.

But memetic expression is not created from a singular perspective, and memetic prepatterning can premise texts that are hegemonic, subversive, or any shade in between. For instance, beginning in 2008, a tumblog called "Fuck Yeah Ryan Gosling" paired photos of the actor Ryan Gosling with romantic quips, predominantly hailing the audience with "Hey Girl" (figure 3.12). The images—like the blog itself—range from empathetic to supportive to arguably misogynistic in the heteronormative fantasy they create around images of the actor. Left on its own, "Fuck Yeah Ryan Gosling" would be collective enough, a combination of popular culture images and normative ideas about romance. However, the memetic potential of "Fuck Yeah Ryan Gosling" texts inspired creativity beyond its original

Figure 3.12
Three images from FuckYeahRyanGosling.tumblr.com, which caption photos of actor Ryan Gosling with expressions of heteronormative romance. Posted respectively on October 25, 2010; January 29, 2009; and December 22, 2008.

Figure 3.13
Three images from FeministRyanGosling.tumblr.com, which caption photos of actor Ryan Gosling with expressions of pro-feminist romance. Posted respectively on December 5, 2011; November 20, 2011; and October 10, 2011.

boundaries. In the years since 2008, Ryan Gosling images have been combined with a "Hey Girl" message to bring romance to topics like typography ("Typographer Ryan Gosling"), classic literature ("Shakespearean Ryan Gosling"), and the tech industry ("Silicon Valley Ryan Gosling"). In these new iterations, a familiar corpus of Ryan Gosling images combines with topic-specific language to produce new dimensions on the idealistically romantic meme.

Figure 3.13 is an iteration from a tumblog called "Feminist Ryan Gosling," which ironically combines the heteronormative precedent of "Fuck Yeah Ryan Gosling" with pro-feminist messages. "Feminist Ryan Gosling" images evidence a playful back-and-forth with stereotypical ideals of romantic love. The images in figure 3.13 might challenge or might ultimately reinforce the values of "Fuck Yeah Ryan Gosling," depending on the reader. Regardless, "Feminist Ryan Gosling" is an act of vernacular creativity in conversation with its "Fuck Yeah Ryan Gosling" founder meme.

In memetic participation, vernacular creativity can sometimes work in favor of marginalized perspectives, providing those perspectives a platform for novel expressions. It can sometimes antagonize and silence those perspectives. Sometimes—as is often the case with everyday acts of expression—it does a little bit of both. Collectives coalesce around shared practices, policing boundaries as they do.

Subcultural Standards

The collective dimensions of vernacular creativity fuel many of the "death of the meme" charges discussed in the last chapter. Collective logics allow for both "Dolan" and "Doge," both Black Twitter "signifyin" and its broader, more ambivalent appropriation. These logics therefore facilitate struggles between subcultural identities and mainstream practices. The tug-of-war between memetic texts as esoterically subcultural and memetic texts as massively popular leads to ample identity clashes, both between and within specific participatory media collectives. The story of subcultural slang and style is often the story of creativity, appropriation, abandonment, and new creativity all over again, even if the actuality of this struggle—pitting "independent purity" vs. "mainstream corruption"—is more complicated than death by sellout. However, that tension is real in a social imaginary sense, and carries different degrees of consequence (the "mainstreaming" of "Dolan" comics carries different cultural weight than hegemonic appropriations of "The Harlem Shake"). The very nature of memetic participation exacerbates tensions between subcultural and mass dimensions of collectivism, as the ease of memetic creation, circulation, and transformation pushes resonant esoteric texts to mainstream participation, shifting them from the subaltern to the everyday register. The vernacular of memetic subcultures—specifically the social imaginaries crafted by participants on sites like 4chan, Reddit, Tumblr, and Imgur—facilitates collective participation, but also appropriations of that participation. Therefore, participants invested in these media collectives as social imaginaries police how others use their subcultural texts.

The collectivist dimensions of memetic participation lend themselves in some cases to subcultural identification within specific sites. Participation on sites like 4chan, Reddit, Tumblr, and Imgur coincides with broader cultural engagement, but many active participants on those sites also claim subcultural identification, hailing themselves and others as members of a highly stylized collective. Reddit has "redditors," 4chan has "anons" (among other more specific names for more specific boards), and Imgur has "Imgurians"—all terms that hail active participants as collective citizens. In these practices, "internet as place" metaphors persist, labeling a loose but recognizable social imaginary, premised on its own loose set of characteristics.

The images in figure 3.14 all conceptualize "The Internet" as a place, a social imaginary with its own citizens and customs. The left image in figure 3.14 is representative of a subgenre of memetic texts, all "welcoming" the implied addressee to "The Internet." The family of images often combines the linguistic welcome with a nonsensical visual: an old woman floating through outer space on a surfboard, a man wearing only boxer briefs and a horse-head mask holding a glass of wine and a cigar and lying in a bed full of Cadbury Cream Eggs, or a cat dressed as a sea captain sitting in an office supply box. These absurdist visuals contrast with the polite and sensible tone of the salutary words, "Welcome to the Internet," underscoring the bizarre "place" that is the subcultural internet. The place metaphor is a stand-in for a set of collective practices, histories, and

Figure 3.14
Three images conceptualizing "The Internet" as a subcultural place. Left: a Photoshopped picture of Marvel's Deadpool riding a unicorn; top right: a GIF of a mother cat carrying her kitten across the room; bottom right: protestors wearing Guy Fawkes masks from the 2005 film *V for Vendetta*. Collected between 2010 and 2015.

discourses that memetically connect participants from diverse geographic locations.

Phillips, in her study of self-identifying trolls, explains that through participants' collective communication "a set of shared experiences and expectations emerges; the resulting content feeds into and sustains an interconnected nest of constitutive content" (2015b, 31). Memetic references, jokes, catchphrases, and histories gesture toward shared experiences and knit "the collective subcultural fabric" that connected Phillips's participants. In her study of collective community on Reddit, Adrienne Massanari acknowledges that even if individual subreddits can be vastly different in their language and practices, "certain patterns characterize interactions throughout the site," and "larger cultural mores shape the space" (2015, 14). Even massive, diverse sites like YouTube have a core of self-identifying collectivist participants. Shifman says of memetic remix videos on the site that "uploading such videos may thus serve as another way to maintain the links underscoring a huge and highly heterogenic crowd" (2013, 371). Out of these spaces emerge folktales (like 4chan's "Chip Chan," who broadcasts her life over webcam and is purportedly a prisoner in her own home, monitored by a deranged police officer), landmark events (like Reddit's 2013 "mystery vault," which had participants guessing what could be inside a safe found in a redditor's basement), and even stereotypes (like denigrations of the "social justice warriors" and "tumblrista feminists" associated with Tumblr). These practices intertwine to craft the tapestry of subcultural memetic participation.

In another mark of collectivism, this ingroup identification comes with outgroup othering. Memetic logics, grammar, and vernacular are employed in subcultural conversations to differentiate insiders from outsiders, and to distinguish members of the collective from the uninitiated. Phillips describes her first moments trying to engage with the memetic esotery that categorized the trolling collectives she analyzes:

> Initially I understood nothing; it felt as if I were trying to read a website written in an entirely different language. I could tell that people were making jokes, but I didn't see what was so funny. Still, there was something about the space that intrigued me, so I continued reading and cross-referencing, and eventually the indecipherable chaos gave way to what I could recognize as a surprisingly coherent behavioral and linguistic system. (2015b, 38)

Phillips's experience is more than the inevitable byproduct of a rat's nest of nearly endless collective intertextual reference; it's the result of explicit boundary work.

That boundary work comes across when certain practices are labeled "dead," "overused," or "corrupted" by mainstream enjoyment. Participants on 4chan's /b/ board—its popular and notorious "Random" board, in full view next chapter—are often vocal about this boundary work, embracing the mantle of being the "tastemakers" of memetic subculture. This view of 4chan is conveyed by an annotated Photoshop of Rambo from the 2008 film *Rambo* (figure 3.15). It tells of the grit and grime of 4chan's /b/, suggesting that the board is a memetic crucible, birthing texts that are then cleaned and distilled as they filter out to other participatory media collectives.

This "tastemaker" mantle can lead to resentment when subaltern vernacular becomes common vernacular. A 4chan participant expressed such frustration in a March 2013 post, at least according to a supposed screen capture shared widely since. Next to a reaction shot of a stupefied and scared Bugs Bunny comes the following text:

Figure 3.15
A captioned image, in which Rambo from the 2008 film *Rambo* (representing 4chan's /b/ board) hands a flower (representing a meme) to an elated woman (representing the social imaginary of "The Internet"). Collected in 2011.

Man. Just imagine that. You're on an image board in some thread (or you make one) and decide to do something that you think is funny/clever/ironic or whatever your intention is.

You make just one post, when all of a sudden, the whole thread joins in. You have your laughs and all, and then later, the whole site is doing it. Must be pretty alright, a few decent ones with a few gems here and there, and you have a good laugh.

Then, other sites see this, don't entirely understand it, then shit it up with unfunny bullshit. Whatever, it's not that big.

Then, that whole site does it, and a few more, too. All of a sudden, people are joining in on your fun, not knowing where it stems from, not understanding how they work, and are making terrible, cringe-inducing versions of that one picture you made.

Facebook pages join in, it becomes massive. Then, you start seeing it in real life. Commercials, shirts, notebooks, etc. They're not funny, the concept is ruined, and people have the wrong idea about them, how to make them, where to use them, and how.

It's all everywhere. All because you made

one

single

funny

post.

On a not-so-well-known anonymous imageboard.

Christ, just imagine that …

In the passage are subcultural assessments of an "us" and a "them." And the "them" is a large and nebulous monolith, corrupting the creative expression of the "us" by its lack of proper subcultural understanding.

The "death of the meme" charges that opened the last chapter largely rest on claims that the subcultural vernacular has been appropriated. Even as memetic logics persist (4chan still has plenty of memes), participants on the sites that are most prolific in producing memetic texts often express frustration that "everyone else" participates. Miltner (2014), discussing lamentations about the "death" of "LOLCats" says, "the elements of LOLCats that made them so appealing on a widespread basis—particularly, the ability to use them as emotional conduits—are ultimately what lead to their rejection by the collectives that created them."

Phillips (2015b) saw these charges emerge surrounding stock character macros birthed on 4chan. Initially, Phillips writes, the creation of image macros required at least some proficiency with photo-editing software. By creating a stock character macro, "one was therefore asserting both subcultural knowledge and technological competence" (143–144). However, with the increased popularity of image macros came "meme generating platforms," sites that would make the macro for participants. All participants had to do was click on an image—or maybe upload their own—and type in the text they wanted. According to Phillips, "this resulted in an explosion of participation, as well as an ever-expanding pantheon of templates" (144), much to the dismay of many vocal participants on 4chan's /b/ board. The narrative is one of appropriated vernacular creativity, and of the need to keep up that vernacular creativity in the face of ever-expanding appropriation. From this perspective, the better a meme spreads in the Dawkinsian sense, the worse it becomes to the collectives that popularized it, because the expressions of the imagined broader "them" have encroached on the more esoteric imagined "us."

The outsider enemies in this struggle over memetic vernacular change depending on the site in question, the text in question, the moment in question, and other layers of context. 4chan participants often contrast themselves with "The Internet" as a broader entity, and have taken issue with the practices of many other sites of memetic participation. One well-circulated 4chan screen capture alleges that the way Reddit uses image memes is like making a cake "composed entirely of frosting." In return, some participants on Reddit critique the regressive reputation of 4chan. Others on Reddit critique the progressive reputation of Tumblr (here they're joined by vocal participants on 4chan, which also houses critiques of "tumblristas" and "tumblrinas"). Imgur was created in 2009 by a redditor as "my gift to Reddit" and billed as "an image housing service that doesn't suck." But by 2013, some Reddit participants were worried that image posts from Imgur were "taking over" their site, and moderators on subreddits like /r/Atheism, /r/TwoXChromosomes, and /r/LifeProTips subsequently restricted image posts. Examples of these between-site conversational rivalries could fill volumes of lore. "4chan vs. Reddit," "Reddit vs. Tumblr," and "Tumblr vs. 4chan" are all active discursive rivalries. Even if many of the memetic practices on these sites are similar—and even if many of the participants on these sites overlap—the discursive distinctions are resonant enough to appear time and again in meta conversations on the sites. Vernacular creativity combined with social imaginary creates these well-worn subcultural tensions. Memetic texts and practices fuel such rivalries.

Identities also clash within memetic subcultures. Massanari (2015) catalogs the identity antagonisms inherent to Reddit, which contains pockets of participation consistently antagonizing other pockets of participation (we'll see this in the next chapter regarding gender identities). During these clashes, memetic in-jokes punctuate jabs, providing those initiated into the vernacular a shorthand callback to a mockable moment. Even single words can carry this kind of memetic force. On Reddit, for instance, calling something "euphoric" is almost certainly a callback to a much maligned /r/Atheism post from 2013. In the post (subsequently deleted, along with the account of the poster), a user—identifying as "just an atheist teenager" and not a professional "quote maker"—had just penned "a quote" and wanted to share it. The post read, "In this moment, I am euphoric. Not because of any phony god's blessing. But because I am enlightened by my intelligence." Because of its perceived arrogance, the post became an instant ironic hit. As it spread through Reddit and beyond, the quotation, and even just the word "euphoric," became memetic shorthand for self-importance, hubris, and obliviousness. Ironic use of the phrase entered the collective vernacular.

Just like vernacular conversation, vernacular creativity is not unfettered creativity; collective precedent shades memetic participation. Even as novel iterations themselves shape and expand new expression based on this precedent, memetic participation is never completely open. It's vernacular, and its creativity is situated within the "normal" and the "everyday" as defined by the collectives creating, circulating, and transforming that creativity. There are benefits to this vernacular creativity, as participants can come together through a collective set of texts and contexts to have collective conversations. However, when reappropriation becomes appropriation of marginalized identities or when collective identity becomes othering, the vernacular does exclusionary work. In these tensions are longstanding struggles between the subaltern and the common dimensions of vernacular creativity.

Memetic Lingua Franca

To Tannen, "paradoxically, it is the individual imagination that makes possible the shared understanding of language. Linguistic prepatterning is a means by which speakers create worlds that listeners can recreate in their own imaginations, recognizing the outlines of the prepatterning. Through prepatterning, the individual speaks through the group, and the group speaks through the individual" ([1989] 2007, 100). The vernacular creativity displayed in memetic creation, circulation, and transformation depends on such collectivism. In more bounded collectives like some of the boards on 4chan and some of the subreddits on Reddit, proficiency in fixed conversations and contexts is required for entry into the discussion, and subculturally "appropriate" novelty is required to create and innovate from that proficiency. But memetic logics have proven too prevalent for this policing. Multimodality and reappropriation have come to underscore a vernacular spoken by vast constellations of participants. Larger than site, geography, or individual contributor, the memetic lingua franca makes social worlds.

The interactions between participants within this lingua franca are as varied as their perspectives, relationships, and contexts. Despite the collective identity policing of participants active on sites like 4chan and Reddit, and despite the subcultural standards by which participants on those sites assess the quality of others' contributions, memetic logics and grammar are fundamental to diverse forms of vernacular creativity. As the memetic lingua franca spreads, so do the shared phrases, references, in-jokes, and assumptions that constitute it. Memetic genres, like interior monologue captioning, can be massively public, esoterically subcultural, intimately interpersonal, or can even span all those contexts at once. Participants can apply the memetic lingua franca to their own contexts and needs. Yes, sometimes jokes wear thin, but even "passé" memetic genres like stock character macros and "LOLCats" still inspire mass participation. This tension is inherent to vernacular itself, but also is the strength of a common tongue. Memetic media are essential to both the subaltern and the common dimensions of vernacular creativity. As long as participants employ memetic logics, their creativity is part of popular and populist conversations.

Acknowledging the limitations of participatory media, Burgess (2007) describes vernacular creativity as a "space of hope" for cultural citizenship, and is optimistic about its potential to provide citizens a means for connection and expression. The ultimate public good of vernacular creativity is increased public voice; this is the hope of memetic participation as well. Part II will assess the potential of memetic media to encourage this public connection and expression. It further articulates the ambivalence inherent to a media ecology that facilitates both silencing antagonism and empowering contribution, as memetic media are employed for public expression.

Part II Memetic Public Participation

The second half of this book argues that memetic media evidence *polyvocal* public participation: that is, many voices can connect and converse—as well as argue and antagonize—by employing memetic logics, grammar, and vernacular. Pulling out from the more micro focus that opened this book, chapters 4 through 6 focus on the meso interactional layers and the macro discursive layers of memetic media, assessing how ideas and perspectives spread on a massive collective scale. The expressive strands and interactional threads assessed in part I—the more formal dimensions of memetic media—will come to bear in part II's assessment of the social worlds woven through memetic participation. Memetic media have significant ramifications for civic participation: for representations of diverse identities, for political debate, and for the culture industries central to the contemporary media ecology. Understanding those ramifications requires an assessment of the memetic dimensions of identity antagonisms, political voice, and cultural conversations. The second half of this book therefore articulates the public dimensions of how memetic media matter.

Based on what we've seen so far, the argument that memetic media convey public voice may seem intuitive. After all, the logics of reappropriation, collectivism, and spread are all premised on the power of mediated participants to express their perspectives and engage with the expressions of others. The intertwine of these expressions is central to cultural conversations beyond memetic media. M. M. Bakhtin ([1970] 1986) calls discourse inherently "polyphonic"—comprising "many sounds" created by a multiplicity of unfinished texts overlapping. Memetic media further weave those many sounds—those many public voices—into tapestries that cover a wide spectrum of perspectives. The assumption that participatory media open up new avenues of expression is a resonant one. When I ask my introductory media studies students to extrapolate on the differences between a media studies class in 2015 and, say, a media studies class in 1985, many of their commonsense distinctions come down to voice. The gatekeepers inherent to the "one-to-many" model of broadcast media are less powerful in the presence of "many-to-many" digital communication. Amateurs can get famous on YouTube. Protests can start on Twitter. Previously silenced identities can now be an influential part of cultural conversations. What are memetic media if not a natural outpouring of this shift toward predominant public voice?

But platforms amplifying everyday vernacular are not necessarily liberatory, and an account of polyvocality has to account for the paradoxical tendency of massive popular participation to sometimes drown out perspectives that are not in line with hegemonic ones. To Nick Couldry (2010), empowering public voice happens not when people merely express themselves, but when they express with agency; individual expressions have to be acknowledged, respected, and engaged by others. As we saw in appropriations of African American vernacular in chapter 3—and as we'll see in discussions of race and gender antagonisms in chapter 4—the promise of voice in memetic public participation is an ambivalent one. Collective participation can easily become "mob rule," as dominant perspectives and identities silence subaltern ones.

Part II makes its argument about public participation by engaging with this ambivalent potential for polyvocality. Chapter 4 assesses the race and gender antagonisms prevalent in memetic media, while assessing the potential for memetic media to afford counterpublic contestation of those antagonisms. Chapter 5 applies that ambivalent counterpublic contestation to political commentary and protest. As both chapters will illustrate, memetic media complicate the ways public participants engage with diverse identities and ideas, even if old antagonisms and marginalizations persist. Understanding these complications is essential to understanding what's really different—and what's really not—in a participatory media ecology.

In addition to carrying old identity inequalities, a polyvocal media ecology also invites other ambivalent media practices. In an open media ecology, memetic collectives can turn their attention toward unsuspecting, unconsenting bystanders, and harness their creativity for mockery and abuse. An open media ecology allows rumors and falsities to spread as easily as fact, provided those rumors and falsities resonate; participants must therefore be vigilant about the information they engage and diligent in the information they circulate. An open media ecology is also open to very familiar commercial and political appropriation, to the point that it may not actually be very open at all. With all these pitfalls, it's worth asking whether memetic participation ends up being a net gain for public conversations.

The social worlds made through memetic media are indeed not utopias. Neither, however, are they wholly toxic. To this point, part II will assess the ambivalent identity politics evident in memetic media, as well as the ambivalent relationship between memetic media and existing cultural practices and culture industries. Chapter 6 in particular will address the murky connections between established media industries, established participatory practices, and memetic media. The ultimate outcome of this murky media ecology is an incomplete but promising complication of age-old limitations to public participation.

In all, part II assesses the interactional threads and massive cultural tapestries born out of memetic participation. In its focus on the antagonism, voice, and conversation emerging from the memetic lingua franca, it connects emerging technological affordances with established thought on public participation, complicating our understanding of each. In this way, it's ultimately an assessment of the promises and perils of polyvocality when vast strands of mediated expression intertwine.

4 Antagonism: Race, Gender, and Counterpublic Contestation

Violentacrez, Reddit, and the Counterpublic Sphere[1]

In October 2012, Reddit was embroiled in a controversy that spilled beyond its borders. Adrian Chen, a journalist for the news site *Gawker*, had just revealed the "offline" identity of Violentacrez, one of Reddit's "most reviled characters but also one if its most beloved users" (Chen 2012). Violentacrez, whom Chen calls "the biggest troll on the web," was responsible for subreddits like /r/Jailbait (sexualized photos of young girls) and /r/Creepshots (sexualized photos of women taken in public without their consent). Chen accuses Violentacrez of releasing onto Reddit "an unending fountain of racism, porn, gore, misogyny, incest, and exotic abominations yet unnamed." To Chen, Violentacrez "hacked" social dynamics with his posts, exploiting the Reddit collective for his own amusement.

The unmasking of Violentacrez (who turned out to be an office worker from Texas) inspired extensive debate about the nature and role of public conversation on Reddit. Some condemned Chen for "doxing" Violentacrez. The term—slang for *document* or *doc*—refers to gathering information about the offline identity of a participant in a pseudonymous online collective, documenting information about them that they would not want shared. According to these condemnations, the right to pseudonymity online is equivalent to America's First Amendment right to free expression, and this right should not be undermined, even when someone uses their pseudonymity irresponsibly. Others countered that those posting to /r/Creepshots hadn't bothered with obtaining consent from the women whose images they posted; why should these posters be afforded more control over their mediated presence than their victims?

Figure 4.1

A vertical comic satirizing misogynistic undertones on Reddit, signed by "2k" and sourced to Wopah.com. The alien puppet is Snoo, Reddit's corporate mascot. Collected in 2013.

The debate stirred. Prominent subreddits like /r/Politics responded to Chen's article by banning links to *Gawker*'s network of sites (including *Jezebel*, *Gizmodo*, and *Kotaku*). Parodying that suppression, the metacommentary subreddit /r/CircleJerk began allowing *only Gawker* network links. Accusations bounced back and forth between participants on /r/MensRights (labeled as "a place for those who wish to discuss men's rights and the ways said rights have been infringed on") and /r/ShitRedditSays (which catalogs and aggressively mocks "bigoted, creepy, misogynistic, transphobic, racist, homophobic" content from other subreddits). After much discussion—and little resolution—the controversy eventually quieted and the Violentacrez story retreated from prominence. Left in its wake are persistent questions about the identity antagonisms prominent in an ostensibly "participatory" media collective.

The collectivist vernacular assessed in the last chapter comes with the potential for exclusion and marginalization, as the practices of Violentacrez and others like him demonstrate. Mediated public participation certainly isn't evenly distributed, and this inequality manifests around age-old identity categories like class, race, gender, sexuality, and ability. In particular, race and gender antagonisms abound on participatory media collectives like 4chan, Reddit, Tumblr, and Imgur, as dominant perspectives sometimes silence and sometimes clash with underrepresented perspectives. Figure 4.1, a comic shared on the pro-feminist humor subreddit /r/TrollXChromosomes, addresses the inequalities persistent in participatory media. In the comic, Reddit's alien mascot (trademarked as "Snoo") is a puppet employed by a fedora-clad misogynist. The implication is that Reddit is a bait-and-switch, promising a prosocial agora before revealing the vitriolic hate underneath. The populism of the collective is really antagonistic mob rule.

Still, the existence of this comic, /r/TrollXChromosomes, and even all the intense contestation over the unmasking of Violentacrez are a sign of at least a degree of vibrant, open conversation. After all, Jürgen Habermas's ([1962] 1991) ideal "public sphere" is a conversational space, one that encourages equal discussion of public issues across different perspectives. The collectivism of memetic media doesn't provide that perfect egalitarian ideal any more than Habermas's Enlightenment coffeehouses did, but it may be a start. In the very least, memetic logics may facilitate the participation of *counterpublics*, who use participatory media to find internal support and to challenge dominant antagonisms. Lincoln Dahlberg speaks of the need for "multiple and vibrant" counterpublics within public conversations, which because they stand "in opposition to 'mainstream' or 'dominant' publics can open up deliberation" (2014, 32). The antagonisms perpetuated by Violentacrez are evidence that the collectivism of participatory media hasn't produced the perfect agora. However, the massive debate Chen's (2012) exposé inspired is evidence that counterpublics exist, and can be vocal in their contestation of dominant inequality. If bricolage, poaching, and vernacular creativity are being applied to these ends, then memetic media might be playing a part for public good.

This mediated counterpublic engagement doesn't always manifest as very polite conversation, and it certainly didn't during Reddit's Violentacrez debate. But, even impolite public contestation can serve important public ends. Under a counterpublic model of civic participation, adversarial agonism is a sign of a vibrant democracy, provided that it doesn't devolve into exclusionary antagonism. Chantal Mouffe (2005, 2009) defines *antagonism* as "relations between enemies," but sees a healthier agonism in "relations between adversaries." Counterpublic agonism is essential to public conversation, Mouffe claims, arguing that "conflict in liberal democratic societies cannot and should not be eradicated" (2009, 551). The collective reality of public life necessitates the existence of factionist discourse. For Mouffe, "when dealing with political identities, which are always collective identities, we are dealing with the creation of an 'us' that can only exist by its demarcation from a 'them'" (550). Agonistic conflict is the core of a counterpublic model of public conversation. Dahlberg says counterpublics succeed when marginalized groups can utilize "critical-reflexive spaces of communicative interaction" to "contest dominant discourses that frame hegemonic practice and meaning" (2011, 861).

When it comes to gender issues on Reddit, several subreddits have coalesced into counterpublic constellations, especially in the years since the Violentacrez debate. Many subreddits actively antagonize feminist perspectives and women in general. /r/MensRights—the "Men's Rights Activism" hub mentioned earlier—professes to be a site of measured social advocacy, but other subreddits make little effort to sugarcoat their misogyny, opting instead to engage in open, unapologetic bullying. /r/TumblrInAction mocks the left-leaning, feminist "social justice warriors" said to populate Tumblr. /r/SRSSucks critiques the vocal feminism of

/r/ShitRedditSays. /r/TheRedPill—reappropriating a metaphor for awakening from the 1999 film *The Matrix*—advocates for hegemonic masculinity and a return to traditional gender roles. /r/FatPeopleHate—until it was banned in June 2015—described itself as a space for "shitlords oppressing fatties" and housed photos of individuals deemed worthy of mockery due to their weight. The brunt of the focus was on judging females.

But there are also vibrant subreddits supporting feminist perspectives. /r/ShitRedditSays takes an aggressive approach to calling out sexism on other subreddits. /r/TwoXChromosomes—a sister subreddit to /r/TrollXChromosomes—houses "thoughtful, meaningful content" on gender issues "intended for women's perspectives." /r/TheBluePill—reappropriating the *Matrix* metaphor for staying sedated and tricked—mocks /r/TheRedPill's advocacy. /r/CreepyPMs catalogs unwelcome sexual advances sent through private messages on various sites, most particularly from harassing males.

The predominant discourse on Reddit favors a masculine stance. Still, the prevalence of counterpublic, pro-feminist subreddits means that participants can find support, even while the wider site tolerates the gender antagonisms that Violentacrez embodied most explicitly. Dahlberg writes that counterpublics function as "safe spaces" of "withdrawal and regroupment" that provide a needed respite from hegemonic pressures and antagonisms (2014, 33). Dahlberg's sentiment is echoed in figure 4.2, which collects stills from a pair of GIFs posted to the image-based /r/TrollXChromosomes after its sister subreddit /r/TwoXChromosomes became a "default" subreddit in March 2014. When subreddits are made default by Reddit staff, new users to the site are automatically subscribed to them. Their content is also more likely to reach /r/All, which catalogs the top posts from across Reddit. With default status comes new participants and new visibility, since posts now spread more easily across the broader Reddit collective. In the case of /r/TwoXChromosomes, default status also came with reports of increased combative misogyny. The poster of the GIFs in figure 4.2 compares the antagonistic tone of conversations on /r/TwoXChromosomes with the supportive tone of conversations on /r/TrollXChromosomes. /r/TrollXChromosomes was framed as a counterpublic safe space, a harbor from the broader antagonisms that had captured /r/TwoXChromosomes when it became a default subreddit.

Figure 4.2
Frames from two different GIFs posted to /r/TrollXChromosomes, which capture two scenes from the 1937 film *Snow White and the Seven Dwarves*. The left image represents conversations in /r/TwoXChromosomes after it became a default subreddit; the right image represents conversations in the smaller /r/TrollXChromosomes. Posted on July 2, 2014.

Addressing agonisms and antagonisms like those that have dominated Reddit since well before Violentacrez, this chapter assesses the public and counterpublic potential of memetic participation. Chapters 2 and 3 established the grammar and vernacular prevalent in memetic conversations. The rest of this chapter will focus on the identity antagonisms and exclusions that so often manifest through that grammar and vernacular. As we'll see, when it comes to core identity categories like gender and race, the collectivist conversations in memetic subcultures are not value-neutral. Instead, they disproportionately marginalize minority identities. Minorities are often marked objects of derision and contestation, while dominant identities and ideologies often pass invisible as the accepted, implicit norm.

As I'll argue in chapter 5, there's reason to be optimistic about the power of memetic media to facilitate voice in public conversations about significant social issues. This optimism, however, comes with a caveat. If participatory media systems do not provide spaces for the everyday expressions of marginalized identities, then the transformative civic potential of memetic media remains unfulfilled. Memetic subcultures, as we saw in chapter 3, are policed by collective conversation, and that policing is political. To further that point, the following section will outline the race and gender antagonisms long prevalent on participatory media, before turning to a discussion of the identity politics on sites like Reddit, 4chan, Tumblr, and Imgur. The section after will assess the nature of this counterpublic engagement in a media ecology wrought by ambiguous irony and ambivalent humor. The chapter will end with an articulation of the value of vibrant, agonistic counterpublic engagement, even in the midst of the tensions evident throughout this discussion.

The analysis in this chapter evaluates racism and misogyny akin to the antagonisms at the heart of the Violentacrez debate. To do so, it must engage with explicitly racist and misogynistic discourses. Such an endeavor is inherently fraught; even when done in the service of critical assessment, reproducing these discourses continues their circulation, and therefore may continue to normalize their antagonisms and marginalizations. My goal here is a frank discussion of the ambivalent potential of mediated public conversation, one that assesses problematic communication without glorifying it. Meaghan Morris ([1988] 2007) warns against a tendency within cultural studies to either cynically overemphasize the "banality and fatality" of everyday antagonisms on the one hand or to "ventriloquize the popular" until those antagonisms become detached and benign on the other. The arguments on race, gender, and participatory media herein could lean either way—either to undue hopelessness or to unmerited defense. Therefore, in this chapter, I will assess the exclusions and antagonisms prevalent in everyday texts and conversations, while attempting to avoid the trap of normalizing and sterilizing those exclusions and antagonisms. In so doing, I hope to highlight what Morris calls the "aggressive, critical voices embedded in the grit and hardness of day to day life" (119).

Identity Antagonisms and Counterpublic Contestation

Long before Violentacrez, participatory media collectives have been associated with the white, male, and privileged. In Lori Kendall's (2002) analysis of a multiuser domain called BlueSky MUD, she observes that whiteness is assumed unless explicitly stated otherwise, as is class cohesion. BlueSky participants argue that they are not racist, instead saying that they hardly notice whether anyone they talk to is "black." After all, how could they, in a "disembodied" online environment? But, Kendall points out, "in these statements, the ultimate test of whether race matters online is the ability of black people to pass unnoticed as black. This emphasizes the presumed desirability of hiding blackness and the assumption that people online are white" (210). It also boils race down to an easy binary: white or black, white or not white. This echoes the claims of Ronald Jackson, Chang Shin, and Keith Wilson (2000), who call whiteness a "constructed centrality." The problem is that "if whiteness is unmarked, it becomes distributed throughout social spaces and eventually functions as a 'universal insider'" (72). Because of this, "white people do not have to change who they are, how they talk, or how they behave. The talk and behavior of whites occupy a legitimized cultural space of social interaction, in which the identity of whiteness is acknowledged as normal and standard" (82).

Along with being white, participatory media collectives have also historically been seen as male-dominated. These spaces have been masculine, if uniquely masculine. As Charlie Gere explains, "the early hackers at MIT and Stanford established one of the central archetypes of computing subculture, which continues to this day, that of the intellectually advanced but socially and sexually awkward male, who is prepared to devote most of his time to an engagement with the possibilities of digital technology, to the exclusion of almost anything else" (2002, 132). Examining this alternative masculinity, Kendall (2002) analyzes how participants on the BlueSky MUD joke about their chances with women. She finds that "the joke is intended to be on the participants themselves, regarding their nonhegemonic masculinity, but women are the ultimate butts of the joke" (87). Women are still detached objects, even if they're unattainable ones. Even in these jokes—meant to be commentary on atypical masculinity—inequality is reproduced.

The problem is that masculine forms are—as with whiteness—the constructed centrality dominant in mediated collectives. Feminine forms are the marked minority and are essentialized in ways that masculinity isn't. Even if the participants on collectives like Reddit, 4chan, Tumblr, and Imgur do skew white and male (and the demographic makeup varies by site), the common practice we saw in chapter 3 of labeling memetic subcultural spaces as "The Internet" does the discursive work of covering up the multiplicity and diversity of mediated participation. "The Internet," of course, is an endless series of decentered conversational knots. The metonymy of substituting just a few sites and practices for "The Internet" as a whole reinforces a false standard of white masculinity. Such demarcations can lead to a hostile environment for marginalized groups, souring participatory potential. In this way, a cycle continues which normalizes partial forms of understanding. Engaging in participatory media collectives often means performing whiteness and masculinity, thus embedding the ideologies further. The rest of this section will assess the memetic dimensions of this white, male centrality, before turning to a discussion of its counterpublic contestation.

Identity Antagonisms and Memetic Media

Beyond facilitating an implicit white, male centrality, memetic media can also facilitate explicit identity antagonisms. In these contexts, race and gender minorities are vocally antagonized as a threatening outgroup. A few pockets of Reddit and 4chan have earned a particular reputation for explicit antagonisms of minority identities, but those boards are not the only participatory media collectives antagonizing identities outside of the white, male centrality. Systemic racism and misogyny manifest themselves across media, and the tone of these aggressions precludes the adversarial encounters that Mouffe (2005) finds so essential to counterpublic agonism. Instead, these antagonisms cast outsider identities as enemies, working to push those identities out of public conversations.

Memetic logics guide the flow of these identity antagonisms just as they guide the flow of other texts and ideas. If racism or sexism resonates collectively, then participants can choose to memetically spread dehumanization just as they spread "Sad Batman" or #TBT. In some ways, stereotypes lend themselves readily to this memetic spread. They're a fixed heuristic shortcut for assessing novel information, and they're an unfortunate cultural touchstone for making new quips, observations, and arguments. Figure 4.3 collects three images that perpetuate resonant racial stereotypes, memetically applying them to novel commentary. If racist cultural associations did not exist, these images would not resonate. But stereotypes linking African Americans to monkeys, Jewish people to greed, and Middle Eastern nations to backward savagery are persistent enough that even those who do not sympathize with their stereotypes understand these images. In this way, all three images perpetuate a meme of dehumanization. The easy

Figure 4.3
Three images antagonizing racial minorities. Top: photo-editing software is used to give American President Barack Obama and First Lady Michelle Obama simian features; bottom left: an image of an elephant seal adorned with Semitic stereotypes and the annotation "gief moniez plox," translating to "give money, please"; bottom right: a quotation from the 1977 film *Star Wars* is used to argue that the U.S. government orchestrated the 9/11 attacks on America's World Trade Center, since Middle Eastern "sand people" lack the sophistication needed to carry out the attack. Collected in 2011.

spread of that othering meme only tangles it more thoroughly into cultural conversations; hegemony is exacerbated with every reproduction of the ideas evident in figure 4.3. And in this process, minorities are consistently marked for their minority status in ways that whites are not. Racism, from this read, is itself memetic, and memetic logics underpin its prevalence.

This memetic racism furthers the white centrality long evident in participatory collectives. Minorities are treated as the other across participatory conversations, reifying the implicit understanding that the default participant in the collective is a white male. Figure 4.4 collects two images from a 4chan thread that explicitly hailed a white, male identity, asking that its participants "build your fort" to keep away a horde of minorities; contributors were challenged to fill in the space between the white "you" and the threatening mob with a creative illustration. The premise assumes that participants are white and male (a few images proposed using "white women" as bait to deflect the ravenous black males) and that interaction with the uniform minority masses is undesirable. In the thread, racism became a memetic game. Most solutions played on prevalent stereotypes about African Americans, as in figure 4.4's bottom image. These contributions were premised on racist essentialisms of a homogenized outgroup, and hailed their reader into the ingroup antagonizing that outgroup.

Memetic stereotypes expressing explicit misogyny are as persistent as racist ones. For instance, figure 4.5 collects three images furthering the "women belong in the kitchen" meme. They perpetuate gender roles that cast women as domestic caretakers, making them wards of the men who "provide" for them and—in the case of the bottom image in figure 4.5—punish them when they don't comply. Each image depends on a narrow cultural understanding of "a woman's place," and each image asserts male dominance as it recreates that narrative. The narrative hails women as the other, outsiders who are subject to male critique and control. The addressivity of these images implies that the reader is male, and content of the images furthers the hegemony of that implied reader.

This antagonizing addressivity is also employed in memetic subcultures during interactions with participants declaring themselves to be female. On 4chan's /b/ board—which Whitney Phillips calls "unquestionably androcentric" (2015b, 54)—participants are regularly othered as soon as they announce they're female. On /b/, it's common practice to tell a female participant posting her picture to also show "tits or GTFO" (get the fuck out) (see figure 4.6), a persistent memetic phrase that serves as shorthand for both sexual dominance and subcultural boundary policing. The oft-repeated warrant for the demand is that "there are no girls on the internet," so a female participant wanting to make her gender identity salient during a discussion must make it physically explicit. The demand overtly reifies the board as a male space. The assumption is that if you're specifically

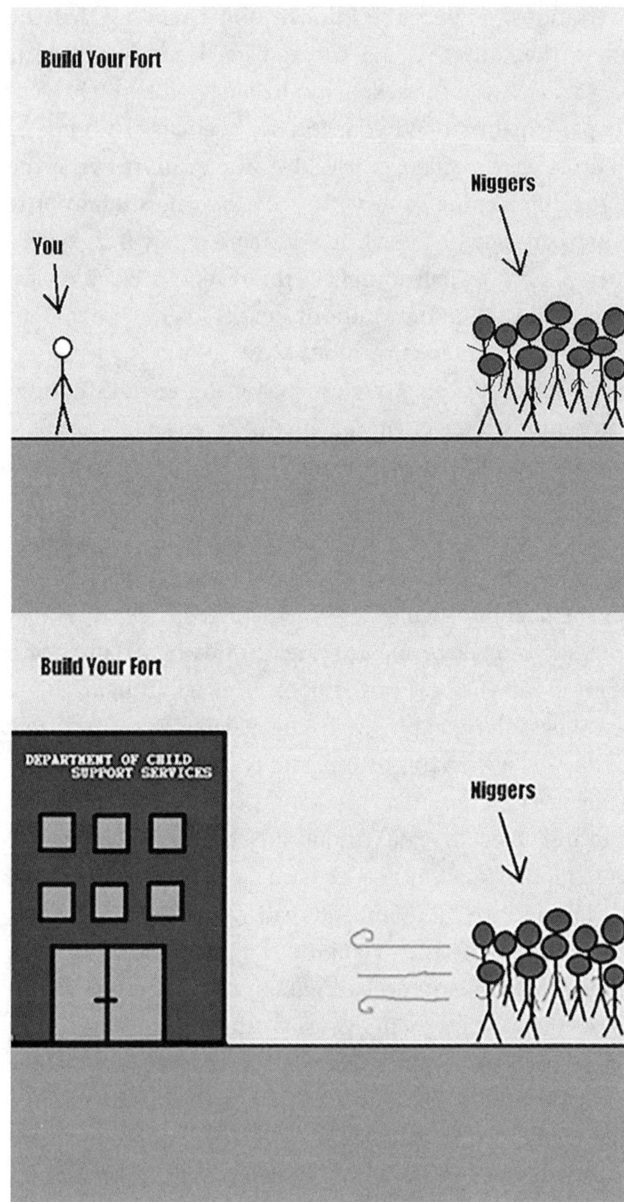

Figure 4.4
Two images from a thread on 4chan's /b/, in which participants annotated a template image with strategies for keeping away a threatening minority mob. The top image is the template; the bottom is an annotation employing a stereotype about African Americans. Posted on December 28, 2011.

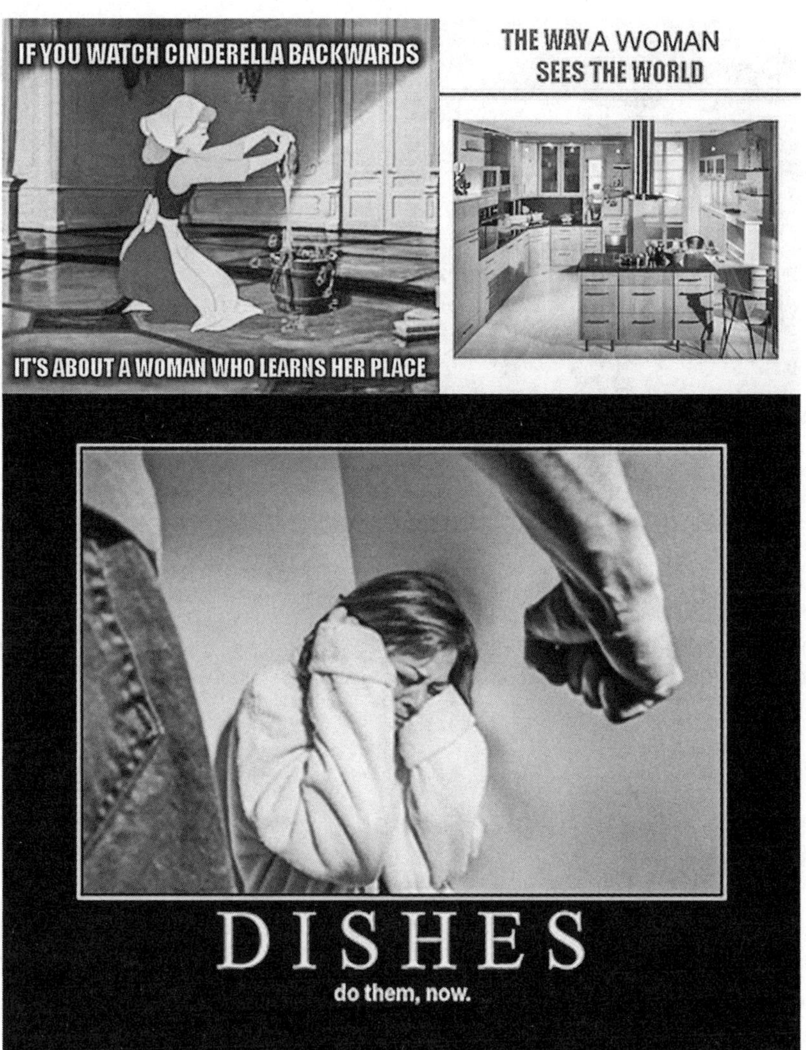

Figure 4.5

Three images antagonizing women. Top left: a sexist joke is applied to a scene from the 1950 Disney film *Cinderella*; top right: the image caption argues that a woman "sees the world" through the kitchen; bottom right: a stock photo portraying domestic violence is captioned with a command to do the dishes. Collected in 2011.

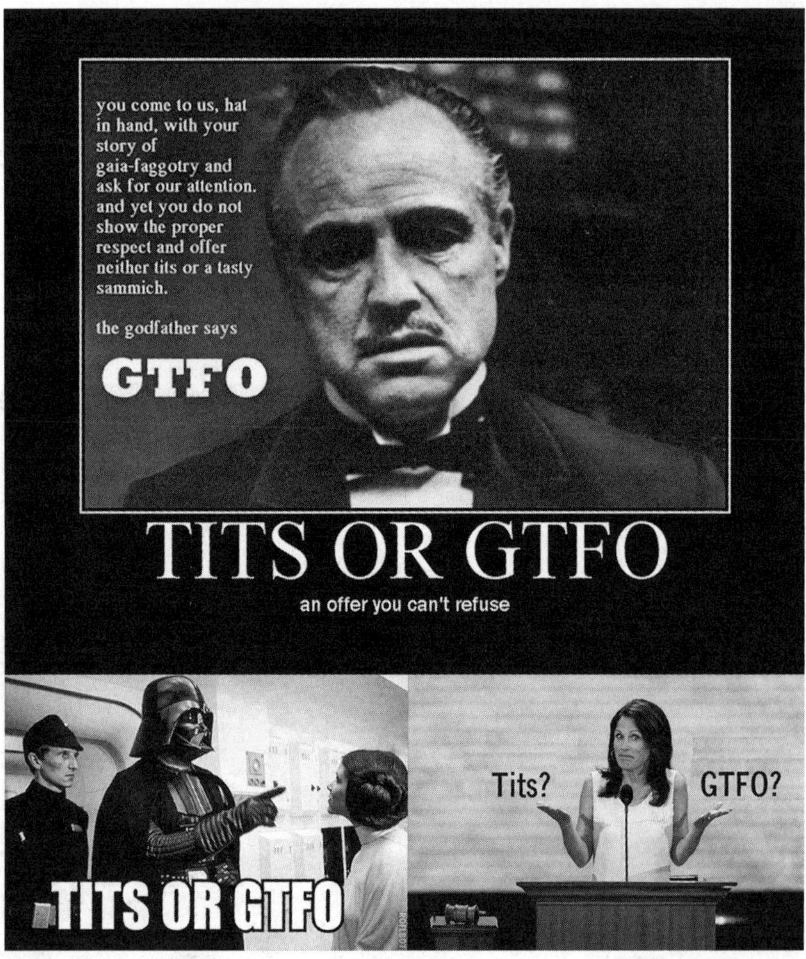

Figure 4.6

Three images demanding female participants show their breasts or leave the conversation ("Tits or Get the Fuck Out"). Top: a parody of Vito Corleone from the 1972 film *The Godfather*; bottom left: Darth Vader threatens Leia Organa in the 1977 film *Star Wars*; bottom right: American politician Michele Bachmann. Collected in 2011.

referring to your female gender (or "your story of gaia-faggotry" in figure 4.6's top image), then you must only be looking for validation (or coming to "ask for our attention").

For participants who "out" themselves as female, displaying their body is the "penance" demanded for the transgression of interrupting the board's normalized masculinity. The process is intentionally antagonistic and coercive. In one oft-shared screenshot, a 4chan participant claims that the only reason to come out as female is to "get your girl advantage back" through sexual manipulation (this statement displays a common tendency to deny male dominance by arguing that "pretty girls" get whatever they want). Therefore, according to the screenshot, displaying female anatomy "is, and should be, degrading for you, an admission that the only interesting thing about you is your naked body." This tendency echoes an established problem. In Kendall's analysis, "the gendered social context on BlueSky casts women as outsiders unless and until they prove themselves able to perform masculinities according to the social norms of the group. Women who are able to do so find acceptance within the group, but their acceptance reinscribes masculine norms, which continue to define women as assumed outsiders and outsiders, by definition, as not men" (2002, 100). On 4chan's /b/, marking gender means marking the "feminine" against a male centrality. To be an "anon" is to be discursively male. To mark one's self as "femanon" means reifying outsider status, linguistically modifying the root word and socially modifying the assumed population. Being female is a transgression punished by coercive and dehumanizing conversation, and a meme of dehumanization spreads.

Stereotypes are leveled against majority populations in memetic collectives as well. However, they still reify the white, male, and Western as the constructed center and implied ingroup of the collective. For instance, a few 4chan boards have conversations about differences between Europe and the United States (the two dominant population centers on the site). In these threads, both sides in the easy binary are critiqued by stereotype. Americans are critiqued for being unintelligent or overweight (a variation of figure 4.4 once asked participants to "Stop the Americans before they reach the McDonald's"); Europeans are critiqued for being weak or pretentious (they're often reminded of America's role in World War II or how many times Americans have walked on the moon). But even in these stereotypical critiques—ones that do feature disparaging images of people with light skin—geographic stereotypes are emphasized, not dehumanizing racial stereotypes. Even in their antagonisms, these conversations keep the white centrality intact. Portrayals of light-skinned people—even negative ones—label their subjects as "Americans," "Brits," "the French," etc., whereas portrayals of dark-skinned people label their subjects as "niggers," "spicks," or "towelheads." In these conversations, the race of minorities is explicitly emphasized, critiqued, and denigrated in ways that the race of whites is not. The idea that people of color are "others" is a resonant one, and it collectively spreads each time it's invoked.

And this white, male centrality still exists in less explicitly antagonistic texts. It can subtly spread even when the conversations don't seem hegemonic. For instance, several stock character macros employ race and gender stereotypes in their memetic premises, and do so in ways that reproduce the invisible insider status of white males (see figure 4.7). In the "Successful Black Man" macro, a racist premise is established in the top clause of the added text; the bottom clause inverts that premise to deliver the punch line. In the "High Expectations Asian Father" macro, stereotypes about domineering Asian parents are lampooned. In the "Sheltering Suburban Mom" macro, hypocritical class comfort is critiqued. Each of these macros exhibits complicated intersections of race, class, and gender. "Successful Black Man" explicitly connects a "black man" with deviance, even as it inverts stereotypes about that deviance. The name of the macro itself creates a racially presumptuous association. If a "black man" is successful, he requires a modifier in front of his name to set him apart from a "normal" black man. His "success"—often a white American version of success—is considered novel enough to premise a joke.

In "High Expectations Asian Father," racial minority and class comfort coexist in a single portrayal. The emphasis is predominantly on education—a class mobility concern—but race is the marked attributive category. Despite the class emphasis of the content, the title of the macro and the nonstandard English often applied as part of the joke foreground race rather than class. As in "Successful Black Man," race is the salient characteristic, even when the premise also relies on class to make its joke. In contrast, "Sheltering Suburban Mom"—with its white subject—isn't marked for race. Even as it critiques a political and social class sheltered from complex inequalities, the macro reinforces the invisibility of dominant whiteness.

Figure 4.7

Six examples of stock character macros emphasizing race, class, and gender identities. Left: two images of a stock character called "Successful Black Man"; center: two images of a stock character called "High Expectations Asian Father"; right: two images of a stock character called "Sheltering Suburban Mom." Collected in 2011.

Instead, "Sheltering Suburban Mom's" female gender is marked, while her race remains the unnamed centrality.

These stock character macros—which spread most prominently between 2010 and 2012 and are still sometimes used in 2015—are less explicitly antagonistic than the texts collected in figures 4.3–4.6. However, there's still danger in the spread of "acceptable" identity antagonisms. The fecundity and longevity of these characters—eclipsing the more explicit antagonisms seen in figures 4.3–4.6—speak to their memetic success, but also to the resonance of their encoded stereotypes. The fact that these images seem so "everyday" helps perpetuate their spread and in the process furthers their skewed representations. Morris writes that the banal intertwines "lordly pronouncement" and "mimetic popular performance" ([1988]

2007, 143); predominant inequalities are thus reinscribed in everyday interactions. Racism and misogyny are in this way memetic, serving as a fixed premise for novel contributions that reinforce the dominance of that premise. The participation structures imbedded in antagonistic texts and conversations work toward exclusion. These images reflect the dominant discourse—the banal standard—and in this way participation can shelter bigotry.

Identity Politics and Agonistic Counterpublics

But everyday texts can challenge these norms as well. Memetic participation can facilitate counterpublic contestation and the creation of counterpublic safe spaces for marginalized identities. In this way, participatory media can evidence vibrant agonism. This, to André Brock (2012), is one of the strengths of the African American perspectives and vernacular prevalent on Black Twitter. Brock argues that "white participation in online activities is rarely understood as constitutive of white identity; instead we are trained to understand their online activities as stuff 'people' do. Black Twitter confounded this ingrained understanding, even while using the same functions and apparatus, by making more apparent through external observation and internal interaction how culture shapes online discourses" (534). Black Twitter—by its mere existence—shines a light on the manufactured, invisible white centrality that dominates participatory media.

Likewise, Frances Shaw (2013)—interviewing feminist bloggers about identity antagonisms—outlines how those bloggers create safe spaces for pro-feminist discussion on their sites. Shaw asserts that "trolling and harassment are both silencing practices" (94) and that feminist bloggers demonstrate counterpublic agency when they vocalize their perspectives and resist silencing practices. These counterpublic spaces challenge hegemony by their very existence. For instance, the /r/TrollXChromosomes subscriber count as of mid 2015 proudly reads that there are "154,667 girls on the Internet." These are 154,667 counters to the silencing logic behind "tits or GTFO."

And those counterpublic spaces and perspectives do not exist on islands. Instead, they frequently engage with broader hegemonies, and do so by employing the same memetic logics that further the hegemonies they counter. Reddit housed not only Violentacrez and his vocal supporters, but his detractors as well. Whitney Phillips and I (forthcoming) discuss how Twitter's #YesAllWomen hashtag connected women sharing stories of discrimination and violence in the wake of a 2014 misogynistic shooting spree near the University of California, Santa Barbara. The hashtag was a reappropriation of the memetic phrase "Not all men," which men's rights activists had previously employed to argue against the idea that gender-based and sexual violence is a systemic, pervasive reality. Not all men may perpetrate gender violence, the #YesAllWomen hashtag granted, but, yes, all women have had to contend with some form of that violence.

Similar memetic contestation came with another hashtag in 2014, as citizens gathered in Ferguson, Missouri, to protest the shooting of an unarmed African American named Michael Brown by a Ferguson police officer. In memetic solidarity with protests over Brown's death—one more minority death at the hands of police in a long line of similar cases—participants on sites like Instagram and Twitter began posting pictures of themselves with their hands in the air, filed under the hashtag "#HandsUpDontShoot." The visual shorthand for surrender—something Brown was reportedly doing as he was killed[2]—was not limited to participatory media. Physical protestors, NFL players, and politicians threw up their hands during street marches, pregame entrances, and Congressional proceedings. In this way, #HandsUpDontShoot ties to other memetic protest iconography, like the Black Panther raised fist that spread in the 1960s and 1970s. #HandsUpDontShoot also connects to the broader #BlackLivesMatter hashtag, which has come to name a broader movement advocating against systemic racism. These rallying cries for racial justice carry counterpublic weight, connecting marginalized participants and bringing attention to their perspectives.

Such acts of counterpublic contestation are not, of course, without pushback from dominant ideologies interested in maintaining that dominance. #YesAllWomen was critiqued by #NotAllMen, which reproduced the memetic phrase as a hashtag response. #BlackLivesMatter was critiqued by #AllLivesMatter and #CopLivesMatter, which sought to rob momentum from the hashtag by appropriating it. But these critiques were met with critiques of their own, creating layered public conversation, even in the midst of dominant antagonism. Figure 4.8 collects panels from two different comics created for a tumblog entitled "Razzytastic." The first comic (the

Figure 4.8

Selected panels from a pair of vertical comics posted to http://Rasenth.tumblr.com. Left: a selection from a comic portraying how unequal gender norms hurt women; right: a selection from a follow-up comic portraying how unequal gender norms hurt men. Posted respectively on May 25, 2014, and June 15, 2014.

left side of figure 4.8)—focusing on how unequal gender norms hurt women—was created in response to the UC Santa Barbara killings. "I drew about my opinions on sexism to channel my rage," the creator wrote in the caption to the post, after providing some context on the killings. "I'm very happy the #YesAllWomen tag is going strong on U.S. Twitter right now." The second comic (on the right)—made a few weeks later—extended the first to show how patriarchy also negatively influences men. The comics resonated in the months after their creation, spreading across Tumblr and beyond.

As the comics spread, they inspired new counterpublic conversations. In March 2015, the second comic—the one focusing on how sexism hurts men—made it to the front page of Imgur as a response to alleged sexism on the site. While many supported the sentiment, some protested that only the male-centered iteration of the original comic was shared. "I need feminism because feminism is only taken seriously when it's explained how and why it affects and benefits men," one commenter posted below the image. "Hey! Here's the source and all the pieces in support of women you left out!" another commented, before linking to the first iteration of the comic. In its resonance, the comic series facilitated vocal engagement with dominant inequalities, both on Tumblr and on Imgur after.

Debates over identity essentialism occur on participatory media through memetic logics. As dominant discourses butt against dissenting perspectives, counterpublic contestation is in evidence. Factions can coalesce around these counterpublic perspectives. In one Reddit post, a participant created a chart that outlined perceived identity differences between Reddit and Tumblr. According to the chart, the Reddit collective saw itself as containing "thought-provoking and serious discussions about science, technology, politics, etc.," while they saw Tumblr as containing "social justice warriors and radical feminists." Conversely, the Tumblr collective saw itself as housing "important social commentary; pro-feminism, anti-racism, pro-LGBT, etc." while they saw Reddit as housing "sexist, racist man children." According to the chart, "anyone else" saw both Reddit and Tumblr as "privileged teenagers whining on the Internet about things they don't even understand." The shorthand, of course, is more social imaginary than factual reality, but it reflects the perception that public conversation on participatory media is not a monolith. It acknowledges that the public sphere has its counterpublics.

Despite evident antagonisms, Dahlberg argues that participatory media—at their best—allow marginalized people "to link up with other excluded voices in developing representative, strategically effective counter-discourses; and subsequently to contest the discursive boundaries of the mainstream public sphere" (2011, 861). Conversations about race and gender on participatory media are problematic because they predominantly further hegemonic antagonisms, just as they so often do beyond participatory media. However, by harnessing these same participatory media, minority perspectives have the power to antagonize in return. In this way, multiple participants can express multiple views, and counterpublics can vibrantly engage with identity issues. Still, we're left with questions on the nature and tone of this engagement, and whether it's closer to adversarial agonism or to the antagonism of enemies. Those questions will be the focus of the next section.

Agonism and the Ambivalence of Irony

The structures of participation on collectives like 4chan, Reddit, Tumblr, and Imgur complicate the agonistic dimensions of public conversation. While agonism embraces adversarial debate, the debates in memetic collectives often come with ambiguities in their tone and tenor, which might mute their vibrancy. For example, the subcultural trolls that Phillips (2015b) studied employ an "adversarial method" of public argument that doesn't seem too far from agonistic engagement. However, this method of engagement invokes a cold and brutal brand of male-gendered "rationality" over what trolls critique as a soft and feminine "emotionalism." It is adversarial engagement that is encoded with marginalizing values, ones that denigrate any signs of "sadness, frustration, or distress" (125) in public conversation. Adversarial or not, this method favors an antagonistic engagement.

Further, while agonistic models assume that counterpublics are invested in their arguments and the identity politics they're engaging, ironic, distanced critique often resonates in participatory media conversations. The shorthand for this distanced, ironic register is *lulz*, from a corruption of the slang acronym *lol* (laughing out loud). Phillips describes the term as labeling an "unsympathetic, ambiguous laughter" (24). As a concept and mode of engagement, lulz are popular both within subcultural trolling circles and more broadly across participatory collectives. This amusement at others' distress shades counterpublic contestation on participatory media. It can be employed both to commit great identity antagonisms and to defend those antagonisms as "just joking." Phillips says that "I did it for the lulz" is a "catchall excuse, explanation, and punch line" (27) for trolling behaviors, one revealing the emotional distance facilitated by such a framing. The rest of this section will assess the implications of similar forms of ironic, adversarial counterpublic contestation that resonates in memetic media collectives.

Identity Antagonism and Lulz

We've already seen how playful vernacular creativity can be employed to further antagonistic stereotypes. The images in figures 4.3–4.7 all depend on marginalization to make their jokes. This constructed centrality is why ironic resonance can reinforce oppressive ideologies and repress minority voice. Lisa Nakamura (2014) makes similar claims about "scambaiting" photographs, a memetic genre born from tricking African "scammers." Scambaiters play along with Africans running phishing scams, often promising to send along financial information after their targets "prove themselves" by dressing oddly, performing bizarre actions, or even tattooing themselves. The game is to collect photo proof of a target doing something as embarrassing as possible and then to share that photo with other scambaiters. To Nakamura, even if scambaiting is ostensibly about "punishing" scam artists, "this 'fun' occurs at the expense of people whose racial and ethnic identities as well as their intention to connect with better-resourced Internet users ... is made violently visible" (261). It is adversarial engagement premised on antagonistic othering.

Playful practices can target vocal counterpublics as well, in attempts to silence and denigrate pushback. Lulz are employed to reduce counterarguments to stereotype. Figure 4.9 collects four frames from a GIF that reappropriates a scene from the 2012 film *The Avengers* in order to mock the "social justice warriors" who advocate for feminist issues. By denigrating the individuals expressing these concerns, and by turning their counterpublic contestations into blanket caricature (in this case, being easily "offended" and "triggered," and angrily "smashing the patriarchy"), the GIF reproduces memetic practices used to marginalize feminist perspectives. Fitting with Phillips's (2015b) observations about the adversarial antagonisms of subcultural trolls, these denigrations critique feminist arguments for being weak and soft compared to the cold rationality of "healthy" public conversation.

But humor, irony, and play can counter dominant antagonisms, even if they also predominantly reinforce those antagonisms.[3] Shaw (2013) outlines tactics "from playful to serious" employed by feminist bloggers to counter harassment (one blogger she interviews changes the spelling of "nasty comments" to make the poster seem less intelligent). Through their use of resonant humor and irony, texts countering racism and misogyny can spread via the same multimodal reappropriations that spread more dominant antagonism. Several GIF sets shared on Tumblr reproduce content from shows like *Last Week Tonight with John Oliver*, *Key & Peele*, and *RuPaul's Drag Race*, all of which have progressive stances or foreground

Figure 4.9
Four frames of a GIF reappropriating a scene from the 2012 film *The Avengers*. In the film, Bruce Banner tells Captain America that his secret for being able to transform into the monstrous Hulk is that he's "always angry." He then turns into the Hulk and smashes an alien invader. In the GIF, Banner is "always offended" instead of "always angry," he is "triggered" instead of hulking out, and he smashes "the patriarchy" instead of an alien. Collected in 2015.

marginalized identities. As an example, figure 4.10 collects four frames from a GIF set reproducing a skit from a 2015 episode of *Inside Amy Schumer*. The skit is a faux birth control ad satirizing reactionary attitudes toward women's sexuality. Humor is a resonate emotion for memetic texts, and that humor can carry both antagonism and its counter.

Sometimes counterpublic contestations explicitly employ the aggressive adversarial humor that characterizes lulz and trolling in order to push against the white, male centrality prevalent in participatory media collectives. On Reddit, /r/ShitRedditSays has long had a reputation for "ruining" Reddit's agora by pointing out its antagonistic white, male centrality. Despite its small subscriber count—only around 68,000 as of mid 2015—its participants have gained notoriety for their brash mockery of mainline Reddit sensibilities and their playfully adamant embrace of the denigrated "social justice warrior" label. The broader Reddit population often accuses

Figure 4.10
Four frames from a GIF set transcribing a skit from a 2015 episode of *Inside Amy Schumer*, satirizing restrictions on access to birth control. Collected in 2015.

/r/ShitRedditSays participants of contributing nothing to productive public conversation, claiming they're as hegemonic as the patriarchal forces they supposedly resist. Figure 4.11—housed at the bottom of the /r/ShitRedditSays front page—might satirize the subreddit's reputation for antagonistic engagement, might flaunt it, or might do both at once. The comic portrays innocent redditors being assaulted by /r/ShitRedditSays members; Reddit's discussions of "funny joeks, post-*ism, logic, reason, and Ron Paul" are all wrecked by flying sex toys.

/r/ShitRedditSays is certainly not an example of narrowly "reasonable" or "polite" public conversation. However, agonistic contestation doesn't always have to be narrowly "reasonable" or "polite." Zizi Papacharissi (2004)—examining political discussion in newsgroup forums—argues that there's a difference between being civil and being polite. Civil conversation can be very *im*polite, but still enrich public deliberation. However, to be civil, counterpublic critique must not include abuse by dominant groups or repression of minority perspectives. To Mouffe (2005), agonism is achieved by embracing adversarial pluralism, acknowledging that disparate perspectives have an equal right to clash. Emphasizing this adversarial pluralism,

Figure 4.11
An image housed at the bottom of the /r/ShitRedditSays front page. Redditors are bombarded with dildos by /r/ShitRedditSays participants, who steal their "internet points" (a reference to Reddit's "Karma" system for tracking how popular posts and comments are). Reddit's mascot, Snoo, weeps over the death of free speech. Collected in 2012.

Adrienne Massanari (2015) contends that agonistic "meta commentary" subreddits like /r/ShitRedditSays serve an essential public function through their parody and critique. Silencing practices are the real threat to agonistic pluralism, not impolite barbs. /r/ShitRedditSays counters silence, and in this way has counterpublic value.

But /r/ShitRedditSays might also be considered counterproductive to agonistic public conversation because it disregards open public debate, implying that it also denies the clash of perspectives central to agonism. /r/ShitRedditSays rules explicitly forbid participants from arguing that a post made to the subreddit is inoffensive or not worthy of its attention. The moderator introducing the rule change expressed frustration because so many comments questioned why something belonged in /r/ShitRedditSays, and insisted that "we are not a debate club." The prevalent perspective on /r/ShitRedditSays is that the subreddit does not exist to explain to nonparticipants why Reddit's hegemonic discourse is problematic. Instead, /r/ShitRedditSays is meant to be a counterpublic space to commiserate about the hegemony that flares up on the mainline site whenever a pro-feminist perspective is espoused. The debate can happen in that mainline space; /r/ShitRedditSays is a counterpublic backstage.

Perhaps /r/ShitRedditSays isn't a space for rational debate, but it is a space for participants to employ criticism, irony, and play to counter the dominant Reddit discourses. Peter Dahlgren sees value in these agonistic practices, arguing that "adherence to what we might characterize as a 'straightjacket' of rational speech for the civic subject ... undermines the potential richness and vibrancy of political discussion in favor of an illusory ideal, and is likely to deflect civic engagement rather than enhance it" (2013, 75). Memetic play can be politically resonant creative expression. For instance, when Erik Martin, then Reddit's general manager, became a candidate for *Time*'s "*Time* 100 Poll" in 2012 (*Time* Staff 2012), participants on /r/ShitRedditSays took the photo accompanying the nomination and added multiple layers of annotation to reflect a sentiment they found appropriate for the site (see figure 4.12).

Figure 4.12
Three iterations of a photo of Reddit's former general manager Erik Martin. Left: an image taken from Reddit content for a *Time* magazine profile; center: a graphic manipulation mocking Martin; right: a macro created in the wake of the Violentacrez debate. Collected in 2012.

Morris ([1988] 2007), borrowing from Michel de Certeau (1984), labels such reappropriations of banal hegemonies "the arts of making do." Working within the lingua franca that predominates mainline Reddit, participants on /r/ShitRedditSays make do with what they have, critiquing collective memetic norms from within. Humor and play can be tools for pluralistic clash and counterpublic recuperation, as much as they can be tools for exclusionary hegemony.

Poe's Law and Ambivalent Irony

But lulz and trolls and the resonance of distanced, mean-spirited humor come with implications for agonistic pluralism. *Troll* itself is an ambiguous term, and this ambiguity is why Chen's (2012) proclamation that Violentacrez was "the biggest troll on the web" could be problematic. As *BoingBoing*'s Xeni Jardin (2012) argues, "posting disgusting sexist shit on the Internet does not make you a troll if you're playing to the home audience: if the people who view that content enjoy it and want more, it isn't trolling." In the case of Violentacrez, the "troll" moniker might have worked to hide very earnest antagonism under a cloak of irony. For these reasons, Phillips advocates against the term's blanket popularity, saying that she prefers "to describe online antagonism in terms of the impact it has on its targets. So, if someone is engaging in violently misogynistic behavior, I call them a violent misogynist, as 'troll' implies a level of playfulness that tends to minimize their antagonistic behaviors" (2015a). Likewise, Christina Xu worries about conflating "people who are actually being aggressive and threatening online with people who are being playful online" (in Hwang and Xu 2014, 386). The space between those two registers—the narrow spectrum between play and hate—can hide multiple silencing antagonisms, even if it can also facilitate healthy adversarial engagement. In that space is the thin line between ironic expression and earnest exclusion. Blurs around that line haunt the agonistic potential of participatory media.

The difficulty in separating "ironic" antagonism from "earnest" antagonism is prevalent enough that it comes with a name in memetic subcultures: Poe's Law. According to Know Your Meme, Poe's Law "is an Internet axiom which states that it is difficult to distinguish extremism from satire of extremism in online discussions unless the author clearly indicates his/her intent" ("Poe's Law" undated). It was named for a 2005 forum thread on Creationism where a poster going by "Poe" declared that "without a winking smiley or other blatant display of humor, it is utterly impossible to parody a Creationist in such a way that someone won't mistake for the genuine article." The term has become a way for participants to express confusion or skepticism over seemingly antagonistic content. Poe's Law indicates the difficulty in parsing out "ironic" and "legitimate" identity antagonism when lulz resonate so powerfully. Know Your Meme also highlights a variation of Poe's Law, which combines it with Arthur C. Clarke's famous aphorism that "any sufficiently advanced technology is indistinguishable from magic"; Clark-Poe's Law tells us that "any sufficiently advanced troll is indistinguishable from a genuine kook."

4chan's /b/ addresses that tension head on; it comes with a boilerplate warning at the top of its page, reminding participants that the board is subject to Poe's Law. The warning proclaims that "the stories and information posted here are artistic works of fiction and falsehood. Only a fool would take anything posted here as fact." In early 2013, a participant on the subreddit dedicated to collecting 4chan content, /r/4chan, shared the suicide note a self-described pilot had posted to /b/. The pilot promised that the suicide would come as a plane crash during a full flight. Participants in the thread wondered if the crash would really occur. When one poster cited the boilerplate warning as evidence the suicide clearly wouldn't happen, another responded by asking, "you don't seriously believe that cop-out disclaimer is always true, do you?" The discussion turned to the difficulties in parsing out the Poe's Law "bullshit" on 4chan.

/r/ShitRedditSays' status as a "troll" subreddit inspires similar debate. In a thread on the subreddit /r/BestOf accusing /r/ShitRedditSays of negatively influencing Reddit, one poster commented that "my take is that SRS is full of people who think they're complete trolls, but don't understand that it doesn't count as trolling if you actually believe the things you say." The next poster speculated that participants on /r/ShitRedditSays really didn't believe anything they posted, and "if that's true, they may well be some of the best trolls Reddit's seen." A third exhibited further confusion: "I don't think even THEY know any more if they're joking or they're not." No matter the message, participants in memetic collectives live in the shadow of Poe's Law.

In Shifman's (2014) terms, Poe's Law is born from a source text's ambiguous stance. Seemingly racist content may be an attempt to "key" satire through a hyperbolic, antagonistic tone, but may also reinforce unequal participation structures while doing so. The banal can carry both simultaneously. When content and form are so grounded in ironic critique, communicative function becomes ambiguous. Shaw echoes this ambiguity in her analysis of harassment on feminist blogs, commenting that some antagonistic participants "couch their comments in civility while simultaneously derailing discussion. For example, a concern troll couches his or her attempts to derail discussion in terms of concern, thereby maintaining 'civility' while also engaging in trolling behavior" (2013, 102). Shaw gives the example of concern trolls antagonizing bloggers in the fat-acceptance community by posting their ridicule under the guise of "health concerns." Though some trolls are more obvious than others, Poe's Law exists because of the blur between ironic creative play and earnest hateful ideology in participatory media collectives.

Sometimes the extent of this blur—and which side of the irony/earnestness spectrum a text represents—is a judgment call. Memetic texts might resonate to a thousand different participants in a thousand different ways. An ambiguous stance toward identity antagonisms means an ambiguous relationship to inequality. For instance, the "Successful Black Man" image macro (figure 4.7) is steeped in stereotype and could therefore further ingrain inegalitarian perspectives. Familiarity with racist tropes is necessary to get the joke. On the other hand, the macro—in its play on stereotypes—might undermine these stereotypes. The turn of phrase that comes with the second clause's punch line lampoons readers for unproblematically accepting negative representations. The humorous incongruity "works" because dominant cultural assumptions lead readers astray. Stereotypes ensure that the prosocial behavior in the second clause creates a clash. That clash works as what Christian Burgers, Margot van Mulken, and Peter Jan Schellens (2012) label an "irony marker," a "meta-communicative clue" that helps readers understand an utterance as ironic. The punch line functions as a "reversal of valence between the literal and intended meaning" (292) of the setup. Readers are taken in by the first clause in the macro, and the bait-and-switch in the second clause reverses a dominant discourse. The mischief might remind us—in a small way—to not take all stereotypes at face value. It might also perpetuate the stereotypes it playfully employs.

Common memetic phrases also demonstrate this ambivalent irony. Pejorative labels for race and gender minorities are frequent in memetic subcultures, often with ambivalent intent (see figure 4.13). On 4chan,

Figure 4.13

Six memetic images employing race and gender epithets, reappropriating (left to right, top to bottom): Catholic Pope John Paul II, Tommy and Chuckie from the 1990s show *The Rugrats*, American President Barack Obama, poet and playwright William Shakespeare, NBA star Yao Ming, and a 1788 painting by Jacques-Louis David entitled *Portrait of Antoine-Laurent Lavoisier and His Wife*. Collected in 2011.

"nigga"—with the soft *a* found in African American vernacular—is often employed in conversations and reaction shots. It might be a nod to the "coolness" of African American vernacular; common memetic phrases like "haters gonna hate," "u mad," and "bae" also find their origins in minority terminology. However—as with the "Medieval Reactions" Twitter account we saw in figure 3.11—such appropriations could also further demarcate African Americans from "normal" participants by distinguishing African American vernacular from "normal" speech. The images employing "nigga" in figure 4.13 also apply the slang to unlikely sources, underscoring an ironic, othering use.

And gendered language can marginalize minority gender and sexual identities just as racial language can marginalize racial minorities. As evidenced in figure 4.13, on 4chan "bitch" is at times an apparently neutral label for a female (as in the William Shakespeare image); at times labels any denigrated other, regardless of gender (as in the Yao Ming image); and at times specifically denigrates a female (as in Jacques-Louis David's painting). Racist and sexist language may spread "playfully," but stereotypes also spread with that play. Pejorative terms—even ironically used—are vehicles perpetuating a history of antagonism and dehumanization.

As we've seen, on many 4chan boards, racism and sexism are memetic ideas themselves. They're a fixed premise by which participants creatively display novel expressions. Invoking "Tits or GTFO" at a humorously appropriate—or, rather, inappropriate—time is a way to further a subculturally accepted in-joke and demonstrate subcultural capital. It's a way to speak in the hegemonic lingua franca. The "build your fort" images highlighted in figure 4.4 use a racist premise to encourage vernacular creativity, and in doing so inspire jokes based on old stereotypes and inequalities. But the consensus "winner" of the "build your fort" thread (figure 4.14) did not explicitly rely on stereotypes to keep away the minority hordes. Instead, it made its joke by presenting the most complex fort possible, one capable of protecting against any invading threat. Figure 4.14 draws its humor not through narrowly racist associations, but by positing the idea that a few stick-figure African Americans deserve this level of extensive defense. The humor is the overkill. In this way, figure 4.14 reinforces oppressive ideologies on a scale even grander than the easier stereotypes. Posters on many 4chan boards operate in an environment where antagonistic stereotypes are an unchallenged assumption. Even in ironic play, the white, male centrality maintains its prominence.

"Lulz" are prevalent enough to blanket a considerable amount of identity antagonism. The racist and sexist texts displayed in this chapter could be the expressions of genuine racists and sexists; they might also be downplayed as a troll on politically correct sensibilities. The line between playful irony, satire, and parody and earnest racist exclusion is a blurry one. This blurriness complicates attempts to gauge the intent of participants who memetically invoke identity antagonisms. The resonance of irony and play in memetic participation means that Poe's Law looms large, and both hegemonic marginalization and agonistic counterpublic contestation exist in its shadow.

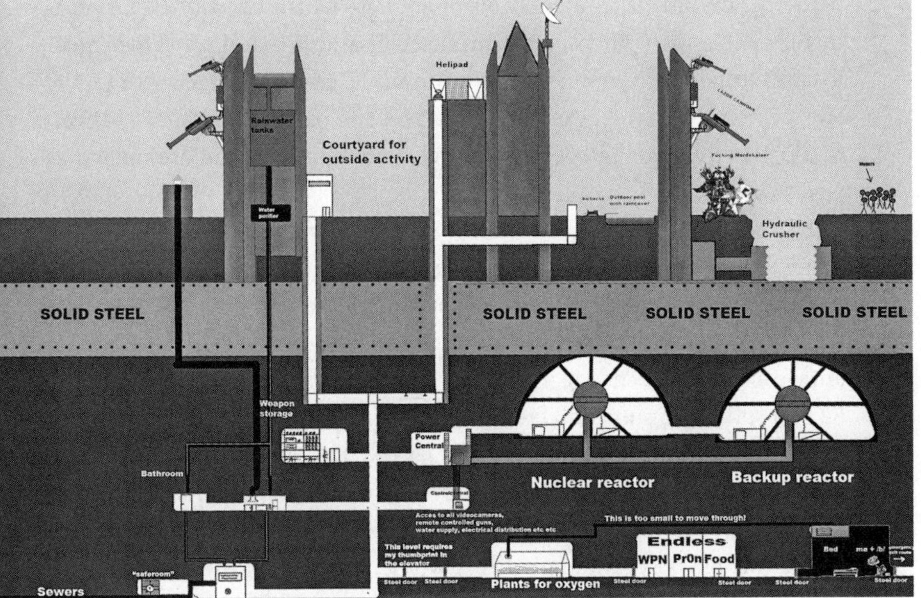

Figure 4.14
A remix on the "build your fort" premise established in figure 4.4's template image. For this poster, the minority threat is sufficient enough to merit multiple towers, lasers, underground bunkers, and solid steel reinforcement. Posted on December 28, 2011.

Phillips (2015b) encounters this same ambiguity when assessing the racist talk of the trolls she studied. That talk, she says, does not prove that "trolls are themselves racist. That particular point is unverifiable, and therefore moot" (96). However, Phillips points out that we can verify "the observable fact that trolls revel in explicitly and unapologetically racist language" (96). Practices that silence or dehumanize minority perspectives—playful or not, ironic or not—perpetuate a white, male centrality in participatory media. Counterpublic contestation comes when these same strategies are turned on their head.

On Countertrolls and Counterpublics

By the standards of agonistic pluralism, memetic subcultures comprise a mixed media ecology. The multimodal grammar that facilitates broad participation also facilitates exclusionary vernacular. Identity exclusion is incompatible with vibrant agonism. Conversations that undermine equality and justice—exception or norm, ironic or earnest—undermine public engagement. The worst examples of racism and sexism in memetic subcultural collectives are antagonistic rather than agonistic, and are uncivil as well as impolite.

Further, antagonism and incivility are still antagonism and incivility when they're presented in a playful register. An ironic stance can perpetuate inequality just as much as earnest racism and sexism can. /r/Creepshots was shut down with Chen's Violentacrez exposé in October 2012, but its antagonisms have not gone away. Instead, /r/CandidFashionPolice, a 52,000-subscriber subreddit created in November 2012, posts the same content as /r/Creepshots and is still active as of 2015. However the creepshots are now veneered with titles like "gurl those are some ugly shorts" and "dayuum, look at dat fabulous dress." The subreddit is labeled as a forum where "people post candid photos of women and then we judge their fashion choices similar to TLC's *What Not to Wear* and E!'s *Fashion Police*."

Reddit's Violentacrez cycle repeated in June 2015, when /r/FatPeopleHate was banned. The ban came shortly after Imgur began removing images linking to /r/FatPeopleHate. The subreddit responded by calling out and threatening Imgur staff, and was subsequently banned. After Reddit's ban, a new subreddit, /r/FatPersonHate, was created and reached 22,000 subscribers within three hours. The subreddit described itself as "a civil place to make fun of fatties," and in its few short hours was full of old content from /r/FatPeopleHate, augmented by critiques of Reddit's practices, and renewed threats to Reddit and Imgur staff. It too was quickly banned, but its marginalizations persist on other subreddits and other sites. These ceaseless antagonisms are serious objectifications and dehumanizations, even when presented with an ironic stance. "Only joking" can be used to whitewash exclusion and to silence countering perspectives, online or off. The memetic spread of partial representations—and the apparent authorlessness of those partial representations—perpetuates inequality. It amplifies the invisible, constructed centrality of dominant identities.

But the resonance of the ironic frame also leads to a lingua franca of contestation. It's a lingua franca that can both broaden and limit voice, even if hegemonic antagonisms seem embedded in its very tone. Phillips grapples with the prospect that the misogynistic "adversarial method" evident in trolling subcultures might be put to use for pro-feminist contestation, explaining, "I too am reluctant to wholeheartedly claim for the feminist cause a rhetorical mode so thoroughly steeped in male domination. On the other hand, if the goal is to dismantle patriarchal structures, and if feminist trolling helps accomplish those ends, then are the means, however problematic, retroactively justified?" (2015b, 168). If they are justified, then counterpublic contestation—even the kind evident on /r/ShitRedditSays—has value when it shakes members of the public into interest, awareness, and engagement over the identity politics significant to everyday life. If ironic, playful, critical contestation ever has agonistic value, it's when that irony, play, and critique couple with pluralistic voice.

Publics need counterpublics; trolls need countertrolls. Participants on /r/MensRights and /r/ShitRedditSays might each label themselves as "counter" and their opponents as "hegemony," but arguments are sharpened and refined when the perspectives of different pluralistic factions can clash. Pluralistic clash is invaluable, given that counterpublics can also create their own backstage safe spaces for recuperation. Even if the relations are between participants who are enemies more than adversaries, contestation is more vibrant than repression; exclusion is always more antagonistic than voice. Thus the danger isn't narrowly "trolling" or "lulz" or impoliteness or irony. The danger is when any of those communicative norms further silence marginalized perspectives.

The next chapter will assesses the potential of memetic media for vibrant public voice, even in the midst of these ambivalent everyday antagonisms. As we'll see, memetic conversations facilitate old inequalities. Those inequalities spread with collective exclusion and antagonism. However, populism can be a widely employed tool. As much as memetic media facilitate old inequalities, they can spark counterpublic voice. That voice—and how it pairs with the dominant antagonisms highlighted here—will be the focus of chapter 5.

5 Voice: Pop and Populism in Public Commentary

Participation and the Occupation[1]

On September 17, 2011, approximately 1,000 protestors descended on New York City's Zuccotti Park, located at the mouth of the famous financial center known as Wall Street. Occupy Wall Street (OWS) was initiated by activists associated with the anticonsumerist organization and "culture-jamming headquarters" Adbusters. The plan was to stage a long-term protest of prevalent social and economic injustices such as income inequality, corporate influence on politics, and unregulated business practices. A contingent of protestors stayed in Zuccotti Park full time, sleeping, eating, meeting, marching, and organizing in order to draw consistent attention to the financial practices that protestors argued were detrimental to social welfare and individual prosperity.

The protest initially garnered little traditional media attention, even though participants on sites like Twitter, Tumblr, YouTube, and Reddit were actively employing memetic logics to disseminate OWS messaging. In the days, weeks, and months that followed, however, media coverage of the protests grew. This was concurrent with an increase in protestors, demonstrations, participating cities (American and international), arrests, and charges of police brutality. While police disbanded the initial occupation of Zuccotti Park on November 15, 2011, OWS has lived on in altered forms across the globe; so has its broader influence on political discourse. "Most significantly," Kevin DeLuca, Shawn Lawson, and Ye Sun note, "in a mere few weeks, OWS changed the national conversation despite the initial neglect and dismissive framing by traditional mass media organizations" (2012, 484). This influence on public conversation may well be the legacy of OWS, and that legacy is largely dependent on memetic media.[2] In the case of OWS, memetic media were vehicles for public voice.

Figure 5.1
An Adbusters OWS promotional poster, depicting a ballerina dancing atop Wall Street's Charging Bull statue. Collected in 2011.

From the beginning of its public-facing campaign, OWS messaging was in the hands of public participants. Even if Adbusters branding, messaging, and influence were evident in the movement, memetic logics allowed the OWS message to spiral out from its Adbusters origins. As OWS messaging resonated in the fall of 2011, dismissiveness by traditional media outlets gave way to a groundswell of memetic voice. So intertwined was OWS with memetic logics that Nathan Schneider, writing for the *Nation*, calls the movement as a whole "the Occupy Wall Street meme" (2013). During the height of the protests, key pieces of OWS content—like the flagship Adbusters poster of a ballerina dancing atop Wall Street's Charging Bull statue (figure 5.1)—spread through participatory media. In the process, the same logics foundational to the Kanye memes discussed in chapter 1 and the identity antagonisms examined in chapter 4 were employed for explicitly political commentary. The images in figures 5.1 and 5.2—shared from OWS media accounts in the fall of 2011—would not exist without a media system premised on memetic logics. They're individual strands contributing to a vast tapestry of political participation.

The images in figures 5.1 and 5.2 employ multiple modes of communication to make their argument. They're simultaneously visual and textual, and point to hypertextual communication (hashtags, Google searches) even though they're static themselves. They're bricolage; they reappropriate found material to craft their message. Fixed icons—like the iconic Charging Bull statue—are poached in service of novel critique. Pop cultural reappropriation is central to the resonance of these images. The bottom right image in figure 5.2, for instance, plays with a popular lyric from hip-hop artist Jay-Z. "I got 99 problems, but a bitch ain't one" becomes "They have 99 problems when we become one," and the familiar cadence of the song's hook is put to civic use. OWS supporters—keeping with the populist aims of the movement—pulled from popular icons and popular tropes to make their arguments. The images hail their readers as common citizens, casting them against powerful capitalist forces. As examples like these spread through participatory media, OWS messaging intertwined with the banal, the popular, and the populist.

In this way, OWS took full advantage of the collectivist affordances of memetic media. Images like those pictured here spread freely among the same networks and collectives housing the everyday expressions, commentary, and even antagonisms we've seen in previous chapters. The relative

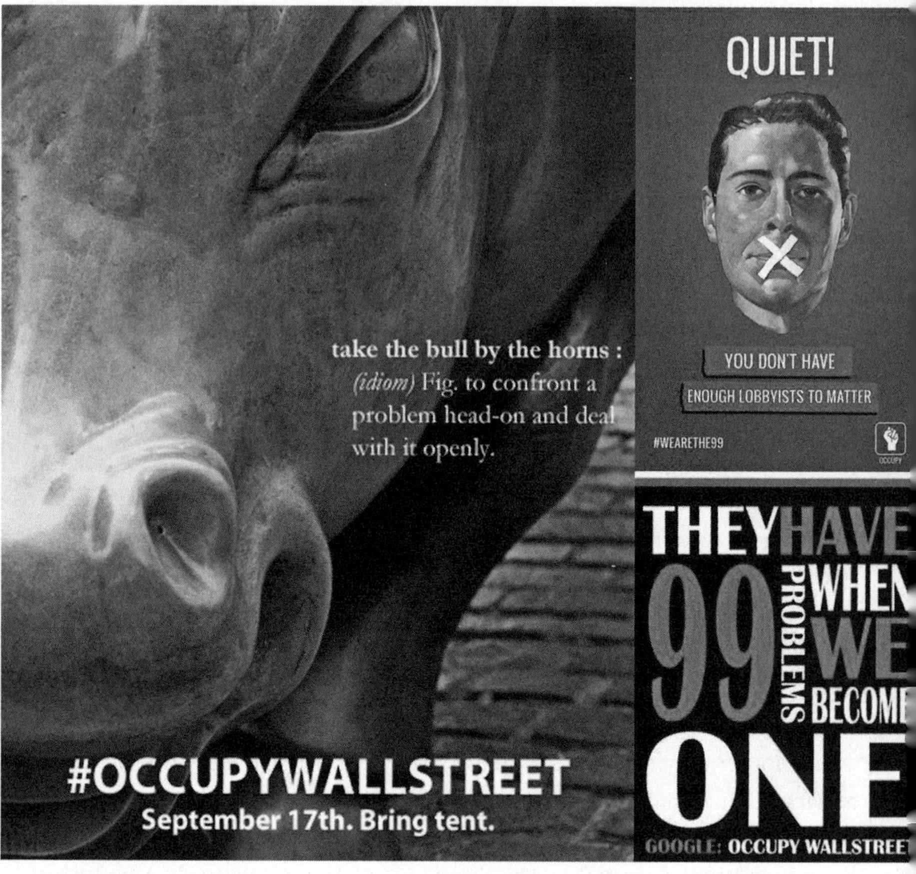

Figure 5.2
Three OWS promotional images, directing readers to hashtags and Google searches. Collected in 2011.

openness of these systems mirrored the openness at the heart of the OWS ethos. Images were shared without signature or citation; Twitter profiles, YouTube accounts, subreddits, and tumblogs affiliated with OWS sprang up with little apparent oversight and no clear single author. However, those critical of the movement could use the same tools and logics to counter the OWS message. Memetic logics opened up the argument to new discussants and new means of discussing, as divergent camps used memetic media to comment and debate. Vibrant public conversations about the movement and its central aims emerged as discursive strands intertwined.

As the last chapter demonstrated, memetic logics can be employed both to denigrate individuals for their core identity categories and to facilitate agonistic counterpublic contestation of that denigration. When /r/ShitRedditSays carves out a space to counter broader conversations on Reddit, or when OWS supporters spread their narratives about the protest on YouTube, memetic logics give counterpublics voice. If the marginalizations we saw in the last chapter are premised on silence, voice—the kind evident in engagement with OWS—is premised on conversation. Without these conversations, there is not much hope for a healthy public sphere.

Participatory media of the sort that carried resonant OWS messaging in September 2011, even as traditional media outlets ignored the movement, can facilitate active, polyvocal citizenship. If more people holding more perspectives can log onto Reddit or Tumblr and engage in political expression and discussion, democracy benefits. The marginalized can use these media to engage in public conversation on more equal footing. Memetic logics—at their worst when they facilitate antagonistic silence—are at their most vibrant when they facilitate open, polyvocal public conversation. The conversational dimensions of citizenship are crucial; civic life is nothing without civic talk. This vibrant public voice has been one of the central promises of participatory media—a promise still largely unfulfilled due to what Nick Couldry calls rationalities and practices "that take no account of voice" (2010, 10). We saw these exclusions manifest in everyday identity politics in chapter 4, but we also saw the counterpublic contestation of those exclusions. Identity antagonisms spread easily through memetic media, and that can't be forgotten. However, even as they facilitate antagonism and silence, memetic logics can also facilitate public voice.

The rest of this chapter will tie memetic media to this polyvocality, evidencing the ways vernacular creativity can be utilized for collective civic talk. It will use memetic participation surrounding OWS as its core evidence, but lessons from the movement apply to mediated public conversations before and since. We've already seen examples of memetic political participation, such as the "It Gets Better" YouTube campaign to combat depression and suicide in LGBT youth, and #YesAllWomen emerging in response to the misogynistic UC Santa Barbara killings. Assessing the political dimensions of this kind of memetic participation, the following section will examine the relationship between popular culture, participatory media, and populist conversation. It will address the vital role of popular culture in public commentary as well as the vernacular creativity evident in this interrelationship. As I'll argue below, memetic media can indeed facilitate vibrant polyvocal participation, and our public conversations are stronger when they do.

As I evaluate the relationship between memetic media and public commentary throughout this chapter, many of the images included are of private citizens captured by amateur photography. Even if those private citizens were photographed at a public protest or if they uploaded a photo of themselves to a public website, I have done my best here—as I have throughout this book—to not reproduce their likeness. This has meant cropping some photos in order to better anonymize them. I recognize the tensions that come with altering photographs during analysis, but have decided to value the privacy of the subject over the sacredness of the text.[3]

Pop and Populism in Participatory Media

Memes—even going back to Richard Dawkins's (1976) concept of cultural replication—are inherently intertwined with the popular. The "best" memes—i.e., the ones that are best at surviving in the cultural soup—are the ones that resonate with the most people for the longest amount of time; the most "fertile" memes are, by definition, the ones that the most people connect with and share. In participatory media, memetic logics are predicated on the popular as well; what resonates with memetic collectives is what spreads. Memetic texts often reappropriate popular media—films, television shows, and song lyrics—in order to produce novel expression. As we saw in chapters 2 and 3, even the most esoteric and subcultural memetic collectives—like the less-trafficked pockets of conversation on 4chan, Reddit, and Tumblr—intricately weave broader popular culture into their in-jokes and insider lingo. The tensions we saw in chapter 3—between the *vernacular* as the subaltern and the *vernacular* as the common—also speak to the interrelationships of memetic media and popular culture.

And this interrelationship can facilitate vast public conversation. As the popular intertwines with the populist in public commentary, participants can make assertions about the social and political issues that resonate with them. Because they facilitate polyvocal participation, pop reappropriations have political potential beyond "mere" entertainment. However, the utility of this relationship can be contested. Pop culture reappropriations used in political discourse may be nothing more than the dumbed-down, imitative pastiche discussed in chapter 2, a commercialized distraction unfit for the hallowed practice of civic talk. Popular culture might be a fine enough inspiration for reaction GIFs, but the stakes may be higher for public protest. Keeping these tensions in mind, this section assesses how memetic media intertwine popular culture and vernacular creativity in the service of polyvocal public commentary, and what this means for broader civic engagement.

Populism vs. Pastiche in Political Commentary

Populist media—which foreground the concerns and struggles of the working class—have long been employed to open up narrow, restrictive public conversations. As Liesbet van Zoonen writes, populism "always involves a protest or policy on account of 'the people' who fall outside the reach of the political system" (2005, 147). She contends that, inherently, "a populist reaction is an inevitable counterforce to the structural contraction of the political field" (147). As populist participation intertwines with popular culture—as more and more people lend their voices to conversations about structural inequalities, about gaps in opportunity, about the haves and have-nots—polyvocal public commentary can flourish. We saw this flourishing expression in the fall of 2011, as participants used memetic media to discuss the OWS movement and spread its core messages.

An example of the counterpublic value of populist media is illustrated by "The Ruling Clawss," a series of editorial cartoons that ran in New York's *Daily Worker* between 1933 and 1935 and were shared in support of OWS in the fall of 2011 (figure 5.3). *New Yorker* cartoonist Syd Hoff penned the cartoons while moonlighting at the *Daily Worker* as "A. Redfield." As Robert Mankoff (2012), the current cartoon editor for the *New Yorker*, explains, Hoff's moonlighting allowed him to express an explicit critique impossible in his regular work for that magazine. In Mankoff's words, "Hoff's *New Yorker* cartoons showed humorous empathy for the lower middle class that he was a member of, but no apparent antipathy for the class that employed and, very often, unemployed them at will. That's not surprising, since Hoff's employer, the *New Yorker*, was actually doing quite well during the Depression, in part by appealing, in its advertising, to that very class."

"Oh, boy, a demonstration today. I'm just itchin'—"

"No doubt, if these 15,000,000 unemployed weren't so lazy they could find jobs."

"Thirty days for picketing! I'll teach you to appreciate a free country!"

"Your grandfather was a victim of the World War—he died on Wall Street."

Figure 5.3

Four editorial cartoons from Syd Hoff's "The Ruling Clawss" series. Published in the *Daily Worker* between 1933 and 1935.

The *Daily Worker*, a more counterpublic populist outlet, gave Hoff a means to comment beyond the constricted scope of the more established *New Yorker*, and in the process facilitated his public expression. This expression resonated almost eighty years after he penned his "Ruling Clawss" comics. At the height of OWS protests in fall 2011, participants spread his comics through participatory media, connecting their Depression-era themes to twenty-first-century income inequality. Their memetic reappropriation bridged decades of distance; new populist outlets spread established populist messages, and Hoff's voice lived on.

By their very nature, memetic media house the potential for populist expression and conversation. Vibrant public conversation depends on more voices having access to channels of interaction, and that's what memetic media provide. Of course, participation in the memetic lingua franca is not wholly open, as this participation is bound both by cultural context and material inequalities. However, the structure is decidedly more polyvocal—more the realm of "the people"—than narrow one-to-many modes of mass mediated communication. Even in restrictive regimes, memetic logics can underscore vibrant public voice, provided cultural participants have some freedom to employ them. To this end, An Xiao Mina analyzes the relationship between memetic media and political subversion in China, arguing that:

> Memes, as micro-actions of media remixing and sharing, are particularly important in a censored, propagandized state, which seeks first to isolate individuals who express opinions contrary to state interests, and then to deaden the sort of public debate that fosters a diverse sphere of opinion. With rich visual language and a culture of creative remix and communal participation, meme culture has provided an outlet for new forms of public conversation and community building. (2014, 362)

Through this conversation and community building, memetic media inspire hope for broader discussion. Populist messages and popular means facilitate and amplify public voice.

Like populism, popular culture—in its most favorable readings—encourages participation in public conversation. Henry Jenkins (2006) argues that as people "Photoshop for democracy" by using participatory media to produce their own populist, political commentary, civic talk is braided into everyday participation. By employing memetic logics, public participants can create, circulate, and transform texts in the name of political expression. And these expressions are not restricted to those who own large platforms or have large audiences. Instead, the vernacular creativity essential to YouTube videos, Twitter trending topics, and Reddit Photoshops depends on memetic participation situated outside of constricted media gatekeepers.

In the case of memetic media and OWS, the reappropriation of popular culture facilitated diverse expressions of citizenship, resulting in the amplification of populist messages. Iconic statues, Jay-Z lyrics, Depression-era comics, quotes from *The Matrix* and *Star Wars*, and other resonant pop media were woven into the OWS conversation, all of which made the political and economic issues at OWS's core more accessible and resonant to a wider range of the population. These populist footholds connected a broad spectrum of participants to the discussion. One prominent example of this intertwine, and one that persisted beyond OWS, is highlighted in the Guy Fawkes masks worn by OWS protestors (figure 5.4). These masks, which reappropriate iconography from the 2005 film *V for Vendetta* (itself based on a 1980s graphic novel), have been associated with the "hacktivist" collective Anonymous since 2008. In that year, as Rob Walker (2011) reports for *Slate*, physical protestors wanted to keep their identities hidden while the Anonymous collective challenged the Church of Scientology over media censorship. The Scientology protestors decided to wear the Guy Fawkes mask because it was already a resonant meme on 4chan (it was worn by a stock character called "Epic Fail Guy" in ironic honor of Guy Fawkes's failed 1605 plot to assassinate England's King James I), and because participating protestors could all find cheap masks in their cities.

As traditional media coverage of the Scientology protests spread, the mask became a memetic touchstone, a loose and ambivalent icon for the loose and ambivalent Anonymous collective. From there, it began to pepper forum threads, physical graffiti, and ambiguous YouTube videos associated with the collective. Its memetic lineage—from a 1605 assassination plot to a 1980s graphic novel to a 2005 film to a 2008 protest—is woven from thread after thread of pop reappropriation. As Whitney Phillips puts it, the Guy Fawkes mask, "once a symbol of failure," was by 2011 "a rallying cry for social justice" (2015b, 150). It spread widely, eventually becoming one more resonant pop icon mobilized for civic use at the height of OWS. Banal bricolage and quotidian reappropriation intertwined with directed protest, facilitating public voice and furthering populist ideals in the process.

Figure 5.4

Three photos of OWS protestors wearing Guy Fawkes masks, reappropriated from the 2005 film *V for Vendetta*. The mask is associated with the "hactivist" collective Anonymous. Collected in 2011.

But the reciprocity between public conversation and populist participation can also inspire worries about a negative "restylization" of politics (see Corner and Pels 2003), especially when that populism is tied to popular culture. These concerns echo the charges of pastiche we saw in chapter 2—charges that civic conversations are cheapened when popular culture and its predominant mass commercial logics become part of political discussion. When popular culture and civic participation intertwine, necessary counterpublic criticism and subversion may be lost. This was an accusation leveled at performer Jay-Z during the height of the OWS protests. As Lauri Apple (2011) reports for *Gawker*, in November 2011 Jay-Z's Rocawear brand started selling an OWS-inspired t-shirt on its site. On the screen-printed shirt, "Occupy Wall Street" was written in white lettering, but red ink scratched out the W in "Wall" and added an S after "street." The new memetic message read, "Occupy All Streets," a sentiment that fits the open OWS ethos well enough. Jay-Z's trouble came, though, when allegations surfaced that Rocawear was not donating any of the proceeds from the shirt to the OWS cause. The brand's appropriation—perceived as purely commercial and therefore absent any political teeth—met resistance, which eventually led to the shirt's removal from the Rocawear site. In this case, opportunistic pop culture appropriation attempted to restyle public activism into a commercial endeavor, and ultimately failed on both counts.

Beyond Jay-Z's transgression, broader arguments were made during the height of OWS that pop cultural iconography undermined the movement's aims and delegitimized its participants, reducing commentary on significant political issues to mere pastiche. For instance, figure 5.5 collects images used to critique the connections between Anonymous, memetic media, and OWS, all implicitly tying the Guy Fawkes mask to a lack of real political efficacy. According to the vertical comic on the left of figure 5.5, even if OWS protestors think they're participating in an uprising as glorious as the French Revolution, they're really just losers quoting denigrated slang and banally parroting toothless platitudes. In the bottom left panel, the middle figure, a bemused green-faced subject wearing a tie, is "Green Man," the face of "Old Anonymous." Before the Guy Fawkes mask became a resonant symbol, Anonymous (or 4chan's /b/, which is deeply, if ambivalently, tied to the origins of the collective) was sometimes portrayed as a man in a suit with a green face free of any defining facial features. In this case, Old

Figure 5.5

Three images critiquing Anonymous and its connections with OWS. Left: a vertical comic that contrasts the French revolutionaries in Jean Victor Schnetz's 1830 painting *Battle outside the Hôtel de Ville* with OWS protestors; top right: an image of protestors points out the irony of Time Warner's ownership of the Guy Fawkes mask; bottom right: a capture of a 2011 episode of *South Park* that spread as a satire of OWS protestors. Collected in 2011.

Anonymous looks on, frustrated with the state of mediated engagement and activism; the pop vernacular of OWS protestors undercut the efficacy of their message.

However, to van Zoonen (2005), calling pop engagement cheapened pastiche is an oversimplification and a way to shut out alternative forms of understanding. Instead, she says that "popular genres and means" allow for richer participation in public conversation. If sharing clips from *The Daily Show* or *The Colbert Report* "can be seen as a political act or a performance of citizenship—a means of engaging with and intervening in matters of personal and public concern"—as Geoffrey Baym and Chirag Shah (2011, 5) put it—then memetic media can be populist tools. Public participants can employ popular culture for multiple ends, and these diverse uses do not preclude civic ones. Memetic media are not, after all, predetermined in content, form, or stance. They do not have a prescribed purpose. Rather, they are a vernacular mode of public conversation; they're dependent on everyday creative expression that can be brought into service for leisure entertainment, for directed activism, and for a whole range of intentions in between. When media created for one purpose can easily be reappropriated for another, the popular is always a breath away from the political.

Vernacular Creativity and Pepper Spray Cop

As we've seen, memetic media—in their popular resonance—can facilitate poignant commentary through creative reappropriation, just as they can facilitate silencing antagonism. This fits well with the counterpublic conceptualizations of public conversation we saw in the last chapter. Far from being mere pastiche, popular culture texts are vibrant with possibility; they can be poached for agonistic political commentary just as easily as they can be poached to make a joke or connect with a friend. The memetic grammar and vernacular we saw in chapters 2 and 3 can transform the populist and popular into the explicitly political, as public participants creatively combine resonant popular texts with resonant political commentary.

The personal and collective resonance that underscores memetic creative expression underscores agonistic politics as well. Chantal Mouffe (2005, 2009) argues that "vibrancy" and "passion" are central to agonistic engagement among political adversaries. Similarly, Peter Dahlgren states, "the life of democracy requires that people be informed, and that they discuss and deliberate, but also that they be emotionally engaged, aroused to involvement, and at some point made to feel that they are sufficiently empowered to make a difference" (2013, 76). This engagement depends on participants crafting messages that resonate with them, but also with other members of the public, who produce their own expressions in kind. The voice we saw exercised by participants on /r/ShitRedditSays in chapter 4 demonstrates this vibrant, passionate, engaged agonism. With a mix of adversarial commentary and ironic play—largely predicated on the resonance of specific phrasal, performative, image, or video memes—the subreddit's participants pushed back against perceived misogyny on Reddit more broadly. Van Zoonen (2005) sees these forms of play and imagination as central to the connection between popular culture and public conversation. Like the "Beyoncé Voters" tumblog highlighted in chapter 1, popular culture texts can help tie "everyday" experience to civics, politics, and the public more broadly. In this intertwine, broader publics can bring shared experiences to political conversations.

One prominent example of the interrelationship between the popular and the political is highlighted in an iconic OWS meme called "Pepper Spray Cop" (see figures 5.6 and 5.7). The meme was inspired by a photo of a police lieutenant named John Pike walking with apparent nonchalance as he pepper-sprayed a group of sit-in OWS protestors at the University of California, Davis, on November 18, 2011. The significant presence of amateur media at the sit-in ensured that Pike's disciplinary action was captured, and the subsequent resonance and spread of the footage drew enough attention to make the incident a landmark OWS moment. Citizens shared videos and images of Pike walking up and down the line of young protestors, their arms linked and their heads down, as Pike's pepper spray can dusted them; in the background, additional officers approached the line to wrench the students apart and drag them away. One image in particular—posted to Reddit on November 19, 2011—resonated enough to explode into mass coverage. As it spread, it inspired extensive memetic remix of its own. Participants wove Pike's likeness into new contexts, crafting commentary about his actions in the process.

In the days that followed the posting of the original Reddit photo, Pike was cut from the background of that original and inserted into several fictional and historical contexts; the "Pepper Spray Cop" meme was thus born. In these images—which spread across sites like Tumblr, Reddit, and Twitter and into traditional media coverage—Pike's police tactics are applied to new contexts, and vernacular creativity is employed for populist commentary. As "Pepper Spray Cop" is Photoshopped into new images, Pike is made to target Dr. Seuss's Cindy Lou Who, the sunbathers in Georges Seurat's painting *Sunday Afternoon on the Island of Grande Jatte*, and even the U.S. Constitution itself. In these reappropriations, participants simultaneously displayed vernacular creativity and evidenced counterpublic commentary.

In particular, "Pepper Spray Cop" was repeatedly portrayed applying his force to innocents from popular texts. Figure 5.6 collects three "Pepper Spray Cop" images that cast the officer against portrayals of cultural heroes. In the top left image, "Pepper Spray Cop" victimizes the all-American little guy George Bailey from the film *It's a Wonderful Life*. The officer is inserted

Figure 5.6
"Pepper Spray Cop" targets cultural innocents. Top left: "Pepper Spray Cop" sprays George Bailey from the 1946 film *It's a Wonderful Life*; top right: he sprays Snoopy from the long-running *Peanuts* comic series; bottom: he sprays Jesus as portrayed in Leonardo da Vinci's c. 1495 painting *The Last Supper*. Collected in 2011.

Figure 5.7
"Pepper Spray Cop" targets antiauthoritarian heroes. Top left: "Pepper Spray Cop" sprays an unknown Chinese protestor in a 1989 Associated Press photo; top right: he sprays civil rights icon Rosa Parks in a 1956 United Press photo; bottom: he sprays an American revolutionary, as portrayed in Emanuel Leutze's 1851 *Washington Crossing the Delaware*. Collected in 2011.

to control an iconic showdown between George and the wealthy town bully, Mr. Potter. His position behind Mr. Potter gives the impression that he is a hired goon, dispelling a man who spoke up for equality of opportunity and transparent business practices. In the top right image, Snoopy—the good-natured troublemaker from Charles M. Schulz's *Peanuts* comic series—is told to "behave" by the staunch authoritarian Lucy. He sticks his tongue out in defiance and is pepper-sprayed for his insolence. In the bottom image—an annotation of Leonardo da Vinci's painting *The Last Supper*—"Pepper Spray Cop" applies his force to Jesus of Nazareth on the eve of his crucifixion. These images reappropriate resonant cultural icons that carry an ethos of innocence and goodwill. That "Pepper Spray Cop" disciplines these subjects is a discursive choice with political undertones made by the citizens doing the Photoshopping; the collective memetic joke comes with an evident critique of Pike's tactics during the UC Davis sit-in.

"Pepper Spray Cop" was made to oppress civic heroes as well. In these iterations, the same populist humor is applied to more explicitly political sources. Figure 5.7 collects "Pepper Spray Cop" images that direct Pike's force at historical antiauthoritarian heroes, victimizing beloved freedom fighters. The top left image in figure 5.7 reappropriates a photograph of an unknown Chinese protestor, called "Tank Man." In the original photo, Tank Man stands resolute in Tiananmen Square, even after Chinese authorities have forcibly removed other protestors and sent their tanks through the square. In this image, "Pepper Spray Cop" joins the tanks. The top right image turns a social justice victory on its head. It reappropriates a 1956 photo of Rosa Parks—who famously refused to give up her bus seat to a white passenger in 1955—riding the newly integrated Montgomery, Alabama, bus system. "Pepper Spray Cop" makes sure that Parks's courage does not go unpunished. The bottom image modifies Emanuel Leutze's painting *Washington Crossing the Delaware*, which valorizes American revolutionary George Washington's surprise attack on British imperial forces in Trenton, New Jersey. The moment is a defining part of the story of early American resilience and independence. "Pepper Spray Cop" revises that history. Each of these historical moments signifies the stern resolution of citizens in the face of oppressive state forces. In these iterations, Pike targets subjects that resonate as heroes.

Taken together, the aesthetic choices made in many "Pepper Spray Cop" remixes make an argument about the events of November 18, 2011.

Participants extended this argument with each new iteration of the meme. Even remembering the ambiguities that exist when reading the stance of memetic media—even acknowledging that we can't read the minds of those creating or engaging memetic texts—a prevalent political narrative emerges across "Pepper Spray Cop" images. Each person who decided to share an image that pricked them spread that commentary further. The collective corpus of "Pepper Spray Cop" images portrays innocents and heroes oppressed and attacked by an instrument of soulless governmental control. Multiple moments from public history and popular culture combine to form mediated, polyvocal commentary.

During the height of OWS, memetic media, pop culture texts, and political engagement intertwined in complex ways, bringing the vernacular creativity always evident in memetic texts directly into civic service. As Dahlgren argues, humorous commentary works to "strip away artifice, highlight inconsistencies, and generally challenge the authority of official political discourse" (2009, 139). In doing so, humor "offers pleasurable ports of entry to current political topics, as it contributes to the evolution of mediated political culture" (139). Whether the end result was pastiche or empowerment, memetic logics facilitated public commentary surrounding OWS, and have facilitated commentary during significant conversations since. Pop texts and participatory media were crucial to the resonance of OWS. They inspired political conversation—the kind we'll see next section—as participants more than made do with the cultural and technological tools at their disposal.

Polyvocality and Public Conversation

Despite concerns about pastiche, the intertwine of popular culture and political commentary is not as dangerous as a system that keeps strands out of the tapestry, keeping some voices out of public conversation. Democracy depends on diverse citizens expressing themselves and having those expressions valued. Civic talk hinges on polyvocality. From this perspective, the agonistic dimensions of /r/ShitRedditSays that we saw in chapter 4 are valuable to vibrant public voice, as are the "Pepper Spray Cop" Photoshops we saw in the preceding section. Memetic logics that foster civic talk—no matter the form—are a net win for public voice, and for democracy in turn. This section will focus on this potential for civic participation. It will explore how memetic media facilitate polyvocal expressions, assessing the conversations born when those expressions intertwine.

Memetic Media and Public Voice

At the height of the OWS protests in the fall of 2011, citizens with a wide range of opinions employed memetic logics in their public conversations about the movement, evidencing polyvocality in the process. In their analysis of OWS Facebook pages, Sarah Gaby and Neal Caren find that the content most shared was not the result of direct framing by anyone in charge of OWS; instead, "those posts that resonated with different audiences became popular through online sharing, while thousands of posts with little appeal were simply passed over" (2012, 372). While Gaby and Caren express concern that this memetic spread may "reduce the power of movements to shape their own frames" (372), Sasha Costanza-Chock (2012) sees such openness as key to the OWS ethos. This memetic participation exemplifies what Dahlgren (2009) calls the "very talkative media culture" essential to polyvocal public participation. Active citizenship demands agile communicative tools, and memetic media were agilely employed to make diverse arguments about OWS.

This added voice helped carry the OWS message across participatory media, which eventually inspired traditional media attention. According to Saki Knafo (2011), writing for the *Huffington Post*, Anonymous hacktivist collectives were part of the reason the OWS message spread, despite the early indifference of mass media outlets. Inspired by faux grassroots "astroturfing" practices, Anonymous collectives reportedly seeded links about OWS into news story comments, connected with sympathetic Facebook groups, and uploaded YouTube videos supporting the movement. In doing so, Knafo says, "Anonymous ensured that news of the scene in Zuccotti Park went viral." Even if "ensure" might be an overstatement, such collectivist participation was significant in furthering awareness of the movement. Using memetic logics, citizens could engage in counterpublic civic talk, sharing their OWS support outside of traditional media framing.

Figure 5.8 collects four images sympathetic to OWS and its aims, each advocating for populist power in the face of repressive practices. The top left image comments on police practices that—as we saw with "Pepper Spray Cop"—were a resonant point of critique throughout the protests. It's a shot of a female protestor—mouth agape—being groped as she's detained.

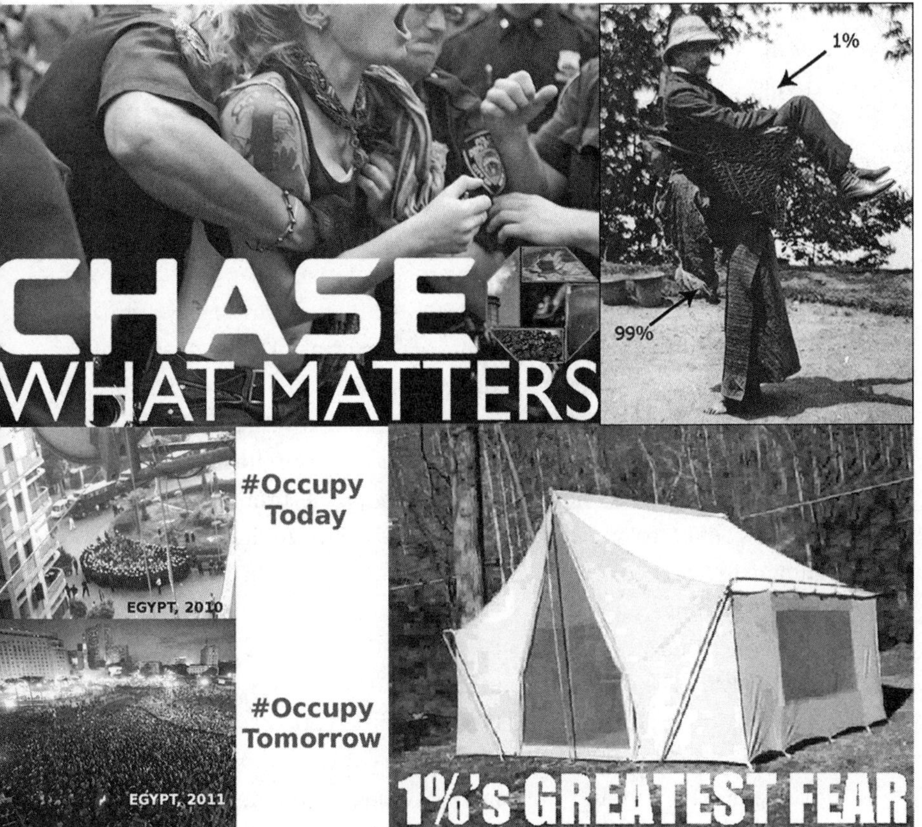

Figure 5.8
Four images sympathetic to OWS. Top left: a capture of a police officer apparently groping a protestor, annotated with the slogan for JPMorgan Chase Bank; top right: a photo of imperialist privilege, annotated with memetic "99 Percent" and "1 Percent" designations; bottom left: images connect OWS protests with "Arab Spring" protests in Egypt; bottom right: image critiques the 1 percent by alleging they're afraid of OWS encampments. Collected in 2011.

No matter how intentional the grope was, or how long it lasted, the fixed image communicates a static violation. The written text adds a pun, overlaying the image with the slogan and font for JPMorgan Chase Bank. Though it was not narrowly tied to income inequality, evidence of police brutality nonetheless provided general sympathy for OWS protestors.

An early memetic critique in this regard was aimed at New York Police Deputy Inspector Anthony Bologna. On September 24, 2011, Bologna pepper-sprayed a young protestor already "kettled" in orange police mesh. As with "Pepper Spray Cop," the incident was caught on amateur photo and video, spreading via sites like YouTube and Twitter. Charges of police brutality were levied, and the incident became an early rallying cry for those supportive of the movement. "Tony Baloney" became a memetic villain critiqued through Photoshop and image macro. Costanza-Chock (2012) claims the social sharing of the Anthony Bologna incident was a catalyst for mass media coverage of the protests. When *The Daily Show* lampooned Bologna on September 29, 2011, the satirical news program simultaneously introduced OWS into its coverage. The resonance of the Bologna pepper spray incident inspired participatory spread, which eventually caught the attention of someone at a massively popular television program, which in turn spread the message even further, among the program's millions of viewers. Charges of police brutality implied that protestors' right to peaceful assembly was being undermined, and that argument resonated beyond direct sympathy with the movement's economic claims.

The other images in figure 5.8 convey other resonant messages sympathetic to OWS. The bottom left image encourages protestors to continue by connecting their populist efforts to those of Egyptian protestors who toppled the Hosni Mubarak regime in February 2011 during the Arab Spring movement. The top and bottom right images both invoke distinctions between the bottom "99 percent" of U.S. income earners and the top "1 percent." These distinctions became the source of the "We are the 99 Percent" memetic phrase employed by those supportive of OWS. The argument implicit in the shorthand is that those at the top of the wealth pyramid have disproportionate opportunity, power, influence, resources, security, and agency as compared to the rest of the population. The references to the "99 Percent" meme in figure 5.8 replicate this populist divide. Each of these images thus uses multimodal shorthand to connect OWS to established populist arguments.

But beyond expressing support for the movement, memetic logics were also employed to express ambivalence, dismissal, and outright disagreement with the goals and methods of OWS protests. Supportive civic talk coexisted alongside critical civic talk, as seen in the memetic images collected in figure 5.9. The top left image contrasts American OWS protestors with Arab Spring revolutionaries, who are portrayed as facing explosions,

Figure 5.9

Four images critical of OWS. Top left: American OWS protestors are contrasted with revolutionaries in "Arab Spring" nations; top right: an image of Humphrey Bogart's Rick Blaine in the 1942 film *Casablanca* is annotated to call OWS protestors "hippies"; bottom left: a stock photo of a crying child annotated to imply OWS protestors are entitled; bottom right: a protest photo annotated to imply OWS protestors are hypocrites. Collected in 2011.

fire, blood, and bullets while OWS protestors sit idly in homemade Guy Fawkes masks. The other images dismiss OWS protestors as hippies, whiny children, or hypocrites.

These images—and the arguments they invoke—charge that OWS protestors are anticapitalist while taking advantage of the fruits of capitalism, are revolutionary without any real consequence, and are complaining about the problems of an entitled leisure class. All these critiques are congruent with complaints levied about OWS across traditional media outlets, indicating a deep interconnection between the arguments being conveyed through memetic media and the broader conversations occurring during the height of the protests. Critiques like these were themselves memetic; they spread via new iterations across participatory media, into embodied conversations, and through pundits addressing massive audiences. In the process, narratives of entitlement and hypocrisy came to dominate perspectives critical of OWS, as much as narratives of inequality and brutality came to dominate perspectives supportive of OWS. Different messages resonated with different publics.

As sites like Reddit, Twitter, Tumblr, and YouTube were mobilized in support of OWS, critiques cropped up in tandem. Just as OWS supporters used participatory media for polyvocal, counterpublic contestation, OWS critics used the same media tools to rebuff supporters' claims. In the fall of 2011, conversations in memetic media collectives and networks were inundated with multiple arguments from multiple perspectives about OWS. Participatory media facilitated polyvocal political assertion. Active citizens produced diverse texts, engaged politically with multiple perspectives, and demonstrated intricate conversational citizenship.

Conversational Citizenship and the 99 Percent

While participatory media can inspire polyvocal engagement with public issues, they also provide enough customizable information to allow users to find whatever they want whenever they want it. "Echo chambers"—the result of collectivism that's too insulated from other perspectives—are the negative corollary to polyvocality. In a boomerang effect, the wealth of public conversation on sites like Twitter, Reddit, Tumblr, and YouTube might lead users to seek and engage only opinion-confirming information. Individuals can create their own metaphoric giant room where they shout an opinion and hear the same opinion bounce right back.

In DeLuca, Lawson, and Sun's (2012) analysis of how right- and left-leaning political blogs covered OWS, they do not find that participatory media resulted in polyvocality. Instead, they write, "in the two alternative worlds of right and left political bloggers, these decentered knots of world-making, the OWS protest is a wholly different event" (492). But there is evidence of polyvocal interaction beyond these political blogs. The sentiment regarding OWS on participatory media collectives was certainly not monolithic. Instead, it was vibrantly (at times ferociously) polyvocal. Sky Croeser and Tim Highfield (2014) speak to the ambiguities that came with the polyvocal dimensions of the "Occupy Oakland" contingent of the OWS protests. In their ethnographic work, Croeser and Highfield find that Twitter helped connect physical protests to mediated messaging, helped spread awareness of Occupy Oakland, and gave protestors an outlet to conversationally engage with the broader public. However, Twitter conversations also meant that protestors had to simultaneously address both insiders and adversaries, and had to debate using both antagonistic and agonistic registers. Polyvocal participation wasn't always easy, but it was a staple of Occupy Oakland both on the ground and through Twitter.

In the case of OWS, one example of memetic conversation was particularly vibrant. In the fall of 2011, the "We are the 99 percent" memetic phrase began to resonate, making its way to protest signs, hashtags, chants, and images shared online. As it did, the "99 Percent" meme spread across OWS protests, moved through participatory media networks, and entered into traditional media coverage. The term has since become common in American vernacular, a memetic shorthand for income inequality. The slogan was powerful, Jenny Pickerill and John Krinsky argue, in that it "immediately created a sense of inclusion and majority" (2012, 281), hailing the vast majority of the population into the OWS ingroup. The phrase owes much of its prominence to a tumblog that featured OWS sympathizers holding up photos with handwritten messages telling why they supported the movement (see figure 5.10). These write-ups became some of the most prominent OWS images shared on Facebook, according to Gaby and Caren (2012). Memetic participation gave force to public argument as participants created, circulated, and transformed personal iterations of collective texts.

However, the shared "99 Percent" aesthetic was not entirely organic. At least on the most prominent "99 Percent" tumblog, WeAreThe99Percent.

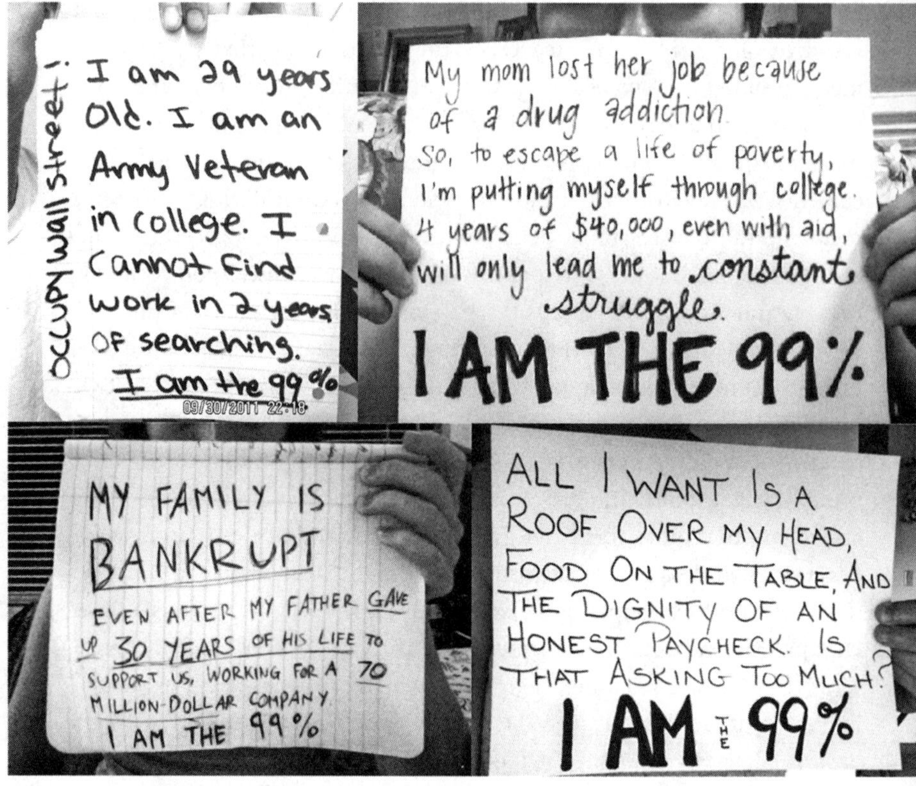

Figure 5.10
Four images from WeAreThe99Percent.tumblr.com, arguing in support of OWS. Posted between October 1 and 2, 2011.

tumblr.com, the rules for remix were made explicit by the curators who were gatekeepers for submissions. The meme's fixed premise was outlined in detail on the tumblog's submission screen:

> Let us know who you are. Take a picture of yourself holding a sign that describes your situation in one sentence—for example, "I am a student with $25,000 in debt," or "I needed surgery and my first thought wasn't if I was going to be okay, it was how I'd afford it." Below that, write "I am the 99 percent." Below that, write "occupywallstreet.org." If you don't want to show your whole face, please show at least part of it. Please have your note be hand written. Please do your best to be concise. Put a face to the 99 percent. Let's get known.

Some of these guidelines were flexibly enforced. Many participants only showed part of their face. A few posts were not handwritten. More than a few were noticeably *not* concise. Instead, some handwritten pages contained words scrawled so tiny they were impossible to read without an accompanying caption. Still, the instructions were followed with enough consistency that the "99 Percent" aesthetic became an immediately recognizable part of the protests. Participants creating and circulating "99 Percent" images may or may not have also been marching down city streets. However, their engagement helped frame the broader political conversation. Long after the physical occupation of Zuccotti Park ended, the "99 Percent" meme was part of public debate. The meme survived years after the occupation.

But—even as it hailed inclusiveness—the phrase was met with polyvocal pushback and ample agonistic conversation. The "99 Percent" meme inspired conversational citizenship, as multiple perspectives used its memetic core to directly engage each other. Figures 5.11 through 5.13 collect memetic variations of the "99 Percent" aesthetic, which reappropriate its form but shift its content and stance. The images in figure 5.11 satirize the "99 Percent" aesthetic, invoking the broader critiques of OWS highlighted earlier: that its message was vague, that it was the product of entitled hipsters, and—as the partial re-creation of Hitler's backstory implies—that it wasn't worth the sympathy it appeared to merit. These satirical takes on "99 Percent" images were conversational in their implicit address of the meme and their explicit appropriation of its form. They are examples of a point-counterpoint that emerged as "99 Percent" messages inspired their own satirical contestation.

Figure 5.11

Three memetic images that reappropriate the "99 Percent" aesthetic in order to satirize it. Collected in 2011.

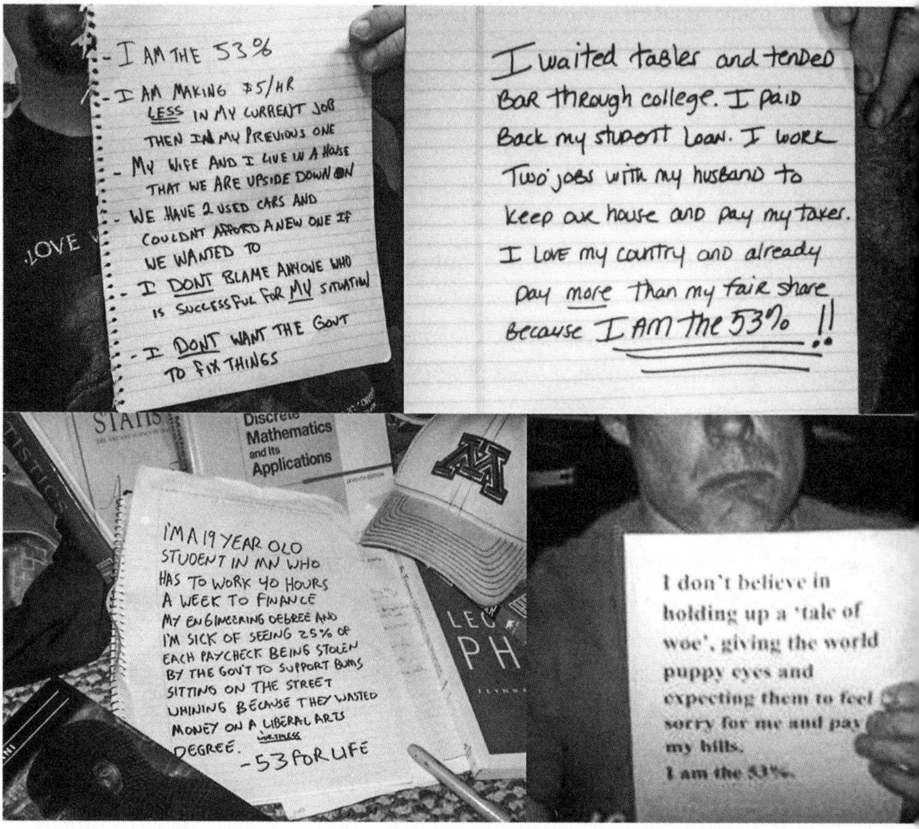

Figure 5.12
Four images from The53.tumblr.com that reappropriate the "99 Percent" aesthetic in order to counter it. Posted on October 11, 2011.

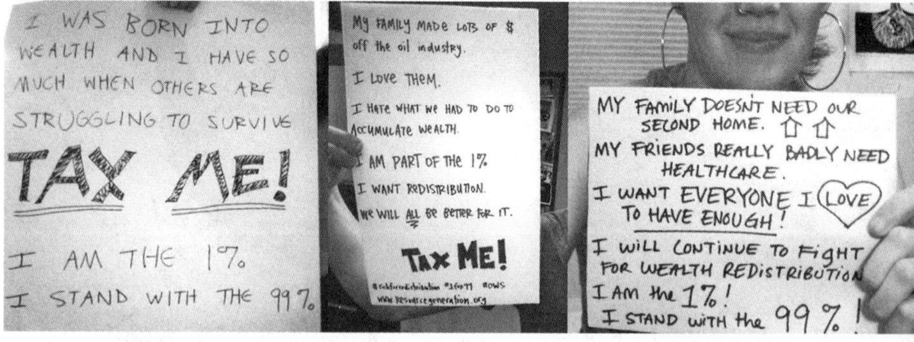

Figure 5.13
Three images from WeStandWithThe99Percent.tumblr.com that reappropriate the "99 Percent" aesthetic in order to support it. Posted between October 12 and 13, 2011.

Along with satire came outright contradiction. Another number-based phrase was employed to counter the "99 Percent" meme as it rose to prominence. Based on the premise that only 53 percent of Americans pay income tax, "53 Percent" images began to circulate in the fall of 2011, responding to "99 Percent" images. The notion resonated as a conservative counterargument to the 99 percent claim.[4] The "53 Percent" meme also had a prominent tumblog, The53.tumblr.com, which reappropriated the "99 Percent" aesthetic in order to make arguments against OWS. The images in figure 5.12 are in their very form a rebuttal to the "99 Percent" meme, and their content responds to "99 Percent" messages as well, arguing by subtext that "99 Percent" images "blame others," "give the world puppy eyes," and are produced by "government-supported bums." While the original "99 Percent" images began as a first-person declaration (a way to "describe your situation," says the "99 Percent" tumblog), the "53 Percent" images attack that declaration, and by extension the resourcefulness, patriotism, independence, intelligence, and overall social worth of those creating "99 Percent" images. While the value of this strategy is up for debate, it's a polyvocal response to a public assertion.

The memetic back-and-forth went even further. There was even a tumblog, WeStandWithThe99Percent.tumblr.com, that purportedly featured members of the top 1 percent of income earners "standing with" the 99 percent. The images in figure 5.13 reappropriate the "99 Percent" aesthetic to express solidarity with its message, even from those who seem to be the outgroup. Repeated on the tumblog are phrases like "TAX ME" and "redistribute." As these examples demonstrate, the hand-drawn, personal aesthetic resonated as a key part of OWS discussions in the fall of 2011. This shared aesthetic gave multiple perspectives a voice and a fixed premise by which to make their own novel assertions in the midst of a buzzing public conversation.

Commentary via the "99 Percent" aesthetic also went beyond single-turn assertion to engage in multiturn civic talk. Arguments emerged across texts and even within texts. In one "99 Percent" image, penned after the rise of "53 Percent" images, the creator uses his handwritten sign to address the countermeme explicitly:

> Since 2008, <u>you</u> have complained about the economy. <u>You</u> have said that big money has corrupted the system. <u>You</u> have worried that your jobs would be outsourced. <u>You</u> have said so ... over and over. Now that people are taking action ... you're suddenly

satisfied with the status quo, accusing others of wanting handouts. YOU ARE THE 99%. Admit it! (Emphasis in original)

The message is a direct address; it is polyvocal beyond single-turn commentary. "You" is repeated five times with underlines, instead of the "I" that signals personal declaration in most "99 Percent" posts. The content, through this second-person address, calls out conservatives who have "complained about the economy" for years, but are "suddenly satisfied with the status quo" when another political group starts "taking action." The last line is another inverse: "YOU ARE THE 99%. Admit it!" The message uses shared aesthetics to argue that there is hypocrisy in "53 Percent" posts. In the post, a citizen directly addresses an implied audience of interlocutors, and in the process memetic reappropriation affords polyvocal, conversational citizenship.

Because of multimodality, multiturn argument could occur even within a single image. For instance, participants sometimes used annotation to argue with a source image right on top of it, circling some passages, crossing out others, and adding their own text to the image they were annotating. The vibrancy inherent to "99 Percent" images didn't demonstrate "echo chamber" parroting or even simple assertion. Instead, citizens engaged in public commentary addressing both implied and specific interlocutors. In this way, they were engaging in conversational citizenship. By participating in memetic commentary surrounding OWS, participants were not just commenting on the activism of others marching in a major city, but were inserting a sliver of their voice into the conversation. Their claims were strands in a discursive thread. Participatory media were mobilized for polyvocal argument.

A More Vibrant Tapestry

This chapter illustrates that there can be a positive relationship between pop-savvy mediation and polyvocal, political conversation. Public perspectives on OWS were articulated vibrantly through memetic logics. The aesthetic practices and humorous tone common in memetic media also carried populist perspectives about the movement. Pop texts and pop networks intertwined as individuals with the literacy to weave discursive strands crafted commentary from everyday sources.

Memetic logics enabled OWS conversations to be widely reappropriated, and, admittedly, not all appropriations shared on sites like 4chan, Reddit, Tumblr, and Twitter were seemingly "productive" commentary on OWS methods or key issues. For instance, figure 5.14 collects politically ambiguous pop uses of the phrases "Occupy" and "99 Percent," ones that might be closer to pastiche, or appropriation without a subversive edge. The most straightforward read is that these images address the core OWS issues only tangentially, and do not explicitly support or deride the aims of the movement. They seem indifferent to any specific political stance, ambivalent at best, trivializing at worst.[5] The images in figure 5.14 seem to be more of a remix for the sake of creative play than explicit political commentary: they take a memetic convention and find new ways to apply it for a humorous effect. But this ambivalence is important too, since it reminds us that

Figure 5.14
Six images employing OWS memes to ambiguous ends. From left to right, the top three apply the movement's "Occupy" signal term to the fictional universes of *Star Wars*, *Harry Potter*, and *The Lord of the Rings*. The bottom three images make jokes by reappropriating the "99 Percent" meme. Collected in 2011.

political participation is not always a simple binary. There are degrees of engagement with political events and popular culture.

Even with these ambivalent texts, those worried about shallow political discourse can take comfort in the intricate multiturn commentary occurring through memetic practices. Even simple images like "Pepper Spray Cop" were premised on intertextual depth. The "Pepper Spray Cop" meme may have been shallow pastiche, or it may have been political commentary that served an important argumentative point, making a visual statement about the nature of police action during the protests. If participants wished to engage the UC Davis pepper spray incident, they could write a long-form textual argument about state control and civil liberties. They could post it to their blog or pass it around to friends and hope they read it thoroughly and engaged it fairly. Or they could produce an image that portrays "Pepper Spray Cop" assaulting George Bailey, negating Rosa Parks's moment of political triumph, or blotting out the U.S. Constitution. Better yet, they could do both simultaneously. They could intertwine pop and the political in order to craft a more participatory argument using more modes of expression. Katy Pearce and Adnan Hajizada (2014) contend that humorous, memetic pop culture texts are essential to public commentary in the repressive state of Azerbaijan. "Memes eschew attribution," they write, "and the anonymity of them enables a type of freedom, especially in cases where a meme is transgressive" (79). In an environment where government-sanctioned media are not trusted, "interpersonally driven, viral narratives can be powerful" (82). Even in explicitly repressive contexts, a polyvocal public sphere has room for diverse perspectives, logics, and ideas.

While chapter 4 points to the significant problems with voice on participatory media, the evidence from this chapter indicates that memetic logics have the means to support a vibrant tapestry of public conversation. Those worried about echo chambers should be encouraged by the multiturn conversations that occurred through the "99 Percent" meme and its iterations. The vibrant collectives highlighted here housed extensive commentary and polyvocal debate from multiple nuanced perspectives. Not only were images used to represent these perspectives, but they spawned intricate text-based discussion on the arguments they presented. The spread of polyvocal assertions through image memes inspired complex public conversation.

Both popular culture and polyvocal conversation were fundamental to the memetic dimensions of OWS. Members of the mediated public produced nuanced commentary and conversation by drawing on a broad range of sources. Alongside the daily deluge of jokes and links, participants on sites like Reddit, 4chan, Tumblr, Twitter, and YouTube shared public perspectives on issues fundamental to democratic rule. Through this activity, one of the core goals of OWS was realized: members of the public had a means to consider and debate issues of wealth, power, and inequality. The polyvocal assertions of mediated citizens intertwined. When memetic media made their perspectives on OWS part of the broader conversation, citizens could engage from many perspectives using many modes of communication. Their voices were amplified as they participated in polyvocal public debate.

However, even the engagement of multiple voices doesn't guarantee truly polyvocal conversation. Unequal power—central to the antagonisms analyzed in the last chapter—means voice can also be tainted with silence. Pearce and Hajizada (2014) make that caveat in their work on memetic logics and public commentary in Azerbaijan. They remind us that—as we saw in chapter 4—"inside jokes that reaffirm a dominant position can in fact reinforce oppressive ideologies" (80). In Azerbaijan, these dominant jokes weren't always the organic outgrowth of participatory media but were the result of memetic logics used by the government to spread messages undermining protestors. Critical, humorous images are planted. Fake Twitter accounts take on the identity of known protestors in order to mock their aims and spread misinformation. Hashtags are hijacked with discouraging messages. Likewise, Mina (2014) argues that the extensive censorship on the Chinese internet necessitates that memetic public commentary be limited to code, innuendo, and pun. Pop savvy mediation is, in China's case, a necessity due to the directed suppression of public voice.

Any opening of public conversation opens it to antagonism, inequality, and manipulation. We saw this in the previous chapter with the identity antagonisms prevalent in conversations on sites like Reddit, 4chan, and Tumblr. We'll see it again in the next chapter in the sway that culture industries hold over memetic media. Voice itself can lead to ambivalent examples of cultural participation, when that voice isn't vibrantly polyvocal. Conceptions of agonistic politics raise questions about how to simultaneously value factionist voice without letting one faction silence another. Even with diverse voices participating, unequal power relations can result in mobs swarming to crush dissent, and agonism drowned out by antagonistic marginalization. When the participation of some silences the participation of others, the agonistic ideal is corrupted. Voice must come with pluralism; diverse perspectives must be in equal conversation for the public to thrive. If there's a Goldilocks "just right" of polyvocality, it is voice that facilitates counterpublic solidarity without trampling opposition.

The OWS protests—at their height in the fall of 2011—evidenced vernacular creativity and conversational citizenship in the participation they inspired. While identity antagonisms still keep the tapestry of public conversation far too muted, polyvocal potential is embedded within memetic logics. We saw bursts of this vibrant color in the fall of 2011. The OWS debates are examples of polyvocal conversation that can occur through memetic media, at least among people well enough situated in the grammar and vernacular to participate. Of course, true polyvocality depends on a much wider contribution to public conversation than the fraction of the population that is active on sites like Twitter, YouTube, Reddit, Tumblr, and 4chan. Gatekeeping practices still exist, and we'll address those practices in the next chapter. But the gates are cracked open, if not flung free. Even in the midst of antagonizing silence, there is ample evidence in memetic media of robust, polyvocal, counterpublic voice.

6 Conversation: Cultural Participation and the Culture Industries

Ridiculously Famous

On March 31, 2012, a user going by the pseudonym King_of_Games posted an album entitled "35th Annual Cooper River Bridge Run" to his profile on the photo-sharing site Flickr. The album contained 112 photos from the yearly 10K Bridge Run, which takes runners over the Cooper River in South Carolina, across the Ravenel Bridge that connects downtown Charleston with its neighboring suburb, Mount Pleasant. King_of_Games had been posting photos to Flickr since early 2011, many from around Charleston, and many only garnering double-digit views. Like so much mediated participation, King_of_Games' contributions were a barely noticed strand in a vast tapestry of conversation. They weren't reaching the whole world, but they were there for those who wanted to engage with their creative expression.

But on March 31, that changed. Or at least it changed for a moment. At least it changed for a photo. Photo 28 of 112 in the Bridge Run album captured runners along Coleman Boulevard in Mount Pleasant at the beginning of the race. Flipping through all 112 photos of the Bridge Run, it may be easy to skip over photo 28. It's just one more collection of pixels, interwoven with the countless others that constitute participatory media. But something in photo 28 apparently pricked King_of_Games. All the other photos in the album are labeled in sequence: "35th Annual Cooper River Bridge Run-26," "35th Annual Cooper River Bridge Run-27." Photo 28 is the sole exception. Photo 28 is labeled "Mr. Ridiculously Photogenic Guy," referring to a prominent subject in the photo, a man in a dark purple shirt looking—gazing even—into the camera with a white-toothed smile and hair that appears to bounce in the sun lighting his back. Far surpassing

Figure 6.1
A capture of Zeddie Watkins Little—dubbed "Ridiculously Photogenic Guy"—being interviewed on *Good Morning America*. Aired on April 11, 2012.

the modest attention garnered by the rest of the album—and the rest of King_of_Games' mediated expression—"Mr. Ridiculously Photogenic Guy" has been viewed 4.2 million times on Flickr alone. In the years since March 2012, the photo has inspired massive media coverage (see figure 6.1) and has cemented itself in public conversation along the way. Its story holds lessons on celebrity, collectivism, and conversation in memetic media. It's a story of the ambivalent connections between polyvocal public participation and predominant culture industries, coexisting in tension as memetic logics become a prominent part of established institutions and infrastructures.

In the case of "Mr. Ridiculously Photogenic Guy," attention from both participatory and traditional media made the photograph and its subject "internet famous" in 2012. The attention began when the subject of that March 31 photo resonated with Flickr's King_of_Games, prompting him to post the image to Reddit's /r/Pics on April 3, 2012, under the title "My friend calls him 'Mr. Ridiculously Photogenic Guy.'" With the attention of participants on Reddit, a memetic text was born (see figure 6.2). Variations of the photo began appearing from its very first Reddit thread. "Ridiculously Photogenic Guy" was cropped and captioned. His face was mapped onto every other runner in the photo. He replaced Marvel's Jean Grey as the

Figure 6.2
Four iterations of the "Ridiculously Photogenic Guy" meme. Top left: a macro commenting on Little's handsomeness; top right: an image that replaces the faces of other runners in the original photo with Little's face; bottom left: Little is inserted into a frame from the 1959 Hitchcock film *North by Northwest*; bottom right: Little is inserted into a scene from a 1992 episode of the *X-Men* animated series. Collected in 2012.

object of Wolverine's unrequited love. He outran a plane with Cary Grant in the Alfred Hitchcock thriller *North by Northwest*. As the unaltered photo went viral, the "Ridiculously Photogenic Guy" meme spread right alongside it.

As "Ridiculously Photogenic Guy" spread through participatory media, traditional media outlets joined the conversation. The coverage began locally. On April 4, 2012, Paul Bowers of the *Charleston City Paper*—a free alternative weekly—outed the subject of the photo as New York's Zeddie Watkins Little and credited its photographer, Flickr's King_of_Games, as Charleston's Will King. King did not hide his identity on his Flickr, but Little's identity was apparently unknown until Bowers identified him by the race bib pinned to his shirt in King's photo. In Bowers's article, King gave some context for the photo, but the *City Paper* hadn't yet tracked down Little for an interview. "We're doing our best to find Zeddie Little," Bowers wrote, "and if he does eventually pick up the phone, we'll barrage him with *Seventeen* magazine-style personal questions."

By April 5, Bowers hadn't got in touch with Little, but had uncovered enough to publish more details about his life. Bowers found Little's father along with a former employer. Together, they confirmed that Little grew up in town, went to the College of Charleston, and worked at a local pizzeria before moving to New York. That same day, Christina Elmore covered Little in the *Post and Courier*, Charleston's major daily newspaper. She interviewed King as well as his friend who had coined the name "Mr. Ridiculously Photogenic Guy." A day later, the story had grown with the meme. It was now receiving national and international coverage. Up to that point—as piece after piece had noted, with a hint of disappointment—Little himself had yet to come forward.

Little's silence was broken on a massive stage a few days later. On April 11, he appeared on ABC's *Good Morning America* along with King (see figure 6.1). After a short background segment on "the man everyone loves," anchor Robin Roberts interviewed Little and King, commending Little for his role in a story that had "made people so happy." She praised King for a photo that "captivated the entire web." Little called the photo a "fluke" and said it had been captured as he was looking at a friend standing near King. He and King said they hadn't known each other when the photo was taken. Roberts also announced—feigning disappointment—that Little had a "beautiful girlfriend" just off camera. When asked how it felt to become so immediately and accidentally recognizable, Little was positive about the experience, saying, "I kinda feel honored to be part of like a joke that's in good spirits, you know, because sometimes the internet can be a little vicious or, you know, jokes can get bent the wrong way. But these are all kinda for the most part positive. ... It's, I guess, the most flattering way to get spread across the internet." Roberts then asked for "one last big smile," thanked him and King for "being such great sports" during the four-minute interview, and moved on to the next segment.

The *Good Morning America* appearance was the height of Little's traditional media coverage, but he wasn't done with participatory media just yet. On April 16, 2012, he took to Reddit for an /r/AMA thread (short for "Ask Me Anything," a subreddit dedicated to notable Q&A sessions). In the thread, he received lots of playful lusting and discussed his celebrity. He said that he found out about his fame when "redditor friends" called him after King's post had reached the front page of Reddit. He said he was initially surprised, but once he saw the photo, he "laughed for about an hour. It was just surreal. It's still surreal." He said that he had stopped looking at memetic iterations of the photo, commenting that eventually "it felt weird looking at a billion pics of myself." When asked how people he knew were taking his newfound fame, he pointed out that "my dad was so proud he would have given away my complete biography, complete with SSN [Social Security Number], to a journalist until I had to ask him to dial it back a little bit." In the end, he expressed appreciation for the site that had pushed an obscure photo into mainstream prominence. "Thanks to all of you for making this random picture such a phenomenon," Little signed off. "It would most likely have gone entirely unnoticed without your collective powers here."

But those "collective powers" ultimately moved their attention to new moments and applied memetic logics to new texts. Roberts said during Little's *Good Morning America* appearance that "the spotlight shining on that high-wattage smile doesn't appear to be fading any time soon." But Google Trends data shows a massive spike in search interest for both "Ridiculously Photogenic Guy" and "Zeddie Little" in April 2012, and a massive drop-off right after. The pattern fits Karine Nahon and Jeff Hemsley's (2013) power-law distribution criterion for viral interest. Little's Reddit account has sat quiet since his AMA. His Twitter account, which has around 5,400 followers as of mid 2015, has only 98 tweets, and none since December 2012. Meanwhile, King—despite Roberts's prognostication on *Good Morning America* that the Little photo "is gonna really help you here"—has returned to small audiences on Flickr, with "Mr. Ridiculously Photogenic Guy" being orders of magnitude more popular than his other work. In fact, the most enduring part of Little's story might be the modifier applied to him. "Ridiculously Photogenic" has become its own memetic label, attached in the years since

Little's glimpse of fame to more and more iterations of unexpectedly "photogenic" icons. Know Your Meme lists "Ridiculously Photogenic Surgery Girl," "Ridiculously Photogenic Metal Head," "Ridiculously Photogenic Syrian Rebel," "Ridiculously Photogenic Prisoner," "Ridiculously Photogenic Jiu-Jitsu Guy," and "Ridiculously Photogenic Running Back" ("Ridiculously Photogenic Guy" undated). In the case of "Ridiculously Photogenic Guy," memetic reappropriation proved bigger than the photo, the photographer, and the subject.

This chapter assesses the ambivalent dimensions of mediated participation as evidenced in Little's case. It explores the pitfalls and promises of social conversations made up of memetic logics, woven by memetic grammar and vernacular, and facilitating both antagonism and voice. This tapestry of mediated conversation—as Little's story demonstrates—is part new precedent and part established infrastructure. The tensions already manifest in Little's case will be the focus of the rest of this chapter. The next section will discuss the interrelationship between memetic media and established culture industries, emphasizing the complicated celebrity and publicity dimensions that arise when figures become "internet famous." The section after will assess the hypermemetic conversations now commonplace in our media ecology, emphasizing the ambivalent network gatekeeping that enables both restrictive commercial control of mediated participation and conversations open enough to cast doubts on the credibility of information. The final section of this chapter will tie together the public implications of memetic media.

Complicating the Culture Industries

The utopian myth of digitally mediated communication was that it would liberate people from hegemony. The industries, institutions, and identities that had held unequal cultural sway could be toppled by a system of tools that put participatory power in the hands of individual users. This potential for mass participation is due to what Jonathan Zittrain (2008) calls a "generative" ethos, one built on an empowering collectivist goodwill, as well as active innovation within and around existing technological and social systems.

But of course utopian promise hasn't completely torn away those industries, institutions, and identities that still hold unequal sway. This reality means to Mirko Tobias Schäfer (2011) that the "participatory media" paradigm is "ultimately rather myopic" when it comes to questions of democracy and voice. Instead of a wide-open agora, Schäfer argues, participatory culture "has to be understood as an extension of the traditional cultural industries into the realm of users" (168). Into this complicated cultural picture enter memetic media. Memetic participation can add democratic voice to mediated public conversations, but can also be appropriated for hegemonic marginalization and institutional influence. Even if the results aren't narrowly anti-empowerment, openness allows massive institutional forces to take advantage of participatory media as much as "everyday" users can.

While participatory media aren't wholly liberatory, they do complicate relationships between media "audiences" and the institutions that have traditionally been seen as the "producers" of media texts. Even if, as Henry Jenkins, Sam Ford, and Joshua Green (2013) contend, we need to recognize those who engage with popular media as active "publics" and not passive "audiences," the conversations occurring across participatory media still exist within established media and social systems. This means old questions emerge anew, even in a hypermemetic media ecology. The rest of this section will address these tensions, connecting memetic logics to established top-down systems of publicity.

Internet Famous, Whether You Like It or Not

As memetic media have become increasingly enmeshed with broader culture industries, the conversations occurring on digital media have increasing influence. For good or for ill, participatory media have become part of the same publicity system that envelops television, film, and print media. "Internet famous" is a shorthand label for individuals—like the "ridiculously photogenic" Little—who have gained fame or notoriety via the support of memetic practices. But "The Internet" cannot be read as a discrete entity; it's not distinct from Schäfer's (2011) culture industries. Mediated messaging persistently includes "participatory" dimensions as well as "traditional" ones. Internet famous doesn't stand alone; it intertwines with familiar practices, even as it introduces its own complications to those practices.

In a persistent example, American President Barack Obama—who from the earliest days of his 2008 presidential run successfully mobilized support through digital media—frequently plays with memetic moments and engages with participatory media collectives. On August 12, 2012—in advance of the November 2012 U.S. presidential election—he took to /r/AMA, where he answered policy questions, joked about the official White House beer recipe, and referenced the "Not Bad" Obama image cataloged in figure 1.4. He returned to Reddit on Election Day, posting a link to his tumblog, and encouraging participants on /r/Politics (American ones, at least) to go vote. Then, on November 15, 2012—a week after winning a second term—Obama welcomed American Olympic gymnasts to the White House. During the meeting, Obama posed with Olympian McKayla Maroney, who in the summer of 2012 had inspired memetic remix by sporting a "not impressed" face on the podium as she received a silver metal. In the White House photo, Obama and Maroney recreated the memetic expression (figure 6.3). The memetic moment, and its subsequent post to the Obama tumblog, were, according to the *Atlantic*'s Megan Garber (2012), both politics as usual and a new take on familiar publicity work. "The image of a

Figure 6.3
American President Barack Obama posing with Olympic gymnast McKayla Maroney, both recreating the "not impressed" face that Maroney wore as she received a silver medal at the 2012 Olympics. Official White House Photo by Peter Souza. Released on November 15, 2012.

meme-faced Commander-in-Chief, cheeky and epic at the same time," Garber says, "was—or at least, seemed—tailor-made for social media."

Obama's playful engagement with memetic moments carried on through his second term. On March 11, 2014, he appeared with comedian Zach Galifianakis on his *Funny or Die* web video series, "Between Two Ferns." In the six-minute video, Obama discussed—or tried to discuss—the Affordable Care Act in between trading non sequitur barbs with Galifianakis. Likewise, on February 12, 2015, Obama made a short video with *Buzzfeed*, again encouraging audiences to sign up for health insurance through the Affordable Care Act.[1] Then, on March 12, 2015, he appeared on the ABC late-night variety show *Jimmy Kimmel Live* for a segment where he read "mean tweets" about himself. On both *Buzzfeed* and *Jimmy Kimmel Live,* Obama referenced the popular "Thanks, Obama" memetic phrase, which ironically blames random problems on the president. In a *Buzzfeed* GIF, Obama says, "Thanks, Obama" when his cookie is too big to dunk in his milk, and in a segment from *Jimmy Kimmel Live,* he reads a "Thanks, Obama" tweet with an exasperated stare as R.E.M.'s forlorn "Everybody Hurts" plays in the background (figure 6.4). To Garber, the Obama campaign's mastery of participatory platforms is political strategy "without being obviously strategic," and its use of memetic media

Figure 6.4
Two images capturing American President Barack Obama reproducing the "Thanks, Obama" memetic phrase. Left: a capture from a *Buzzfeed* GIF set; right: Obama participating in a regular segment on *Jimmy Kimmel Live* where celebrities read "mean tweets" about themselves. Posted and aired respectively on February 12, 2015, and March 12, 2015.

represents "a significant shift in participatory politics. Which is to say, in politics." The Obama administration's appropriation of existing culture industries extends from established traditional media to emergent participatory media, mixing established publicity techniques and emergent practices. The generativity of memetic participation became one more publicity tool in the Obama toolbox.

But the controlled engagement with memetic moments exhibited by President Obama is a far cry from the accidental fame of the "ridiculously photogenic" Little, who had a decidedly more positive experience than some others who have become famous via the attention of participatory media collectives. Memetic media and internet fame inspire questions of hyperpublicity and denied privacy, in addition to the familiar tensions that already exist within established media systems. Zittrain worries about the implications of a cultural landscape where "ubiquitous sensors threaten to push everyone toward treating each public encounter as if it were a press conference" (2008, 212). The concerns are with a system that is not just public, but *hyper*public.

Memetic media sometimes apply this hyperpublic attention to figures considered public already (though the line between "public figure" and "private citizen" is, of course, a blurry one). When Obama plays with *Buzzfeed*, or Maroney poses "meme-faced" with the president, we might not be worried, or even really surprised. These are politicians and athletes; they are members of professions that have long had to balance the benefits and detriments of media attention. But collective memetic interest is not only given to individuals deemed "public figures." Instead, reappropriation and vernacular creativity can pull figures from obscurity and privacy into the collective spotlight; they can make a citizen public or amplify a small public audience into a massive one.

Sometimes individuals made "internet famous" embrace the mantle, as we saw with Little and King. Another example is Blake Boston, who gained attention in January 2011 when a photo of him wearing a fur coat and a backward baseball hat was taken from his MySpace profile. It was captioned with rude social behaviors in standard macro format ("Borrows your lighter ... permanently"; "Sold you weed ... hangs out and smokes it all with you"; "You buy the liquor, I'll buy the beer ... case of Natty Light"). Those images were posted to /r/Funny with the title "I Hated This Dude." The top comment read, "We all hate Scumbag Steve!" and a stock character was born. "Scumbag Steve"—and the "Scumbag" iterations it inspired—became one of the most popular macros of 2011 and 2012. Despite the apparent invasiveness of the macro and the negative connotations of its premise, Blake Boston embraced the fame. He has spent the years since 2011 making appearances, giving interviews, and performing as his crowd-sourced doppelganger. In an interview with Rough Draft TV posted to YouTube in March 2011, Boston reflects on the tensions that came with his unexpected fame. "Blake Boston is my real name," Boston begins in the interview. "Scumbag Steve is a meme. So he's like a character. Like an alter ego."

Boston is one of a rank of individuals who have gained memetic prominence and embraced their anointed alter egos, parlaying them into more established personas. The popular 2012 stock character macros "Overly Attached Girlfriend" and "Bad Luck Brian" have followed similar trajectories. "Overly Attached Girlfriend" (the joke is that she's too zealous in her relationships) had her image taken from her YouTube channel, captioned, and posted to Reddit. "Bad Luck Brian" (the joke is that bad things happen to him) also had his likeness uploaded to Reddit, taken from an unflattering school portrait. In the months after they gained notoriety, both turned their memetic attention into public personas. In August 2013, they produced a YouTube video together—"Overly Attached Girlfriend Meets Bad Luck Brian"—playing their characters on a blind date (see figure 6.5). The video has been viewed 3.4 million times on the YouTube account of "Overly Attached Girlfriend" (where she goes by "Laina").

By embracing roles crafted by collective vernacular creativity, these unlikely celebrities furthered the memetic premises attached to them. In the process, they blurred the components of their public identity that they could control with the collective attributions provided for them on participatory media. Jessica Contrera (2015), writing for the *Washington Post*, profiles the modest capitalization by "Bad Luck Brian" on his fame. She highlights the tensions between "Bad Luck Brian," the character, and Kyle Craven, the teenager whose goofy picture became a macro. "He appears at conferences such as VidCon and Indy Pop Con, where he sells t-shirts," Contrera writes. "They look at the photo, look at him and squeal as if they've just won a backstage pass to the Internet. He takes pictures with thousands of these fans, and they tell him things like, 'When my grandpa was really sick, I always looked at Bad Luck Brian photos to make me laugh.'

Figure 6.5
A capture of the memetic characters "Bad Luck Brian" and "Overly Attached Girlfriend" from a YouTube video entitled "Overly Attached Girlfriend Meets Bad Luck Brian." Posted on August 1, 2013.

They thank him, as if he were the one writing and posting the memes." To Blake Boston, aka "Scumbag Steve," the identity tradeoff that comes with collective attention is worth it. "That's the beauty of the internet," he tells Rough Draft TV. "You can find something so simple, so plain, and then you just write one thing on it and then everybody goes fucking nuts."

The Downsides of Generativity

The collective resonance that generates memes can indeed, as Boston says, be beautiful. There's something populist and democratic in the ability to reappropriate widely, to do the work of the poacher, the bricoleur, to make media texts into something unintended and new. But vernacular creativity can also leave real individuals in its wake. Tim Hwang (in Hwang and Xu 2014), speaking of his work with the ROFLCon internet culture conference, addresses these tensions. He recounts inviting the internet famous "Tron Guy" to a ROFLCon. Tron Guy earned the name in 2004 for uploading photos of himself in a cosplay outfit inspired by the 1982 film *Tron*. To Hwang, the Tron Guy invitation prompted "a lot of stress." Hwang's tension came because "Tron Guy became famous on the internet largely because he was mocked at scale … and we thought it would be terrible if we brought him and that experience was replicated" (382). In thinking through the implications of what participants create, circulate, and transform, Hwang comments, "you realize that the internet is made of actual people" (382). In the end, Tron Guy—who has also embraced his given persona—accepted the invitation and became a ROFLCon participant. By interacting with the person behind the character, Hwang says, conference participants gained insight into their own practices:

> What's interesting is: he came, people really liked him, and people treated him with a lot of respect. In 2012 he even ended up being this odd, "elder statesman" character. A lot of people told me they took away from the experience this realization that, "yeah, this colossal amount of human effort and experience is going into the generation of the internet every day," and you sometimes don't think about it because your experience of it is just a wall of images. (382)

That "wall of images" is the result of social actors, and their vast interrelationship is both the promise and the peril of memetic conversation.

To Zittrain (2008, 2014), persistent mediated communication—and the memetic remix that comes with it—is a double-edged sword. To that end, he compares "Disaster Girl" images (spawning from a photo featuring a little girl smiling in front of a house fire) with the viral "Star Wars Kid" video (a clip of a teenager fighting with a pretend *Star Wars* light saber). Zittrain posits that the cases show different shades of unexpected memetic notoriety. "It is one thing to be famous for being a serendipitously adorable little girl," he writes, "but it's quite another to be Star Wars Kid, who gained notoriety for embarrassing himself as an awkward teenager to the tune of 28 million hits on YouTube" (2014, 390).

Alex Pasternack (2010), writing for *Motherboard,* estimates the total views of "Star Wars Kid" iterations to be over one billion (and that was a half decade ago). He also charts the extensive harassment, and subsequent depression, of its subject, which concurred with his rising notoriety. Whitney Phillips (2015b) chronicles similar harassment faced by a preteen who posted a combative video to YouTube in 2010, met with unfavorable attention from participants on 4chan's /b/, and thereafter received a slew of threats, including the public posting of her home address and phone number. Her father appeared on her tearful response video, told trolls they had "done goofed," that he'd contacted the "cyberpolice" to "back-trace" them, and that "consequences would never be the same" after their actions. All four phrases have become memetic touchstones in the years since. Their antagonistic origins may have been dulled by persistent use, but Phillips reminds us that "by intervening on his daughter's behalf" (30) a concerned father attracted further harassment to them both. In these cases—and in many beyond—"lulz" came at the cost of unwelcome collective attention.

The story of Little and his "ridiculously photogenic" smile is a more ambivalent example of this unsolicited attention. On the one hand, Little embraced his memetic interest, and seemed grateful for the collectives that brought him his taste of fame. On the other hand—whether or not Little appreciated that attention—a stranger posted his picture to a public forum without consent, and a local paper subsequently outed him, going so far as to contact his family and former employers. As Little's image spread across participatory and traditional media, his likeness became public domain; he had no control over that likeness or how it was employed. My inclusion of his story here is another step in this cycle of unexpected fame, just as the story of harassment I included in the last paragraph draws attention back to the harassed individuals. Even though I've done my best to treat issues of representation in this book with ethical care, Little's story carries on because I made the decision that Little had volunteered to be "public" enough to merit specific analysis.

And all this says nothing of the ten other people whose faces are visible in King's original photo, none of whom have the social benefit of being deemed "ridiculously photogenic." They're collateral damage in Little's viral success. Though they were participating in a very public event, very few likely expected they'd end up as set dressing on *Good Morning America* when they signed up for a neighborhood 10K. And even as *Good Morning America* put their likeness on national TV, and uploaded that likeness to YouTube for permanent posterity, Roberts assured Little that the broadcast would keep his girlfriend off camera. Her identity was protected in a way that the others in King's image were not. Protecting the identities of people who did not consent to memetic attention motivates my decision not to include King's original "Mr. Ridiculously Photogenic Guy" photo, as well as my decision in the paragraph above to limit the identifying details about the preteen harassed.[2]

In Charleston's *Post and Courier*, Elmore (2012) acknowledges the ambivalence of this unwelcome attention, even as her coverage perpetuates Little's unexpected—and to that point unconsented—fame. "Browse photos from past Cooper River Bridge Runs and you're likely to spot thousands of people gasping for air, grimacing from the sweat dripping in their eyes or pleading for dear life while in the midst of a leg cramp," Elmore writes. "At those moments runners are thankful they'll blend into the rest of the crowd. Little, however, wasn't so lucky." This framing is sympathetic, but it's sympathetic within old inequalities. Across multiple stories, Little's conventional attractiveness—and the subsequent fact that the attention he received was positive—was a justification for spreading his likeness. Little's favorable attention, even if he did vocally appreciate it, came because of the problematic identity politics wrapped up in his image. Little was happy that he had sidestepped "vicious" interaction with the collectives who became interested in him. Other internet famous figures have not been so lucky.

Zittrain (2008) calls this potential for unsolicited attention one of the downsides of generativity. Even as he argues for solutions that don't "unduly dampen" the power of collective voice in participatory media, he worries that participatory media allow "individuals in many cases to compromise privacy more thoroughly than the government and commercial institutions traditionally targeted for scrutiny and regulation" (200). As this tension plays out, old notions of celebrity, publicity, and privacy will have to consistently account for new social conversations and technological platforms. Old culture industries will intertwine with new tools, raising new concerns of their own. We'll see this ambivalent mix in the next section.

Gatekeeping the Open Internet

For those seeking to capitalize on memetic fame, the road still goes through traditional culture industries. As Jean Burgess and Joshua Green argue of YouTube, "even when ordinary people become celebrities through their own creative efforts, there is no necessary transfer of media power: they remain within a *system* of celebrity native to, and controlled by, the mass media" (2009, 23, original emphasis). This power structure is so ingrained that YouTube success is measured not only by popularity on YouTube itself, but by the "subsequent ability to pass through the gate-keeping mechanisms of old media—the recording contract, the film festival, the television pilot, the advertising deal" (24). At the same time, the system is open enough to encourage expression outside of these traditional gatekeepers. Little's fame is equal parts Reddit and *Good Morning America,* equal parts participatory conversation and old-school agenda-setting. His is a story of what Nahon and Hemsley call "network gatekeeping," which occurs as media participants "link networks together, allowing information to travel far and fast" and, in the process, to "connect people to information and ideas" (2013, 48). Nahon and Hemsley argue that this gatekeeping—not wholly distinct from, but not wholly dependent on traditional culture industries—"is the key to social transformation in networked societies" (48).

The existence of network gatekeeping means that the open internet is at times very closed; the "right" participants have to engage with content for that content to spread. It's a system where institutional forces—with all their familiar commercial goals and organizational infrastructures—can prop up some moments and dampen others. But it's also a system where those forces have no direct control over the participants in their sphere of influence. They can't control what resonates, why it resonates, or how it's reappropriated, but they can guide the collectives that participate through their platforms. As *Buzzfeed*'s editor-in-chief Ben Smith told *USA Today,* "we try to create memes and also curate them, but we don't get to decide what goes viral" (quoted in Singer 2012).

An example of the reciprocal relationship between traditional and network gatekeepers came in 2010, with the memetic fame of YouTube user Hungrybear9562, also known as Paul Vasquez and—more prominently—the "Double Rainbow Guy." On January 8, 2010, Vasquez uploaded a three-minute video of a double rainbow over his home near Yosemite National Park in California. There the video sat for months, relatively unknown, much like King's Flickr albums. But, on July 3—as happened with King's photo—that changed. Vasquez's commentary during the video—humorous in its seemingly earnest philosophical awe at the appearance of a double rainbow—resonated with someone enough to send it to *Jimmy Kimmel Live* host Jimmy Kimmel. It resonated enough with Kimmel for him to share the YouTube link with millions on Twitter. After that tweet, it apparently resonated with millions more, and "Double Rainbow Guy" became a memetic hit.

By July 22, 2010, Kimmel was telling his live television audience the story, recounting how he found a video with 800 views and turned it into

Figure 6.6
A capture of Paul Vasquez, YouTube's "Double Rainbow Guy," being interviewed by Jimmy Kimmel on ABC's *Jimmy Kimmel Live*. Aired on July 22, 2010.

a viral hit with 7 million views in less than two weeks. He then had Vazquez on for an interview (figure 6.6), further amplifying the video's attention. By 2015, the original video had over 41 million YouTube views, and had inspired its own memetic flurry of remixes, Auto-Tunes, Photoshops, image macros, and catchphrases. As far as we can know, Jimmy Kimmel didn't produce Vazquez's video or upload it, and he certainly didn't produce the memetic content that came after its collective discovery. But without him, the chances that "Double Rainbow Guy" would have received any kind of media attention—participatory or traditional—are slim.

As we'll see below, network gatekeeping systems ensure that memetic conversations are at times still dependent on age-old culture industries. They also ensure that conversations are at times the result of vibrant collectives spreading information without signature or citation, to the point of difficulty in assessing accuracy and credibility. The subsections to follow will address this paradox in network gatekeeping, assessing both its institutional control and its complications for informational attribution.

Commerce, Control, and the Collective

In the midst of memetic participation, a familiar shadow looms. The same culture industries that capitalize on publicity and celebrity in memetic participation also contribute to its increasing commercialization. These gatekeepers are often familiar corporate entities. To Hwang (in Hwang and Xu 2014), the influence of culture industries in participatory media became more and more apparent as ROFLCon grew. Hwang describes the moment he had to talk to an agent to book "Grumpy Cat"—the pet cat who received memetic attention because of its resonant scowl. From Hwang's perspective, the moment signaled a big shift in the memetic media system:

> In 2012 we were on the phone with Grumpy Cat's agent, and it was like, "This cat has an agent." I think that fact alone was a really big indication of how the space of internet culture had changed in a four-year time period. I don't want to say, "Ah man it was so punk back then and now it's less punk," because the original conference was sponsored by the Barbarian Group, an interactive marketing agency. But I think the "profession" of internet culture was something that you could say changed quite a bit. (379)

"Grumpy Cat's" agent is Ben Lashes, who has also represented a slew of other internet famous figures, including Little and Boston. Beyond organizing appearances and inking merchandise deals, he has brought lawsuits to content creators who profit from his clients' likeness without compensating them (see Robertson 2013). This treatment may seem paradoxical and maybe even hypocritical. After all, it was open sharing that made these figures famous in the first place. And as Max Read (2013) reports for *Gawker*, even one of the most profitable "Grumpy Cat" t-shirt slogans—"I had fun once; it was awful"—was lifted from an image macro that itself reappropriated a comic by artist Kate Beaton. This ambivalent commercial appropriation is an essential part of a memetic media ecology in step with broader culture industries.

This intertwine is an unsightly knot to Christian Fuchs, who says that those who praise participatory media "advance an ideology that simply celebrates capitalism without taking into account how capitalist interests dominate and shape the Internet" (2013, 215). Fuchs contends that "Web 2.0 is not a participatory system, and it would be better understood in terms of class, exploitation, and surplus value" (215). Evidence mounts supporting Fuchs's claims. To be internet famous almost always entails engagement with traditional culture industries. Capitalizing on the attention requires national TV appearances, local commercials, reality series, autograph sessions, and more. Commercial appropriations of memetic content are now rampant. Memetic images and catchphrases are plastered on clothes at Urban Outfitters and Hot Topic, as well as notebooks at Target and even stuffed animals at tourist shops (see figure 6.7).

Beyond merchandising, brands take to Tumblr to converse with publics by using hip-hop slang and playful GIFs, mirroring the perceived communicative content and form of their target demographics. In February 2015, when participants on Twitter erupted in conversation about whether a striped dress in a viral photo was white and gold or blue and black (the conflicting perceptions were an optical illusion inspired by the white balance in the photo), brands played with the premise for promotion. *Adweek* (Maskeroni 2015) catalogs replies to the debate from companies like Denny's, Pizza Hut, JCPenney, M&M's, Miller Lite, Guinness, Dunkin Donuts, Lego, and even Hellmann's Mayonnaise. All tried to connect a memetic moment to a positive mention of their brand, and all appropriated vernacular creativity for corporate promotion. Similarly, a Delta flight-safety video, entitled "The Internetest Safety Video on the Internet" and posted by the company to YouTube on May 20, 2015, playfully surrounds the airline's typical flight-safety information with

Figure 6.7
Physical merchandise that capitalizes on memetic media. Left: "Grumpy Cat" merchandise for sale at a tourist shop; right: a notebook invoking the "Hey Girl" Ryan Gosling meme (see figures 3.12 and 3.13) for sale at Target. Photos taken by the author in 2014 and 2015, respectively.

references to memetic jokes and cameos by internet famous figures (figure 6.8). Both "Double Rainbow Guy" and "Overly Attached Girlfriend" make appearances as Delta appropriates collective texts for their brand. In these examples, memetic practices are noticed by and hailed into existing culture industries.

All of this fits Schäfer's (2011) account of culture industries, which he says have long adapted to changing cultural practices in order to earn new revenue. In this process, "new enterprises emerge and gain control over cultural production and intellectual property" (11), and often do so right alongside folk expression. In 2013, the Dr Pepper Snapple Group produced a collection of image macros that attempt just such an appropriation of vernacular creativity (figure 6.9). As part of a deal signed with gymnast McKayla Maroney, the parent company to Sunkist Soda sought to capitalize on memetic catchphrases and in-jokes popular in the years leading up to 2013. The images, shared on Sunkist's Facebook and Twitter profiles, were part of a marketing campaign that included the "unimpressed" Maroney endorsing the company's new line of ten-calorie sodas. According to an interview with the *New York Times* (Elliott 2013), Regan Ebert, senior vice president for marketing at Dr Pepper Snapple, wanted to "leverage the meme" by using Maroney in the campaign. Sunkist is "finally getting her impressed," Ebert assures readers, after so many memetic examples have not. Ebert hoped the move would "get digital buzz across the Internet."

What Ebert calls "buzz across the Internet," Fuchs (2013) calls "surplus labor," which he says manifests when cultural participants create, circulate, or transform participatory media content for the benefit of commercial organizations. Even under the best of circumstances, Fuchs argues that "prosumers" labor for corporations when they contribute to participatory platforms like Reddit, YouTube, Twitter, and Tumblr. As they work, these participants "are sold as a commodity to third-party advertisers" (219). The images produced by the Dr Pepper Snapple Group are an even more pronounced dimension of this relationship, since they're a direct appropriation of the creativity generated by participatory media collectives. That appropriation was then fed back into the memetic media ecology in the hope of drumming up surplus labor through its circulation.

As these practices become more predominant, noncommercial dimensions of collective public conversation risk being squeezed out. An example

Figure 6.8
Two stills from a Delta flight-safety video entitled "The Internetest Safety Video on the Internet." Top: "Double Rainbow Guy" stows two rainbows in the overhead bin; bottom: "Overly Attached Girlfriend" grips a flight attendant. Posted on May 20, 2015.

Figure 6.9
Six memetic images produced by the Dr Pepper Snapple Group to market their Sunkist Soda brand. Each references memetic subcultural jokes or memetic phrases. Collected in 2013.

comes from the endeavors of 4chan founder Christopher "moot" Poole, who has seen the platforms he's built struggle. Despite its cultural significance, 4chan has long been—as Parmy Olson phrased it in *Forbes* (2012)—a "web giant run on a shoe string." This is in part because of the kind of content housed on the site—it's not very easy to monetize the blatant antagonisms described in chapter 4—but also perhaps in part because of Poole's vocal opposition to the persistent identity, sponsored content, and data-mining practices on which other sites capitalize. Poole retired from 4chan in 2015, but assured participants that the site would keep running for the foreseeable future. For Fuchs—who lauds platforms like Wikipedia and Wikileaks as "shining beacons of a commons-based Internet and a political, networked public sphere" (2013, 221)—monetization shouldn't be necessary for vibrant participatory conversations. Instead, he argues, "the communicative commons of society should be available without payment or other access requirements for all and should not be privately owned or controlled by a class" (221).

But the relationship between memetic participation and commercial appropriation may not be as simple as either/or. Indeed, the collectivism and reappropriation foundational to memetic participation can both facilitate and critique hegemony, as multiple participants embrace memetic logics for multiple ends. Bricolage and poaching are at their core subtle subversions to dominant culture industries; vernacular creativity is likewise situated within everyday folk practices. Even within an increasingly corporatized and commercialized media ecology, participants can critique the practices ingrained all around them almost as easily as they can implicitly support them.

For instance, Reddit's system affords political publicity and viral marketing as much as it affords the policing of those practices. /r/HailCorporate is a watchdog subreddit, cataloguing alleged corporate content on the site. Likewise, when the Sunkist images in figure 6.9 surfaced, they were posted to /r/CringePics and /r/TerribleFacebookMemes, both of which focus critical attention on participatory media content deemed oblivious to the collective sensibilities of the Reddit social imaginary. On Twitter, accounts like "Brands Saying Bae" ("@BrandsSayingBae")—whose description satirically reads, "It's cool when a corporation tweets like a teenager. It makes me want to buy the corporation's products"—do similar work. Burgess and Green argue that YouTube's commercial dimensions aren't clear-cut either: "To understand YouTube's popular culture, it is not helpful to draw sharp distinctions between professional and amateur production, or between commercial and community practices. These distinctions are based in industrial logics more at home in the context of broadcast media rather than an understanding of how people use media in their everyday lives, or a knowledge of how YouTube actually works as a cultural system" (2009, 57). For this reason, Jenkins, Ford, and Green (2013) speak of participatory media collectives in terms of "engaged" labor rather than "exploited" labor. Their choice of the word "engagement" recognizes the active public dimensions of mediated participants, even as they produce content within commercial systems.

The culture industries that produce and exploit celebrity and commercialism beyond digital media are knotted up with the participatory practices that make up memetic media. Neither wholly liberating nor wholly hegemonic, memetic conversations balance antagonism and voice, and in doing so complicate existing culture industries without upending them.

Attribution and Authenticity in Memetic Media

Network gatekeeping practices can facilitate not only institutional control, but open participation as well. Due to their folk dimensions, memetic logics can facilitate the spread of both information and misinformation. Cultural participants create and transform content with inconsistent accuracy and credibility, and network gatekeepers circulate both in kind. Nahon and Hemsley warn that "viral events can spread ill-intentioned and deceptive content as easily as scandalous and humorous content. Virality's speed means people's lives, careers, and social statuses can all be compromised in a matter of days or hours" (2013, 103). Because memetic conversations are embedded in existing culture industries, publicity and commercialism are constant concerns; because memetic conversations spread through folk collectives, attribution and authenticity are struggles as well.

Sometimes—as with any good folk story—this dubious credibility is part of the fun. 4chan's /x/ board, housing discussions of paranormal phenomena, is ripe with entertaining and playful conversations about fantastic topics. There are threads speculating that pop star Miley Cyrus was killed and replaced with a duplicate (annotated photos circle differences in her facial structure through the years). There are threads urging participants to "ask a time traveler anything" (wherein the "time travelling" poster replies in character, navigating both an onslaught of skepticism and questions posed in apparent belief). There are also threads claiming that the 9/11 terrorist attacks on the World Trade Center were perpetrated by the U.S. government (which also turn out apparent believers and debunkers in equal measure). But as we've seen throughout this chapter, these open conversations come with tensions of their own.

After all, memetic participation exists within a media ecology where Poe's Law looms large, one where lulz are an integral component of vast conversations, and where participants can use anonymity to perform multiturn conversations with themselves. Earnestness, satire, and outright deceit are hard to parse out in the midst of memetic spread, especially given the diverse communicative goals of those creating, circulating, and transforming memetic texts. "You really think someone would do that," a popular refrain ironically asks, "just go on the internet and tell lies?" It's frequently employed as a sarcastic response when participants in forums speculate on the authenticity or credibility of what they're seeing. The actual pervasiveness of deceit through memetic media may be hard to verify, but the threat of such deceit is resonant enough to merit ample conversation. As we've seen, questions often arise about whether participants on ideological subreddits—like /r/ShitRedditSays—are perpetuating a subtle and complex satire or earnestly endorsing partisan views. We may be better off asking if motives matter at all when the conversations seem to come out the same regardless. The subreddit description for /r/MURICA—a house for hyperbolic American patriotism—underscores how unfruitful distinguishing ironic intent from earnest intent in memetic play can be. According to the description, /r/MURICA is "a parody subreddit (except when it's not) to celebrate freedom. If you don't like that then get the fuck off out of my country." The quasi disclaimer allows brash jingoism to thrive on the subreddit, a space where it's hard to tell the line between earnest fanaticism and satire of that fanaticism.

A redditor provided another example of this ambiguity on March 25, 2015, the day Zayn Malik left the pop group One Direction. In an /r/Videos post entitled "I made a video pretending to care about One Direction. CBS aired it," the poster linked to a YouTube video capturing a CBS report on Malik leaving One Direction. The CBS report included footage from the participatory media posts of several teenagers who had recorded videos lamenting Malik's departure. Included was a video of a teenage boy crying while holding a picture of Malik. After kissing the picture, he crumples it and presses it against his face. "That's pretty much how I reacted when I heard," the anchor jokes as the segment ends. The poster's insistence that his contribution was satirical met with playful barbs on his thread. There was also a charge that the thread's original poster wasn't even the teenager from the CBS video (the poster responded with a time-stamped photo of himself holding up a middle finger and a paper that read "Here's your damn proof"). All of this buzzing paratext was inconsequential to the message of the CBS video, which merely took advantage of a particularly colorful reaction for its human-interest segment. To CBS and its primary audiences, the memetic dimensions of what the footage represented (i.e., the "teenage overreaction to a pop culture event" meme) were more likely resonant than its specific factuality.

Much like folk texts more broadly, memetic media often walk a tense line between the discursive truth and the actual facts behind that truth. An example came with Obama's /r/AMA thread on August 29, 2012. Obama—as per /r/AMA custom—publically verified the authenticity of his identity to the Reddit community. That verification consisted of a tweet from the official "@BarackObama" Twitter account and a photo (figure 6.10). Neither was explicit proof that Obama himself was sitting at the keyboard responding to participants. The president's "verification" photo did nothing to demonstrate that he was on Reddit at that moment, or even that he was aware the photo was being used to say he was. And Obama's Q&A—consisting of ten fairly textbook answers to tightly screened policy and social questions—could have been copied right from his campaign website or easily penned by a staffer. All of this is not to suggest that Obama wasn't the one behind the keyboard during his /r/AMA thread. Rather, I mean to suggest that the discursive truth—the messaging of a president "participating" on Reddit—is what resonated. Whether or not it was actually Obama

Figure 6.10
American President Barack Obama's "verification photo" for his /r/AMA thread. Posted on August 29, 2012.

himself participating is less significant than the impression that a president engaged "the people" using this medium.

The narrative fit, just as the "bad yearbook photo" narrative fit the "Bad Luck Brian" meme. However, in his interview with Contrera (2015), Kyle Craven, the real "Bad Luck Brian," said the "goofy" portrait that made him a macro star never even appeared in his school's yearbook. He took the unflattering picture as a joke; administrators made him do a reshoot, but he got to keep prints of the rejected image. When his friend uploaded that joke photo to Reddit years later, the ironic dimensions of the original picture were washed away by its memetic resonance. The only thing evident in the text is its unflattering aesthetic, and so Craven became associated with a socially awkward stock character. The playful connotations that existed at the photo's genesis didn't spread with the photo itself; it became an apparently earnest premise for ironic play of its own.

These decontextualizations and recontextualizations make it easy for partial information and outright deceit to spread in participatory networks, provided the partial information or outright deceit fit the sentiment supported by network gatekeepers. James Estrin (2014) examines the story behind a set of memetic photos demonstrating this tension. The photos—of young, somber-looking African women—were superimposed with the hashtag "#BringBackOurGirls" and shared on Twitter in mid 2014. The hashtag campaign emerged in response to the kidnapping of 276 female Nigerian students by the Islamic militant group Boko Haram. Admirable as the campaign was, the popular images Estrin profiles weren't photos of the kidnapped girls, or even of girls from the same country. Instead, they were from a 2011 photo series profiling girls from Guinea-Bissau. The sentiment that made the images resonate won out over the fact that they weren't connected to the actual kidnappings. Their use, Estrin comments, "raises troubling questions of representation, and misrepresentation" in mediated participation. As they were memetically reappropriated, the individuals in the images were misappropriated, and two different nations were combined under the same mistakenly singular "African" mantle.

Along with sharing inaccurate photos, participants also commonly share quotations from famous figures—Abraham Lincoln, Albert Einstein, Thomas Jefferson, Marilyn Monroe, George Carlin, etc.—across mediated networks and collectives, a practice that also leaves itself open to ambiguous recontextualization. Often shared in image form (as decorative text next to a photo of the supposed originator of the quotation), these inspirational or apropos maxims are often memetically healthy—that is, they spread well to new participants and new moments—but they're also at times factually dubious.

Megan McArdle (2011), writing for the *Atlantic*, traced the "anatomy" of one such fake quotation, attributed to civil rights leader Martin Luther King Jr. It circulated across participatory media in the wake of the U.S. assassination of al-Qaeda leader Osama bin Laden in May 2011. In the midst of celebrations over bin Laden's death came more somber reflections on the senselessness and sadness of any form of violence, and of a global climate that premised such action. Some expressed that counterpoint in the form of a quotation supposedly written by King:

> I will mourn the loss of thousands of precious lives, but I will not rejoice in the death of one, not even an enemy. Returning hate for hate multiplies hate, adding deeper darkness to a night already devoid of stars. Darkness cannot drive out darkness; only light can do that. Hate cannot drive out hate; only love can do that.

McArdle—saying she agreed with the sentiment but was bothered by the misrepresentation—shows that the quotation is only half accurate. King did pen everything in the passage from the word "Returning" forward, but the first sentence wasn't his. McArdle traces the confusion back to a Facebook status that introduced King's quotation with a personal annotation, tying King's words to celebrations over the death of bin Laden:

> I will mourn the loss of thousands of precious lives, but I will not rejoice in the death of one, not even an enemy. "Returning hate for hate multiplies hate, adding deeper darkness to a night already devoid of stars. Darkness cannot drive out darkness; only light can do that. Hate cannot drive out hate; only love can do that." MLK Jr.

Somewhere in the process of that status being shared, the quotation marks separating King's words from their introduction fell off, as did the attribution to King at the end of the quotation, making it easier to spread the whole chunk of text as his. McArdle explains that the altered form was amplified when comedian Penn Jillette posted it for his massive audience. A few small mutations in the memetic spread of the message, and the inaccurate version became the standard. However dubious their factuality, though, the resonance of these aphorisms is what inspires their spread. And that resonance is tied to a discursive truth beyond specific facts.

But of course the internet didn't invent inaccuracy, and these issues have long been part of public conversation across all manners of mediated communication. Paul Martin Lester (1995) points out that photo manipulation is as old as photography itself; early photo retouchers would use brushes and ink to add hue to cheeks and color to dresses, and skilled photo engravers could even remove subjects from photos entirely. A pair of photographs taken during the Crimean War in 1855 by the famous photographer Roger Fenton (figure 6.11) provide an example of early photo manipulation.[3] They're a historical mystery and the subject of analysis by Errol Morris (2011). The two photos, which are largely the same, have one key difference between them. The conspicuous presence of cannonballs on the road in one image and their absence in the other have led to speculation that Fenton may have staged or otherwise altered elements of the photos for a desired aesthetic. The consensus—one supported by Morris—is that Fenton found a road with cannonballs along its edge and moved them to a position of prominence in the middle of the path for the second photo in figure 6.11. As Morris points out, Fenton exhibited both photos when he returned to London from Crimea, so deception may not have been his goal. However, the subtle aesthetic differences between the photos resonate in distinct ways, and therefore could very well demonstrate Fenton's play with different iterations of the same fixed content in order to produce different emotions in viewers.

Traditional gatekeepers have been known to spread inaccurate information as well, and participatory media can be a check to that inaccuracy as much as they can perpetuate it. One case, reported by Shawn Pogatchnik (2009) of the Associated Press, involves Wikipedia edits that a Dublin University student made to the page of late composer Maurice Jarre. Hours after the composer's death, the student took to Jarre's Wikipedia page and attributed to him a fabricated quotation about the power of music. Wikipedia editors quickly removed the fake sentiment, but not before journalists reproduced the falsity in their own reports. The quotation—which has Jarre stating, "When I die there will be a final waltz playing in my head that only I can hear"—was apparently too apropos to pass up. After a few outlets reproduced the quotation, other publications—caught in a journalistic echo chamber—could "fact check" its authenticity by citing other publications that had already reproduced it. The quotation circulated in this way for almost a month before the student went public, calling what he had done a "sociological experiment." For those circulating the quotation

Figure 6.11
Two iterations of a photograph by Roger Fenton entitled "Valley of the Shadow of Death." The top image portrays an empty road after a battle; the bottom image portrays that road littered with cannonballs. Taken on April 23, 1855.

without checking its attributions, the memetic resonance of its message was powerful enough to sustain its spread.

The culture industries that shade and shape memetic conversations are not to be underestimated. The systems that perpetuate celebrity, orchestrate publicity, and commodify culture are alive and well in participatory media. Our public conversations include their practices as much as they always have. But these practices are now themselves in conversation with more open expression, creativity, and debate. Because of the network gatekeeping foundational to memetic conversations, mediated interaction is not wholly open, but it's not wholly closed either. The reality is a media ecology displaying familiar restriction, even as it fosters innovation.

Public Conversations and Participatory Media

In the end, memetic media intertwine with the culture industries that have long dominated mediated participation. The texts that participants create, circulate, and transform exist within the cultural contexts that birth them, and are limited by the rules that govern those contexts. An example of this interdependence occurred when an unexpected hit was performed in orbit 250 miles above earth. Chris Hadfield, of the Canadian Space Agency, recorded a cover of David Bowie's 1969 "Space Oddity" while onboard the International Space Station, and posted it to YouTube in May 2013. Despite the 23 million views the video received in the year that followed, it was removed in May 2014. When he produced the cover, Hadfield only made a one-year deal with Bowie's publisher; he could leave the link active until May 2014, but then it had to come down. On his website, he recounts the moment of his video's demise:

> Thus it was with some regret that we took the "Space Oddity" video off YouTube last May. David Bowie and his publisher had been very gracious. They had allowed his work, his intellectual property, to be made freely available to everyone for a year, and had in fact worked with us and the Canadian Space Agency to make it happen. There was no rancor, and we removed it from YouTube to honor that agreement. (Hadfield undated)

Hadfield's play on Bowie's track—made all the more epic by his soaring setting—could only publicly, legally exist at the pleasure of the musician and his record label. The noncommercial nature of Hadfield's cover didn't matter, nor did the fact that it promoted not a corporate entity but a public agency (along with arguably drawing interest to Bowie's work itself). It couldn't exist on YouTube without the blessing of Bowie's label. Even though, according to Hadfield, Bowie called the video "possibly the most poignant version of the song ever created," the use of Bowie's intellectual property was subject to the culture industries that governed it.

The story does have a happy ending. At least for now. After the initial takedown, Hadfield petitioned to renew his copyright permissions. After communicating with Bowie's representatives, Hadfield received permission to upload the video again, this time for a two-year duration. Hadfield's memetic take on Bowie's "Space Oddity" is live on YouTube as of mid 2015, sitting at 25 million views and counting.

But his case—like every case we've seen in this chapter—raises questions about the nature of public conversations as they shift under the pressure of participatory media. We could rightly question the ethics of Hadfield's need for any sort of label permission to noncommercially share a song cover. Our memetic media ecology complicates issues of privacy, credibility, attribution, and ownership, with easy legal and ethical solutions often proving evasive. Debates over representation and appropriation will likely continue, and their resolution mandates, as Zittrain argues, "threading the needle between needed change and undue closure" (2008, 151). To Zittrain, participatory media need to remain generative, even if this complicates public conversations. The benefits of generativity outweigh potential risks, especially for public voice, which is sustained by the vibrancy that comes with generativity.

If memetic media are any indication, the generativity of public participants isn't going anywhere, even if it's inextricably intertwined with powerful culture industries. Memetic media are now under the purview of brands, managers, and merchandisers. They're used for campaigning and protest. They're the subject of gatekeeping and control. Our public conversations evidence this uneasy coexistence. This is the legacy of a conversational system built on memetic logics, implemented through memetic grammar and vernacular, and facilitating both antagonism and voice. The conclusion that follows will make an ultimate assessment of this world made meme.

Conclusion: The World Made Meme

Once in class—with the Photoshopped picture of Kanye West interrupting Martin Luther King, Jr. (figure 1.1) on the screen behind me—I asked my students to define *internet meme*. There was the usual desk staring and head scratching, until a student in the back spoke up. "It's like ... a nationwide inside joke," she said. Her unconventional definition inspired chuckles. But as the hours wore on, I realized its poignancy. Like inside jokes between friends, internet memes—the multimodal texts created, circulated, and transformed by countless cultural participants—balance the familiar and the foreign. And like inside jokes, internet memes are at once universal and particular; they allow creative play based on established phrasal, image, video, and performative tropes. The difference, of course, is the scale of these inside jokes. Assessing that scale, this book has charted the vibrancy that emerges when expressive strands become interactional threads, which in turn weave vast cultural tapestries. In the end, Richard Dawkins's (1976) genes may be selfish, but his memes are social.

The logics central to this book underscore the social significance of memetic media, and signify shifts in mediated public conversation. The memetic practices that came to define the subcultural in-jokes emerging out of esoteric forums in the early 2000s have proven applicable to conversational dynamics on a much grander scale. Multimodality, reappropriation, resonance, collectivism, and spread made "LOLCats" an early touchstone and propelled "Rickrolling" into mass attention. They guided massive playful invocations of "Imma let you finish" and the significant conversational threads around #YesAllWomen. But the spread of a specific meme isn't why memetic media are—on the whole—significant. Whether an individual meme lasts a night or a week or a year, whether it's shared on one thread, one site, one hashtag, or spirals out to millions of users in thousands of contexts, it is animated by the memetic logics explored in this book. By these logics media are made memetic, and by these logics public participants memetically make their social worlds.

Multimodality—in its intense integration of word, image, audio, video, and hypertext—facilitates the vibrant creative expression and conversation at the heart of memetic media. Some forms of this expression—like participating in a hashtag or uploading a photo—are widely accessible. Some forms—like Photoshopping or Auto-Tuning—are more specialized. Through these practices, mediated conversations are not just linguistic, or even just visual. Instead, these conversations rely on an array of communicative forms. And commentary spills out from these multiple sources. A captioned photo can be a conversational turn or a political argument; a GIF can express an emotion or spread an idea. With the ease and prevalence of multimodal communication, the lines between media texts and mediated conversations further intertwine, as do the lines between vernacular conversation and creative expression.

Within this multimodal vernacular, participants weave novel expression out of found material. As digital technologies have evolved, so too have participants' options for "making do" beyond the parameters of traditional culture industries. It is now easier than ever to transform texts that have come before, whether the source is a candid photo or a scene from a film or a music video from the 1980s. In the contemporary media ecology, reaction GIFs can poach popular source texts to make new statements, and even the tiniest photo edit can turn dominant reads into oppositional ones. As a result, the bricolage long common in folk expression is now even more thoroughly knotted up with the culture industries at the helm of popular media. Despite expressive shifts, those culture industries are not completely undone by participatory media. Reappropriation is such a persistent logic precisely because media industries still control the bulk of media content. Working within a system they don't own, cultural participants have found new ways to express themselves and engage with the expressions of others. Culture industries subsequently appropriate memetic material in turn, creating a tense relationship between populist participation and commercial commodification. In this reciprocal system, the dominant reading of a media text must contend with vocal oppositions and negotiations, as the reappropriation of the bricoleur becomes a staple of mediated public conversation.

Resonance is central to this memetic reappropriation. Through humor, irony, and wit, participants play with resonant texts, whether that resonance is a studium affiliation or a punctum prick. The motives and meanings of this play are not always straightforward. Memetic participation enables the ambivalence of Poe's Law. The fact that memetic irony and humor can both forward racist and misogynist perspectives and critique racist and misogynist perspectives—often without any way to demarcate which is which—illustrates this tension. But even in this ambivalent lingua franca, memetic media can resonate in the service of polyvocal public commentary. Empathy, anger, and sentimentality can resonate like play, and memetic media can help spread those emotions as well. The resulting "nationwide inside jokes" aren't always narrowly jokes, even if they do depend on the same self-referentiality and context as jokes. The nonchalance of a police officer pepper-spraying college students and the genuine frustration, sadness, and despair animating #BlackLivesMatter and #HandsUpDontShoot resonated deeply enough to inspire an outpouring of memetic media. Even in the most harrowing cases, memetic engagement follows familiar patterns; hefty conversations can resonate right alongside cute cats and "Sad Batman." Memetic media do not follow a specific template; they circulate when they connect with the participants who circulate them.

And individual resonance spirals into collective participation. Memetic media are the result of folk and populist—if not always inclusive—practices that give mass perspective priority over individual expression. This collectivism certainly isn't entirely harmonious or universal. Polyvocal expression and counterpublic contestation can be collectivist, but factionist too. When "We are the 99 Percent" becomes "We are the 53 Percent," for example, collectivism is evident both within and between agonistic public factions. The memetic lingua franca connects participants to both affiliation and contestation. But this collectivism is also imperfect because it leaves groups of people out. The white male centrality presumed by participants on forums like 4chan and Reddit can preclude the full participation of women and minorities. And this says nothing of those individuals who do not have access to the technologies or the cultural literacies that provide entry into collectivist spaces. Even if the inside jokes are "nationwide," there's still a whole world outside of their purview. Still, memetic media exist beyond individual signature or citation; they're collectively created, circulated, and transformed by those who can engage with them. The collective isn't necessarily the whole world, and it isn't always egalitarian and empowering, but it's more open than the gatekeeping practices associated with traditional mass media.

As these collective texts spread, participants memetically make their world. Memetic commentary moves through media systems woven together from the contributions of millions of unique participants. By adding a new bit of creativity to a fixed premise, participants are a generative part of a broader conversation. Their strands help craft vast cultural tapestries. Infrastructures and platforms matter to these tapestries, and to the spread of the ideas that weave them. Age-old gatekeepers have the power to pluck a YouTube video up from obscurity; new gatekeepers have the power to keep a hashtag off a "trending topics" list. However, in the midst of this gatekeeping, participants can create, circulate, and transform what matters to them. Multiple perspectives blend to shade broad conversations, even as frictions and factions emerge. As commentary spreads, strands intertwine, even if not always smoothly.

The tapestry can be vibrant even in its chaos. When participants punctuate a text message with "Imma let you finish," when they caption a work of art with their own inferred dialogue or use a GIF to tell a new story, when they employ a stereotype to make a joke or edit a photo to comment on an injustice, they do their part to make the social world they inhabit. Their contribution adds its particular color and texture to the broader tapestry. At the smallest level, the messages we spread are of our choosing. Even if we can't control collective sentiment—even if we can't control culture industries—we can decide what resonates with us and what bit of conversation we'll contribute. We have the power to weave our own strand into the tapestry. It's a small power, but it's ours, and it's more vibrant when it intertwines with the vibrant strands all around us.

Appendix: Methods and Ethics

This book is the result of a half-decade of participating in the vast collectives that create, circulate, and transform memetic media and analyzing their discourse. Beginning with preliminary Ph.D. dissertation work in late 2010, the research presented here is the culmination of consistent engagement with memetic texts, moments, and trends. This book's analysis is the result of thoughts refined through multiple presentations and publications over five years. My overarching research question has been—in one variation or another—the question presented in the introduction of this book: how do cultural participants weave memetic media into tapestries of public conversation? With every iteration of this project, I've worked to get closer to an appropriately nuanced analysis of that question.

However, during these years of research, the best methods for how to do that analysis haven't always been clear. Memetic media comprise vast tapestries of innumerable braided strands of text and context, and much of my analysis has focused on finding the right angle from which to see those tapestries. Early on, I found critical discourse analysis to be a helpful perspective for discerning the interrelationships essential to memetic media. Even the weaving metaphor that frames this book—strands, threads, knots, tapestries, braiding, intertwining—is developed from the work of critical discourse analysts Siegfried Jäger and Florentine Maier (2009), who employ it in their methodological guide. Understanding the implications of memetic media for public conversation has required a method that appreciates multimodal, intertextual connection, even while focusing on a corpus of individual texts.

And just as the best methods for analysis haven't always been clear, neither have the best ethics for how to conduct that analysis responsibly. Memetic media trouble easy answers to questions of attribution, authorship, privacy, and intellectual property. What resonates and spreads among cultural participants very often isn't limited to what's appropriate to include in a published analysis. As my own research has continued over the years, I've refined what I am willing to reproduce as part of my scholarship. I've also come up against ownership and distribution concerns that transcend my own personal values.

Even after this half-decade of research, I still don't have the best answers for all the methodological and ethical questions that arise from an extensive analysis of mediated cultural participation. My goal in this appendix is to present my thoughts so far, with the hope that they may be helpful to those planning to undertake similar projects with texts so fraught with tension. Below, I'll outline my methods for the critical discourse analytic study of memetic media, followed by the ethical considerations I've come to embrace during this analytic work.

Critical Discourse Analysis and Memetic Media

From the beginning of my collection of memetic media, I wanted to follow the advice of Christine Hine (2009), who asks those researching online communication to be mindful of how conversations, norms, values, practices, and patterns flow between sites, instead of just within them. While I knew in late 2010 from my own mediated cultural participation that sites like 4chan, Reddit, and Tumblr could all be fruitful to explore in depth, I opted instead to focus on the discourses that flowed between these sites. For all the memetic media that participants on 4chan, Reddit, and Tumblr produce, my goal wasn't an analysis of any one of these sites. My goal was, instead, an analysis of the conversations and practices that exist between and beyond these epicenters of memetic participation. All three feature prominently in this book, but all three exist interdependent with each other and with conversations outside them.

From the beginning of this study, I also followed the advice of Gerlinde Mautner (2005) and tried to establish a comprehensive picture of the "range of voices" significant to my questions about memetic media and public conversation. This meant more ambiguity and more vigilance, as I did my best to follow and collect resonant memetic moments across multiple contexts. The end result was a vibrant corpus, of which this book's examples are only a part. This corpus focused not only on prominent memetic collectives like 4chan, Reddit, and Tumblr, but also on memetic trends evident on larger sites like Twitter and YouTube, as well as on news and commentary about those trends from the journalistic outlets covering them.

Instead of narrowing my corpus by specific sites of interaction, I narrowed by what Jäger and Maier (2009) call discursive "strands," interconnected groups of texts connected by a common topic or context. As my collection and analysis of various discursive strands led to my framing of memetic media in terms of their predominant logics (multimodality, reappropriation, resonance, collectivism, and spread), I more purposefully honed collection and analysis around those thematic threads. As it became evident that specific media moments were culturally resonant and theoretically fruitful (Kanye West's interruptions, Occupy Wall Street, Reddit's Violentacrez debate, Barack Obama's engagement with memetic media), I more purposefully honed in on those contextual threads. I wove those threads together, knitting what I hoped would yield an ever-tighter argument as I forged ahead. Through the years, and across multiple publications, collection moved from broad and exploratory to intentional and purposeful as my ultimate argument became clearer.

From the beginning of this project, collection and analysis occurred simultaneously; analysis drove the flow from exploratory to purposive collection of discursive strands. When analyzing the images, forum threads, videos, tweets, and articles I collected, I kept focused on Teun van Dijk's maxim that the heart of a discourse analytic method is the study of "talk and text in context" (1997, 3). In fact, this emphasis was the foundation of the analytical work in this book. The critical dimensions of this analysis come from the insights of scholars such as Norman Fairclough and Ruth Wodak (1997), who argue that power relations are both reproduced and challenged through that talk and text. In particular, Fairclough's emphasis on discursive dimensions of inequality and "the many ways in which the dominant logic and dynamic are tested, challenged, and disrupted" (2009, 164) suited the questions of antagonism and voice I have addressed.

Implied in the maxim "talk and text in context" are multiple levels of emphasis in critical discourse analysis. "Talk and text" refers to a micro analysis of specific communication, the small strands formed by, say, individual posts, tweets, or articles. "Context" refers to the intertextual and interdiscursive tapestries those strands form through their more macro interconnection. The meso labels the liminal interactional space between micro strands and macro tapestries—the threads of conversation. Critical discourse analysis provides tools for each of these dimensions of talk and text, and all of them are essential to analyzing how small memetic texts weave big collective conversations. Van Dijk (1995) provides a few methodological tools for analyzing the social realities embedded in specific utterances. Syntax, structure, lexicon, semantics, organization, and style all carry value beyond the neutral conveyance of meaning. Likewise, Martin Reisigl and Ruth Wodak (2009) argue that ideologies are reproduced when topics are referenced, named, evaluated, and framed. Gunther Kress and Theo van Leeuwen (2006) provide a framework for understanding the multimodal dimensions of this talk and text, focusing on compositional and representational elements of visual texts like shape, perspective, color, movement, actors, and gaze. They show how multimodal texts can carry narratives and concepts in ways that are both familiar and unique when compared to spoken and written texts. Combining these different emphases, this study conceptualized its mediated texts as "single, multimodal communicative acts" (van Leeuwen 2004, 7), and applied this diverse range of analytic tools to their deconstruction.

Critical discourse analysis also provides tools for assessing the contextual relationships between texts, which are useful in assessing how ideologies and perspectives are normalized when strands intertwine. To Fairclough (2009), individual texts are consistently recontextualized as they spread across new contexts. Since broad social realities and individual stylistic tendencies intertwine in specific texts, Fairclough contends that discourse analysis should oscillate between analyzing individual expression and analyzing social practice. Reisigl and Wodak (2009) describe intertextuality as the bridge by which statements flow from one setting to another when participants create a juxtaposition, invoke a metaphor, or posit a truth, something consistently evident in the reappropriations prevalent in memetic media. Further, Mautner (2005) says text and discourse can intermingle in new ways thanks to the multimodality and hypertextuality of online communication. Because of digital technologies, texts can intertwine with more regularity, ease, and proficiency. This study kept those interrelations at its forefront.

An eye for intertextuality is helpful when analyzing ideologies. Jäger and Maier (2009) argue that ideological associations are made through "entanglements" of discursive strands, which knot up abstract values and specific conversations. To Ruth Wodak and Michael Meyer, "people with diverse backgrounds and interests may find themselves thinking alike in startling ways. Dominant ideologies appear as 'neutral,' holding on to assumptions that stay largely unchallenged" (2009, 8). Van Dijk is mindful that "to 'read off' ideologies from discourse is not always possible, precisely because ideologies need to be very general and fairly abstract" (2009, 79). However, he provides some methodological insight into just how we might connect discourse and ideology. When we look at the discursive actions of a collective—membership devices, "typical" acts, explicit aims, relations to others, and resources used—we can get empirical clues to the dominant ideologies of that group. In this way, we are able to not only "*describe* text and talk, but also to *explain* how real language and socially shared beliefs affect discourse production and how these are in turn affected by discourse" (79, original emphasis). This ideological work happens multimodally as well. Kress and van Leeuwen (2006) argue that images interweave "cultural and social histories" into new contexts and therefore carry ideologies in their dominant readings. This is the ideological power in the "stance" dimension of memetic texts identified by Limor Shifman (2013). While the content and form of a multimodal text can be read denotatively at face value, understanding stance—which voices are included and silenced, whether the text keys irony or earnestness, what communicative function it serves—requires connotative nuance. Interpreting stance helps interpret embedded ideologies.

These methodological insights were invaluable as I made my way through the vast discursive tapestry constituted by memetic media. An eye for "talk and text in context" helped me understand the social dimensions and ideological implications of the countless conversational turns that craft the vibrant participatory media ecology. Applying the micro-textual, meso-interactional, and macro-cultural insights of critical discourse analysis to memetic participation provided perspective as I assessed the conversations woven by collective contribution. The next section will discuss the ethical considerations of this analysis.

The Ethics of Visual Representation and Reproduction

As my years of work on memetic media have worn on, I have had to grow more intentional in my thinking about the ethical implications of that work. In particular, my perspectives on the ethics of visual representation have evolved, and the way I conduct my analysis has changed right alongside those perspectives. I've grown more reflective about the implications of a massive, vibrant, buzzing multimodal media ecology, and more reflexive about my role as a researcher in reproducing parts of that ecology. Memetic media—in their reappropriation, collectivism, and spread—often propagate without the consent of their subjects or attribution to their source texts. As we saw in chapter 6, a joke yearbook photo, a playful video from adolescence, or a candid shot snapped by a stranger on the street can have massive long-term consequences if the text resonates enough to spread. Even beyond all the established ethical considerations necessary during any kind of internet research—questions addressed in sources like Annette Markham and Nancy Baym's (2009) *Internet Inquiry*—the visual analysis central to this work deserves its own considerations. As Gillian Rose (2012) points out, visual research merits most of the same ethical considerations that are merited when working with interviews, ethnographic observations, or elicited data. However, visual research also carries "specific ethical dilemmas" (329), which I have had to reckon with. Over the years, I have had to reflect on both the prevalence of visual representations and on my reproduction of them in my work.

In my earliest work on memetic media, I was cavalier about the visual material I reproduced. I was largely oblivious to my role in spreading a person's likeness or their intellectual property without consent or attribution. That early work is brimming with candid photos and unsourced creative work. I was studying memetic texts, after all, and if it was a memetic text, then, I believed, it was fine to reproduce it in my work. It was already "public" anyway, I reasoned; it was already "up on the internet" for everyone to see. But after years of stories about unwanted fame and misattributed material—after years of thoughtful editors and reviewers challenging this unreflexive stance—I have refined my thoughts on visual representation. Charles Ess's (2014) consideration of the privacy and distribution issues complicated by digital media have helped this refinement, as have Rose's (2012) discussions of consent and copyright in visual research, particularly when it comes to "found materials." I have also consulted the ethical recommendations of the Association of Internet Researchers (Markham, Buchanan, and the Association of Internet Researchers Ethics Working Committee 2012), the International Visual Sociology Association (Papademas and the International Visual Sociology Association 2009), Britain's Economic and Social Research Council and its National Centre for Research Methods (Wiles et al. 2008), the Society for Cinema and Media Studies (Society for Cinema and Media Studies 2010), and the International Communication Association (Jazi, Aufderheide, and the International Communication Association 2010). In particular, I focused most intently on issues of privacy and intellectual property, two prevalent ethical concerns in visual analysis.

Concerns about privacy in visual representations emerge from the perspective that individuals with a reasonable expectation of privacy—an admittedly murky category—should not have their likeness reproduced without their expressed consent. Dianna Papademas and the International Visual Sociology Association (2009) point to our ethical obligation to protect "confidential information" in photo reproduction. Britain's National Centre for Research Methods (Wiles et al. 2008) advise that "consent, confidentiality, and anonymity" should guide the reproduction of images in research. Annette Markham, Elizabeth Buchanan, and the Association of Internet Researchers Ethics Working Committee are mindful of the blurry line between "personal and private" and "public and freely available" content in internet research (2012, 9). A reasonable expectation of privacy—as we saw in chapter 6—is often ignored in memetic participation, but I became convinced I needed to make adjustments in my own work so as not to perpetuate likenesses and representations when privacy might be expected.

Of course that stipulation is ambiguous. Is a face "confidential information"? Do you have a "reasonable expectation of privacy" if you post your image to your public MySpace profile as chapter 6's Blake Boston did? Did Boston have a reasonable expectation of privacy before he embraced the public persona of his "Scumbag Steve" stock character, but not after? Did the public appearances of Boston or "Ridiculously Photogenic Guy" or "Overly Attached Girlfriend" or "Bad Luck Brian" transform them into "public figures" that I could therefore responsibly include? After all, as the National Centre for Research Methods states, "personal information should be treated confidentially and participants anonymized unless they choose to be identified" (Wiles et al. 2008, 8). While the sentiment is normally applied to informed consent, do public appearances constitute a choice to become open to reproduction? These figures were all certainly the subjects of journalistic attention, but what about the standards of scholarly attention?

The criteria are imperfect, but I did make distinctions between "public" and "private" figures, and chose not to include in this book the likenesses of "private" figures. In particular, I followed the advice of Papademas and the International Visual Sociology Association (2009) when it came to reproductions that require "special sensitivity" because they disrupt seclusion, disclose embarrassing facts, put figures in a false light, or unreasonably appropriate their likeness. Since much memetic reappropriation could easily commit any of these injustices, I erred toward caution in the likenesses I included here. I made the decision to focus on reproducing images I deemed "public" because of their popular media source material, their reproduction of public figures, or their origin as stock photos, which are produced to be spread. For instance, the three stock character macros in figure 4.7—"Successful Black Man," "High Expectations Asian Father," and "Sheltering Suburban Mom"—each fit these criteria. The image for "Successful Black Man" comes from a widely used stock photo; "High Expectations Asian Father" captures an actor in the 2007 South Korean film *Epitaph*; and "Sheltering Suburban Mom" reappropriates a publicity photo of a novelist. While probably none of these figures imagined their likeness would become a stock character macro, I (however imperfectly) deemed the images public enough to merit inclusion. I chose to reproduce their likenesses—while choosing to remove some others—as part of a difficult ethical choice about a reasonable expectation of privacy.

A potential loophole exists when it comes to reproducing the images of "private" citizens. As Papademas and the International Visual Sociology Association (2009) argue, consent for reproduction might not be required for images captured in "public places." This means that while, say, the protest photos in figures 5.4, 5.8, and 5.9 contain images of "private" citizens, they were at a "public" gathering, and so their inclusion in this book might be defensible. Same with the background individuals in Will King's original "Mr. Ridiculously Photogenic Guy" photo I chose not to include. Even further, if participatory media sites are metaphorical "public spaces," then perhaps the faces of individuals in "99 Percent" images (figures 5.10–5.13) might be considered public. After all, they were posted about a public issue to a public site with the expectation of publicity. However, in these cases I was mindful of the advice of Markham, Buchanan, and the Association of Internet Researchers Ethics Working Committee, who point out that "while a participant might not think his or her information is sensitive now, this might change in five years" (2012, 10). This book will continue to exist long after a rally in 2011; the work carries its message beyond the tumblog that housed "99 Percent" images that same year.

Therefore, I wanted to respect figures who were "public" only by nature of their likeness being photographed at a public protest, and I appreciate that uploading content to a tumblog in 2011 is not necessarily granting consent to be included in a book published in 2016. My decision for these images, then, was to crop out background participants and identifying features (cropping faces from the eyes up was an admittedly imprecise way to diminish "identifying features"). Cropping, though, is an imperfect solution. As Britain's National Centre for Research Methods puts it, "the purpose of visual images is that they can portray something additional to that of text alone; so to tamper with images in ways that obscure certain important details, such as people's facial expressions, makes the purpose of collecting visual images questionable" (Wiles et al. 2008, 23). Instead, they claim that "the more common approach favoured by social researchers is to present visual data in its entirety, with consent, and not to attempt to anonymise individuals" (27). However, this ideal becomes difficult when dealing with a protest photo taken in an unknown city and posted to Reddit, or a "99 Percent" image uploaded to Tumblr without contact information. My decision to crop these photos was a compromise born out of the nature of the texts I was analyzing.

Decisions about whose identity to reveal and whose identity to protect also required a series of judgment calls, which I made as thoughtfully as possible as I tried to balance insightful analysis with ethical analysis. I didn't reproduce the likeness of protestors, but I did reproduce the name and likeness of University of California, Davis, police officer John Pike, whose actions while in the line of duty unexpectedly made him a public figure. I didn't reproduce the original "Ridiculously Photogenic Guy" photograph to protect the privacy of the other runners in the image, but I didn't crop the people out of the background of Peter Souza's photo in figure 6.3, who were included in an official White House image posted for publicity purposes. These decisions about privacy and representation—while certainly open to critique—were my best attempt to produce valuable scholarship that also protected the dignity of those at the heart of its analysis.

A desire to protect reasonable expectations of privacy also guided my decision to include so many pop cultural texts as examples in this book. The reproduction of Kanye West in figures 1.1–1.3 or Barack Obama in figures 1.4, 6.3, 6.4, and 6.10 is defensible on the grounds that those individuals have come to expect this kind of visual reproduction as part of their status. However, my decision comes with its own ethical complications, given the ambiguous nature of intellectual property and memetic reappropriation. As Daphne Keller argues of mashup music, "the cultural practice of sampling meshes very poorly with copyright, the body of law which turns creative expression into private property" (2008, 136). Those tensions carry over into visual representations and research on those representations. To Ess, the present ease of capturing and transmitting images means that "the ethics of both consent in photography and copyright in publication are now conjoined in new ways that we simply have not had to think through before" (2014, 13). The source texts for the memetic images presented in this book ranged from iconic to obscure to downright unverifiable. I did my best to provide attribution when texts had an identifiable source, but many included here were so nebulously created and spread so widely that I decided listing the year of collection provided sufficient enough context.

I also opted for the most part not to include the given names or screen names of specific public participants, instead attributing content to the sites that curated texts: individual subreddits, 4chan boards, Imgur galleries, tumblogs, and Twitter accounts. I did this both in the name of privacy and in the name of not conflating "curator" with "creator." However, I acknowledge that—particularly on more individualistic sites like Twitter and Tumblr—the line between "creator's screen name" and "curating site" is a blurry one. Saying "this came from /r/TheWalkingDead or /co/" provides less identifying detail than saying "this came from KanyeWesAnderson.tumblr.com or @ZackSnyder." In decisions about attribution, the desire to protect participant privacy and the desire to credit creative expression often butted heads.

But even perfect attribution wouldn't solve all the complications that come with reproducing visual content. The legality and ethicality of reproducing images are murky even within my home nation of the United States, to say nothing of the complications that come from the global dimensions of memetic imagery. On the one hand, it would be easy to invoke the perspectives of what Hector Postigo (2012) calls the "digital rights movement," which uses the ambiguous legal concept of "fair use" as a symbolic "master frame" underscoring the ethicality and necessity of openly reproducing information. On the other hand, I recognize that fair use is a complicated concept, as evidenced by the copyright restrictions placed on this very book—perhaps paradoxical for an analysis of open media texts. As I made decisions about what material was fair to include without permission or payment, the fair use guides of the Society for Cinema and Media Studies (Society for Cinema and Media Studies 2010) and the International Communication Association (Jazi, Aufderheide, and the International Communication Association 2010) were particularly helpful.

It was help I certainly needed when considering the ethical and legal ambiguities inherent in the reproduction of popular culture texts. By including the Kanye Wes Anderson images in chapter 1, was I required to retain rights from Kanye West's label for his lyrics? Wes Anderson's studio for his films? The managers of the tumblog for their reappropriation? Or no one, because of the noncommercial, transformative nature of the images and the scholarly nature of their inclusion here? These questions came up time and again. The reappropriation essential to memetic media made it impossible to conduct analysis without reproducing remixes on journalistic photos, screen captures from popular media, and even classic works of art. The "Pepper Spray Cop" images in figures 5.6 and 5.7 include all three. The annotated images in this book are born from a chain of reappropriations, and the protocols for their reproduction are unsettled. This is especially true in the case of "orphan works," creations and transformations that cannot be easily traced back to an owner for attribution or permission.

I also included several unannotated images that reproduce popular media texts with no transformation at all. Does the reproduction of still images captured from animated GIFs—which themselves reproduce scenes from TV shows and films—constitute an intellectual property violation? What about the pop cultural ephemera of promotional photos (figures 2.4, 2.11, 6.3)? Screenshots taken from videos posted to YouTube by both massive corporate entities (figures 6.1, 6.4, 6.6, 6.8) and smaller "amateur" participants (figure 6.5) are of issue too. In a media ecology premised on reappropriation, a rigid conceptualization of the ethics of reproduction would mean no text would be reproduced, especially if amateur and candid visuals were also removed for the sake of privacy.

It is for these reasons that I chose to reproduce pop cultural reappropriations—citing and attributing their source material as best I could—premised on the "master frame" of fair use. The reappropriated pop media in this book, I argue, do not harm the commercial value of their original (not all of which were commercial products to begin with). The Society for Cinema and Media Studies endorses the fair use of intellectual property in the name of "historical, theoretical, or aesthetic arguments" (2010, 182), and the International Communication Association endorses it in the service of "analysis, criticism, commentary" (Jazi, Aufderheide, and the International Communication Association 2010, 9). My goal was a mixture of all of that. And even beyond my analysis, when memetic texts are annotated and altered (and perhaps even when they're not), their use is in service of transformative creative expression that is shared openly across participatory media collectives. Both at the level of creative expression and at the level of scholarly investigation, I stand by the argument that images reproduced here are fair use. However, I also acknowledge that fair use does not mean unfettered use. During my analysis, I was mindful of my obligation to reproduce only what was needed for that analysis. I was also mindful of my obligation to attribute and cite source material when possible, even if—in line with the best practices above—I felt no particular obligation to seek permission when reproducing that source material.

Fair use does not mean carte blanche for completely open appropriation; it does mean the freedom to conduct the kind of analysis I've attempted to model. Decisions on what texts to include in this book and how to include them weren't always easy, and my thoughts on how to ethically treat the creative expressions analyzed here have evolved over time. My ultimate hope for this work is that it balances thorough analysis with a respect for the vibrant individuals and collectives that produce memetic media.

Notes

Introduction

1. For a book called *The World Made Meme*, it's perhaps ironic to focus largely on U.S. and Western examples. I acknowledge this limitation, but also acknowledge the factors that generate it. This limited focus is due in part to the fact that the only cultural analysis I can fully undertake is of my own cultural context. Given how intensely intertextual and referential memetic media are, trying to disentangle the knots of callback and allusion for a cultural context not my own would be irresponsible, if not impossible. Fortunately, others are applying memetic study to collectives outside of Western contexts (see Mina 2014; Pearce and Hajizada 2014). Another reason for this book's U.S.-centered perspective is that memetic media have long been what Giselinde Kuipers (2002) calls "blandly global," largely spreading in English and largely furthering Western perspectives, no matter who's interacting. Limor Shifman, Hadar Levy, and Mike Thelwall find that as internet jokes spread, they "serve as powerful agents of globalization and Americanization" (2014, 739), since they globally carry American cultural contexts without much "localization" into the cultures they spread to along the way.

Chapter 1

1. For more on my decisions about image attributions in the very murky context of memetic media analysis, see the appendix for a discussion of the methods and ethics of visual representation and reproduction.

2. *Tumblog* is a term for personal blogs curated on Tumblr, combining the two words.

3. *Original content* (often shortened to "OC") is a contested term on participatory media collectives like 4chan, Reddit, and Tumblr. Sometimes it's used to denote something never published before, such as a new piece of fan art or a new set of photographs. Sometimes it's used to mark newly reappropriated material, such as a new conversion of a film segment into a GIF file, or a new caption on an old image.

The conflicting use of this term speaks to the tensions in memetic media between imitation and transformation, between creativity and pastiche. These tensions will be addressed in chapter 2.

4. I recognize that—semantically and theoretically—the line between *appropriation* and *reappropriation* is blurry. For instance, my use of *reappropriation* here might by some definitions be closer to *appropriation,* since appropriation can mean "taking from one context to another." Likewise, reappropriation is sometimes used to narrowly describe the act of marginalized groups positively employing a derogatory label previously employed by dominant groups. Here—and blending bits of both—the "re" in *reappropriation* is like the "re" in *reciprocal* or *recursive.* It acknowledges that as individuals take from one context to another to craft their shared texts, even the texts they're taking from have borrowed from cultural contexts that have come before. Further, accounting for power dynamics as Michel de Certeau (1984) does, I argue that appropriation occurs when dominant discourses, institutions, and industries take from populist practices, and reappropriation occurs when public participants craft their texts by taking from those dominant institutions. By this read, Kanye West and Wes Anderson might be said to appropriate cultural tropes and artistic forms to craft their products; "Kanye Wes Anderson" might reappropriate those products for their folk expressions. Or perhaps "Kanye Wes Anderson" stereotypically appropriates African American vernacular as the source of its humor. Regardless, the process is reciprocal, and the power dynamics of that reciprocity will feature heavily in the last half of this book.

5. I originally conceptualized this logic as centering on "humor," as humor was the most obviously resonant part of many of the memetic texts I was studying. I would like to thank Michelle Forelle for encouraging me to think about the larger concept behind that humor, since memetic media don't really have to be funny. Likewise, I'd like to thank Kate Miltner for setting my thinking toward "emotional resonance" instead. Last, I'd like to thank Whitney Phillips for honing that thinking by helping me connect Roland Barthes's (1981) studium and punctum with the idea of resonance. The thought in this section is iterative and collective in these ways.

6. The tumblog was reportedly created in response to a term coined by *Fox News* host Jesse Watters. Watters used the term "Beyoncé Voters" to describe the "single ladies" (a Beyoncé track) who Hillary Clinton would be wooing for the 2016 American Presidential election. The tumblog's intent is to reappropriate the essentialism of the label (see Schroeder 2014).

Chapter 2

1. *Subreddit* is the name given to Reddit's participant-created pages, which function as interdependent forums. They're accessible through their own URL and also via a newsfeed cataloging all of a subscriber's chosen subreddits. Their shorthand label

comes from their URL. The atheism subreddit is located at https://www.reddit.com/r/Atheism/, so its shorthand label on the site is /r/Atheism.

2. *Dank* could also imply its more literal definition: cold, damp, and musty. The common reappropriation of slang in participatory media collectives convinces me that the intended use here is an ironic invocation of the slang for marijuana. However, it's possible that the creator of the image is simply comparing memes to a moldy old basement. But both the ironic slang and the literal dictionary definitions of the term bring one to the same assessment: memes are past their prime.

3. As critical discourse analysts, Kress and van Leeuwen (2006) stress that these culturally specific systems of meaning have the power to both privilege and silence certain perspectives, conversations, and identities. Chapters 4 and 5 will specifically address this potential.

4. The resonance of these sorts of anachronistic reappropriations is also evidenced by the "Fly Art Productions" tumblog analyzed in chapter 1, the "Medieval Reactions" Twitter account analyzed in chapter 3, and the "Ruling Clawss" comics analyzed in chapter 5.

5. As of 2015, some of these limiting factors are evolving with new takes on the GIF premise. Reddit users are turning to http://gfycat.com, which presents GIFs as HTML5 video files, allowing higher definition at smaller file sizes and control over playback. On 4chan, participants can upload WebM files, which also have playback control and can carry sound. Imgur introduced a higher-definition GIFV format to allow clearer or longer looped videos. The popular Vine app allows participants to share short videos—with full audio—on a loop as well. Older GIF files still have a place in this more diverse ecology, and the existence of all these new options for looped videos is a testament to the resonance of the stalwart format.

6. Like subreddits on Reddit, the shorthand label for *boards* on 4chan comes from their URL. The "Comics and Cartoons" board is located at http://boards.4chan.org/co/, so its shorthand label on the site is /co/.

Chapter 3

1. I'm less concerned with the idea of an "aesthetic good or bad" when it comes to popular culture texts. Prescriptive formalism fails to account for the diverse perspectives, backgrounds, goals, and motivations that constitute popular culture. Jean Burgess (2007) insists that the "creativity" in "vernacular creativity" does not prescribe a standard of quality, but rather describes the creation of cultural texts, objects, and performances. That being said, I am convinced that assessments of "ethical right and wrong" when examining populist participation are essential. Chapters 4, 5, and 6 will undertake this assessment when it comes to memetic participation.

2. Before lamenting the "corruption" of language that occurred between 1939 and 2015 as evidenced by the "textspeak" in figure 3.10, we should note that the 1939 version of the line inspired its own pearl-clutching concern. "Damn" was an obscenity frowned upon by the motion picture industry at the time. The 2015 version, to its credit, omits this once-salacious swear word.

Chapter 4

1. Portions of this chapter were originally published as "Hacking the Social: Internet Memes, Identity Antagonism, and the Logic of Lulz," *Fiberculture Journal* 22. Available at http://twentytwo.fibreculturejournal.org/fcj-156-hacking-the-social-internet-memes-identity-antagonism-and-the-logic-of-lulz/.

2. On March 16, 2015, Jonathan Capehart of the *Washington Post* reported that "Hands Up, Don't Shoot" was "built on a lie." A newly released Department of Justice report on Brown's death provided strong evidence that the story of Brown's attempted surrender "isn't corroborated by ballistic and DNA evidence, and multiple witness statements." But even with this evidence, the phrase "Hands Up, Don't Shoot" and the related "Black Lives Matter" still carry memetic value. Beyond the specifics of Brown's death, the memes resonate because they connect to more systemic social inequalities, ones not dependent on how Brown died. As Capehart himself explains, the Department of Justice report "does not diminish the importance of the real issues unearthed in Ferguson by Brown's death. Nor does it discredit what has become the larger 'Black Lives Matter.'" Capehart says "the false Ferguson narrative stuck because of concern over a distressing pattern of other police killings of unarmed African American men and boys." In other words, it resonated because of the larger injustices it represented.

3. As evidence of the ambivalent, polysemic nature of memetic irony, a friend of mine reacted to the characterization of feminist anger in figure 4.9 by saying, "Actually, I do find righteous anger to be an effective tool for fighting patriarchy." To her, the Hulk comparison was a favorable one.

Chapter 5

1. Portions of this chapter were originally published as "Pop Polyvocality: Internet Memes, Public Participation, and the Occupy Wall Street Movement," *International Journal of Communication* 7. Available at http://ijoc.org/index.php/ijoc/article/view/1949.

2. In an interview with *Grist* (Cortes 2014), former Adbusters editor and OWS organizer Micah White calls the movement a "constructive failure." Rather than emphasizing shifts in public conversation, White points to electoral success as an indicator of progress, and laments that OWS did not produce such success. "We believed that

people's assemblies were enough to gain political sovereignty," he told the site. "This turned out to not be true. To gain political sovereignty we must win elections." To White, the OWS message didn't have the longevity or fecundity to formally influence political power.

3. The issue of photo representation and the control individuals should have over their likenesses is an ethical gray area. See the appendix for a discussion of that ambiguity and the decisions made about photo representations for this book.

4. Of course, even if the contested "53 percent" fact is accurate, it is as fallacious to imply that all of those sympathetic to OWS do not pay income tax as it is to assume that "99 percent" of the population is in the OWS ingroup.

5. This point can be argued, and there may be cases where connecting OWS to *Harry Potter*, *Star Wars*, and *Lord of the Rings* is intentionally, narrowly political. The fact that the top three images in figure 5.14 pull from such beloved texts might be evidence of more than indifference. See Henry Jenkins (2006) for memetic uses of fictional pop culture narratives in public conversation.

Chapter 6

1. Engaging with audiences on *Funny or Die* and *Buzzfeed* is smart political messaging. If Obama's goal is to promote the Affordable Care Act—a controversial healthcare policy on which his presidential legacy could very well rest—then catering to uninsured youth through the media platforms they regularly visit may be the best approach. Fitting the Affordable Care Act message into a communicative mold already established on those sites—if done well—results in a message that reaches a demographic with a high percentage of uninsured voters. In both cases, the successful spread of the videos—even as they attracted some negative commentary for being "beneath" the presidential office—implies that something in their form, content, or both resonated with participants.

2. See the appendix on the methods and ethics of visual representation and reproduction for more on my own tensions about representation, publicity, and consent.

3. I would like to thank Jacob Steere-Williams for introducing me to Roger Fenton's "Valley of the Shadow of Death" and for helping me develop its connections to memetic media during a class we co-taught on media history.

References

Alfonso, Fernando, III. 2014. "The Internet Meme Is Dying, and Reddit Is Killing It." *Daily Dot*, May 15. http://www.dailydot.com/lol/internet-memes-future-reddit/.

Appadurai, Arjun. 1996. *Modernity at Large: Cultural Dimensions of Globalization*. Minneapolis: University of Minnesota Press.

Apple, Lauri. 2011. "Jay-Z Not Selling His Controversial 'Occupy All Streets' Shirts Anymore." *Gawker*, November 12. http://gawker.com/5858978/jay-z-not-selling-his-controversial-occupy-all-streets-shirts-anymore.

Aunger, Robert. 2000. Introduction. In *Darwinizing Culture: The Status of Memetics as a Science*, ed. Robert Aunger, 1–23. Oxford: Oxford University Press.

Bakhtin, M. M. 1986. "From Notes Made in 1970–71" (1970). In *Speech Genres and Other Late Essays*, ed. Caryl Emerson and Michael Holquist, 132–158. Austin: University of Texas Press.

Barthes, Roland. 1977. *Image, Music, Text*. New York: Hill and Wang.

Barthes, Roland. 1981. *Camera Lucida: Reflections on Photography*. New York: Farrar, Straus, and Giroux.

Baym, Geoffrey, and Chirag Shah. 2011. "Circulating Struggle: The On-line Flow of Environmental Advocacy Clips from *The Daily Show* and *The Colbert Report*." *Information Communication and Society* 14 (7): 1–22.

Bennett, Andy, and Keith Kahn-Harris. 2004. *After Subculture: Critical Studies in Contemporary Youth Culture*. Basingstoke, UK: Palgrave Macmillan.

"Best Memes of 2013: Editorial Choices | Know Your Meme." 2013. Know Your Meme, December 13. http://knowyourmeme.com/blog/meme-review/best-memes-of-2013-editorial-choices.

Bowers, Paul. 2012a. "Got Questions for the Ridiculously Photogenic Bridge Runner?" *Charleston City Paper*, April 4. http://www.charlestoncitypaper.com/

charleston/got-questions-for-the-ridiculously-photogenic-bridge-runner/Content?oid=4049186.

Bowers, Paul. 2012b. "Ridiculously Photogenic Guy Is a Local Boy." *Charleston City Paper*, April 5. http://www.charlestoncitypaper.com/charleston/ridiculously-photogenic-guy-is-a-local-boy/Content?oid=4050179.

Brideau, Kate, and Charles Berret. 2014. "A Brief Introduction to Impact: 'The Meme Font.'" *Journal of Visual Culture* 13 (3): 307–313.

Brock, André. 2012. "From the Blackhand Side: Twitter as a Cultural Conversation." *Journal of Broadcasting and Electronic Media* 56 (4): 529–549.

Burgers, Christian, Margot van Mulken, and Peter Jan Schellens. 2012. "Verbal Irony: Differences in Usage across Written Genres." *Journal of Language and Social Psychology* 31 (3): 290–310.

Burgess, Jean. 2007. "Vernacular Creativity and New Media." Ph.D. diss., Queensland University of Technology, Australia.

Burgess, Jean, and Joshua Green. 2009. *YouTube: Online Video and Participatory Culture*. Malden, MA: Polity.

Capehart, Jonathan. 2015. "'Hands Up, Don't Shoot' Was Built on a Lie." *Washington Post*, March 16. https://www.washingtonpost.com/blogs/post-partisan/wp/2015/03/16/lesson-learned-from-the-shooting-of-michael-brown/.

Carbone, Nick. 2013. "Top 10 Memes." *Time*, December 4. http://newsfeed.time.com/2013/12/04/pop-culture-and-social-media/slide/top-10-memes/.

Chen, Adrian. 2012. "Unmasking Reddit's Violentacrez, the Biggest Troll on the Web." *Gawker*, October 12. http://gawker.com/5950981/unmasking-reddits-violentacrez-the-biggest-troll-on-the-web.

Contrera, Jessica. 2015. "Being Bad Luck Brian: When the Meme that Made You Famous Starts to Fade Away." *Washington Post*, January 15. https://www.washingtonpost.com/lifestyle/style/being-bad-luck-brian-when-the-meme-that-made-you-famous-starts-to-fade-away/2015/01/05/07cbf6ac-907c-11e4-a412-4b735edc7175_story.html.

Corner, John, and Dick Pels, eds. 2003. *Media and the Restyling of Politics*. London: Sage.

Cortes, Amber. 2014. "An Occupy Founder Says the Next Revolution Will Be Rural." *Grist*, April 28. http://grist.org/politics/an-occupy-founder-says-the-next-revolution-will-be-rural/.

Costanza-Chock, Sasha. 2012. "Mic Check! Media Cultures and the Occupy Movement." *Social Movement Studies* 11 (3–4): 375–385.

Couldry, Nick. 2010. *Why Voice Matters: Culture and Politics after Neoliberalism*. Los Angeles: Sage.

Croeser, Sky, and Tim Highfield. 2014. "Occupy Oakland and #oo: Uses of Twitter and the Occupy Movement." *First Monday* 19 (3). http://firstmonday.org/ojs/index.php/fm/article/view/4827/3846.

Dahlberg, Lincoln. 2011. "Re-constructing Digital Democracy: An Outline of Four 'Positions.'" *New Media and Society* 13 (6): 855–872.

Dahlberg, Lincoln. 2014. "The Habermasian Public Sphere and Exclusion: An Engagement with Poststructuralist-Influenced Critics." *Communication Theory* 24 (1): 21–41.

Dahlgren, Peter. 2009. *Media and Political Engagement: Citizens, Communication, and Democracy*. Cambridge: Cambridge University Press.

Dahlgren, Peter. 2013. "Tracking the Civic Subject in the Media Landscape: Versions of the Democratic Ideal." *Television and New Media* 14 (1): 71–88.

Dawkins, Richard. 1976. *The Selfish Gene*. Oxford: Oxford University Press.

Dawkins, Richard. 1982. *The Extended Phenotype: The Gene as the Unit of Selection*. Oxford: Oxford University Press.

De Certeau, Michel. 1984. *The Practice of Everyday Life*. Berkeley: University of California Press.

DeLuca, Kevin, Shawn Lawson, and Ye Sun. 2012. "Occupy Wall Street on the Public Screens of Social Media: The Many Framings of the Birth of a Protest Movement." *Communication, Culture and Critique* 5 (4): 483–509.

Douglas, Nick. 2014. "It's Supposed to Look Like Shit: The Internet Ugly Aesthetic." *Journal of Visual Culture* 13 (3): 314–339.

Elliott, Stuart. 2013. "Soft-drink Giant Wants Consumers to Be 'Impressed.'" *New York Times*, February 25. http://mediadecoder.blogs.nytimes.com/2013/02/25/soft-drink-giant-wants-consumers-to-be-impressed/.

Elmore, Christina. 2012. "Really Photogenic Guy in Cooper River Bridge Run Goes Viral." *Post and Courier*, April 5. http://www.postandcourier.com/article/20120405/PC16/120409571/1165.

Eppink, Jason. 2014. "A Brief History of the GIF (So Far)." *Journal of Visual Culture* 13 (3): 298–306.

Ess, Charles. 2014. *Digital Media Ethics*. 2nd ed. Cambridge: Polity.

Estrin, James. 2014. "The Real Story about the Wrong Photos in #BringBackOurGirls." *New York Times*, May 8. http://lens.blogs.nytimes.com/2014/05/08/the-real-story-about-the-wrong-photos-in-bringbackourgirls/.

Fairclough, Norman. 2009. "The Dialectical-Relational Approach to Critical Discourse Analysis." In *Methods of Critical Discourse Analysis*, ed. Ruth Wodak and Michael Meyer, 162–186. Los Angeles: Sage.

Fairclough, Norman, and Ruth Wodak. 1997. "Critical Discourse Analysis." In *Discourse as Social Interaction*, ed. Teun van A. Dijk, 258–284. London: Sage.

Fleming, Juliet. 2001. *Graffiti and the Writing Arts of Early Modern England*. London: Reaktion Books.

Fonarow, Wendy. 2006. *Empire of Dirt: The Aesthetics and Rituals of British Indie Music*. Middletown, CT: Wesleyan University Press.

Fuchs, Christian. 2013. "Class Exploitation on the Internet." In *Digital Labor: The Internet as Playground and Factory*, ed. Trebor Scholz, 211–224. New York: Routledge.

Gaby, Sarah, and Neal Caren. 2012. "Occupy Online: How Cute Old Men and Malcolm X Recruited 400,000 U.S. Users to OWS on Facebook." *Social Movement Studies* 11 (3–4): 367–374.

Gal, Noam, Limor Shifman, and Zohar Kampf. 2015. "'It Gets Better': Internet Memes and the Construction of Collective Identity." *New Media and Society*. http://nms.sagepub.com/content/early/2015/01/24/1461444814568784.

Garber, Megan. 2012. "The Campaign Tumblr Is Dead! (Long Live the Campaign Tumblr)." *Atlantic*, November 28. http://www.theatlantic.com/technology/archive/2012/11/the-campaign-tumblr-is-dead-long-live-the-campaign-tumblr/265688/.

Gere, Charlie. 2002. *Digital Culture*. London: Reaktion Books.

Godwin, Mike. 1994. "Meme, Counter-meme." *Wired*. http://www.wired.com/1994/10/godwin-if-2/.

Habermas, Jürgen. 1991. *The Structural Transformation of the Public Sphere: An Inquiry into Bourgeois Society*. (1962). Cambridge, MA: MIT Press.

Hadfield, Chris. Undated. "Space Oddity | Chris Hadfield." Official Chris Hadfield. http://chrishadfield.ca/space-oddity/.

Haig, David. 2006. "The Gene Meme." In *Richard Dawkins: How a Scientist Changed the Way We Think*, ed. Alan Grafen and Mark Ridley, 50–65. Oxford: Oxford University Press.

Hall, Stuart. 1993. "Encoding, Decoding." In *The Cultural Studies Reader*, ed. Simon During, 90–103. (1973). London: Routledge.

Hebdige, Dick. 1979. *Subculture: The Meaning of Style*. London: Methuen.

Hine, Christine. 2009. "How Can Qualitative Internet Researchers Define the Boundaries of Their Projects?" In *Internet Inquiry: Conversations about Method,* ed. Annette Markham and Nancy K. Baym, 1–20. Los Angeles: Sage.

Howard, Robert Glenn. 2008. "The Vernacular Web of Participatory Media." *Critical Studies in Media Communication* 25 (5): 490–513.

Hwang, Tim, and Christina Xu. 2014. "'Lurk More': An Interview with the Founders of ROFLCon." *Journal of Visual Culture* 13 (3): 376–387.

"Interior Monologue Captioning | Know Your Meme." Know Your Meme. Accessed January 28, 2016. http://knowyourmeme.com/memes/interior-monologue-captioning.

Jackson, Ronald L., II, Chang In Shin, and Keith B. Wilson. 2000. "The Meaning of Whiteness: Critical Implications of Communicating and Negotiating Race." *World Communication* 29 (1): 69–86.

Jäger, Siegfried, and Florentine Maier. 2009. "Theoretical and Methodological Aspects of Foucauldian Critical Discourse Analysis and Dispositive Analysis." In *Methods of Critical Discourse Analysis,* ed. Ruth Wodak and Michael Meyer, 34–61. Los Angeles: Sage.

Jardin, Xeni. 2012. "Disgraced Reddit Mod Violentacrez on CNN." *BoingBoing,* October 19. http://boingboing.net/2012/10/19/disgraced-reddit-mod-violentac.html.

Jazi, Peter, Pat Aufderheide, and the International Communication Association. 2010. "Code of Best Practices in Fair Use for Scholarly Research in Communication." *International Communication Association*: 1–16. http://www.cmsimpact.org/fair-use/best-practices/code-best-practices-fair-use-scholarly-research-communication.

Jenkins, Henry. 1992. *Textual Poachers: Television Fans and Participatory Culture.* New York: Routledge.

Jenkins, Henry. 2006. *Convergence Culture: Where Old and New Media Collide.* New York: New York University Press.

Jenkins, Henry, Sam Ford, and Joshua Green. 2013. *Spreadable Media: Creating Value and Meaning in a Networked Culture.* New York: New York University Press.

Jewitt, Carey. 2004. "Multimodality and New Communication Technology." In *Discourse and Technology: Multimodal Discourse Analysis,* ed. Phillip LeVine and Ron Scollon, 184–195. Washington, DC: Georgetown University Press.

Keller, Daphne. 2008. "The Musician as Thief: Digital Culture and Copyright Law." In *Sound Unbound: Sampling Digital Music and Culture,* ed. Paul D. Miller, 135–150. Cambridge, MA: MIT Press.

Kemp, Martin. 2011. "In and Out of Time: Is There Anything New under the Cyber-sun?" In *Imagery in the Twenty-first Century*, ed. Oliver Grau and Thomas Veigl, 377–398. Cambridge, MA: MIT Press.

Kendall, Lori. 2002. *Hanging Out in the Virtual Pub: Masculinities and Relationships Online*. Berkeley: University of California Press.

Knafo, Saki. 2011. "Occupy Wall Street and Anonymous: Turning a Fledgling Movement into a Meme." *Huffington Post*, October 20. http://www.huffingtonpost.com/2011/10/20/occupy-wall-street-anonymous-connection_n_1021665.html.

Knutilla, Lee. 2011. "User Unknown: 4chan, Anonymity, and Contingency." *First Monday* 16 (10). http://firstmonday.org/ojs/index.php/fm/article/view/3665/3055.

Kress, Gunther, and Theo van Leeuwen. 2006. *Reading Images: The Grammar of Visual Design*. 2nd ed. London: Routledge.

Kruse, Holly. 2003. *Site and Sound: Understanding Independent Music Scenes*. New York: Peter Lang.

Kuipers, Giselinde. 2002. "Media Culture and Internet Disaster Jokes: Bin Laden and the Attacks on the World Trade Center." *European Journal of Cultural Studies* 5 (4): 450–470.

Lamb, Chris. 2004. *Drawn to Extremes: The Use and Abuse of Editorial Cartoons*. New York: Columbia University Press.

Leaver, Tama. 2013. "Olympic Trolls: Mainstream Memes and Digital Discord?" *Fibreculture Journal* 22. http://twentytwo.fibreculturejournal.org/fcj-163-olympic-trolls-mainstream-memes-and-digital-discord/.

Lester, Paul Martin. 1995. *Visual Communication: Images with Messages*. Belmont, CA: Wadsworth.

Lévi-Strauss, Claude. 1966. *The Savage Mind*. (1962). London: Weidenfeld and Nicolson.

Malone, Ailbhe. 2014. "Sad Batman Is the New Meme that Gotham Deserves." *Buzzfeed*, May 17. http://www.buzzfeed.com/ailbhemalone/sad-batman-is-the-meme-that-gotham-deserves.

Mankoff, Robert. 2012. "The Ruling Clawss." *New Yorker*, September 19. http://www.newyorker.com/cartoons/bob-mankoff/the-ruling-clawss.

Markham, Annette, and Nancy K. Baym, eds. 2009. *Internet Inquiry: Conversations about Method*. Los Angeles: Sage.

Markham, Annette, Elizabeth Buchanan, and the Association of Internet Researchers Ethics Working Committee. 2012. "Ethical Decision-making and Internet Research:

Recommendations from the AoIR Ethics Working Committee." *Association of Internet Researchers*: 1–19 http://aoir.org/reports/ethics2.pdf.

Maskeroni, Alfred. 2015. "Every Brand Wanted a Piece of #TheDress, but Who Wore It Best?" *Adweek*, February 27. http://www.adweek.com/adfreak/every-brand-wanted-piece-thedress-who-wore-it-best-163176.

Massanari, Adrienne L. 2015. *Participatory Culture, Community, and Play: Learning from Reddit*. New York: Peter Lang.

Mautner, Gerlinde. 2005. "Time to Get Wired: Using Web-based Corpora in Critical Discourse Analysis." *Discourse and Society* 16 (6): 809–828.

McArdle, Megan. 2011. "Anatomy of a Fake Quotation." *Atlantic*, May 3. http://www.theatlantic.com/national/archive/2011/05/anatomy-of-a-fake-quotation/238257/.

Meyer, John C. 2000. "Humor as a Double-edged Sword: Four Functions of Humor in Communication." *Communication Theory* 10 (3): 310–331.

Milner, Ryan M., and Whitney Phillips. 2014. "Why We're Never Gonna Give Up on the Rickroll." *Conversation*, July 29. https://theconversation.com/why-were-never-gonna-give-up-on-the-rickroll-29864.

Miltner, Kate. 2014. "'There's No Place for Lulz on LOLCats': The Role of Genre, Gender, and Group Identity in the Interpretation and Enjoyment of an Internet Meme." *First Monday* 19 (8). http://firstmonday.org/ojs/index.php/fm/article/view/5391/4103.

Mina, An Xiao. 2014. "Batman, Pandaman, and the Blind Man: A Case Study in Social Change Memes and Internet Censorship in China." *Journal of Visual Culture* 13 (3): 359–375.

Morris, Errol. 2011. *Believing Is Seeing (Observations on the Mysteries of Photography)*. New York: Penguin.

Morris, Meaghan. 2007. "Banality in Cultural Studies." In *The Cultural Studies Reader*. 3rd ed., ed. Simon During, 119–144. (1988). London: Routledge.

Mouffe, Chantal. 2005. *On the Political*. London: Routledge.

Mouffe, Chantal. 2009. "Democracy in a Multipolar World." *Millennium* 37 (3): 549–561.

Murphie, Andrew, and John Potts. 2003. *Culture and Technology*. New York: Palgrave Macmillan.

Nahon, Karine, and Jeff Hemsley. 2013. *Going Viral*. Malden, MA: Polity.

Nakamura, Lisa. 2014. "'I WILL DO EVERYthing That Am Asked': Scambaiting, Digital Show-space, and the Racial Violence of Social Media." *Journal of Visual Culture* 13 (3): 257–274.

Newitz, Annalee. 2013. "We Who Spoke LOLCat Now Speak Doge." *io9*, December 11. http://io9.com/we-who-spoke-lolcat-now-speak-doge-1481243678.

Olson, Parmy. 2012. "How 4chan's Chris Poole Runs His Web Giant on a Shoestring." *Forbes*, October 18. http://www.forbes.com/sites/parmyolson/2012/10/18/how-4chans-chris-poole-runs-his-web-giant-on-a-shoestring/.

Papacharissi, Zizi. 2004. "Democracy Online: Civility, Politeness, and the Democratic Potential of Online Political Discussion." *New Media and Society* 6 (2): 259–283.

Papademas, Dianna, and the International Visual Sociology Association. 2009. "IVSA Code of Research Ethics and Guidelines." *Visual Studies* 24 (3): 250–257.

Pasternack, Alex. 2010. "After Lawsuits and Therapy, Star Wars Kid Is Back." *Motherboard*, June 1. http://motherboard.vice.com/blog/after-lawsuits-and-therapy-star-wars-kid-is-back.

Pearce, Katy E., and Adnan Hajizada. 2014. "No Laughing Matter: Humor as a Means of Dissent in the Digital Era: The Case of Authoritarian Azerbaijan." *Demokratizatsiya (Washington, DC)* 22:67–85.

Phillips, Whitney. 2013. "In Defense of Memes." *Spreadable Media: Web Exclusive Essays*. http://spreadablemedia.org/essays/phillips.

Phillips, Whitney. 2015a. "Let's Call 'Trolling' What It Really Is." *Kernel*, May 10. http://kernelmag.dailydot.com/issue-sections/staff-editorials/12898/trolling-stem-tech-sexism/.

Phillips, Whitney. 2015b. *This Is Why We Can't Have Nice Things: Mapping the Relationship between Online Trolling and Mainstream Culture*. Cambridge, MA: MIT Press.

Phillips, Whitney, and Ryan M. Milner. Forthcoming. "Decoding Memes: Barthes' Punctum, Feminist Standpoint Theory, and the Political Significance of #YesAllWomen." In *Entertainment Values: How Do We Assess Entertainment and Why Does It Matter?* ed. Stephen Harrington and Tanya Nitins. London: Palgrave.

Pickerill, Jenny, and John Krinsky. 2012. "Why Does Occupy Matter?" *Social Movement Studies* 11 (3–4): 279–287.

"Poe's Law | Know Your Meme." Undated. Know Your Meme. Accessed February 26, 2016. http://knowyourmeme.com/memes/poes-law.

Pogatchnik, Shawn. 2009. "Student Hoaxes World's Media on Wikipedia." *Associated Press*, May 12. http://www.nbcnews.com/id/30699302/ns/technology_and_science-tech_and_gadgets/t/student-hoaxes-worlds-media-wikipedia.

Postigo, Hector. 2012. *The Digital Rights Movement: The Role of Technology in Subverting Digital Copyright*. Cambridge, MA: MIT Press.

Read, Max. 2013. "How to Get Rich from Memes: Steal Other Memes." *Gawker*, September 30. http://gawker.com/how-to-get-rich-on-memes-steal-other-memes-1426797890.

Reisigl, Martin, and Ruth Wodak. 2009. "The Discourse-historical Approach." In *Methods of Critical Discourse Analysis*, ed. Ruth Wodak and Michael Meyer, 87–121. Los Angeles: Sage.

"Ridiculously Photogenic Guy/Zeddie Little | Know Your Meme." Undated. Know Your Meme. http://knowyourmeme.com/memes/ridiculously-photogenic-guy-zeddie-little.

Robertson, Adi. 2013. "Nyan Cat and Keyboard Cat Creators Sue 'Scribblenauts' Studio for Using Their Memes." *Verge*, May 2. http://www.theverge.com/2013/5/2/4293484/nyan-cat-keyboard-cat-creators-sue-scribblenauts-over-easter-eggs.

Rose, Gillian. 2012. *Visual Methodologies: An Introduction to Researching with Visual Methods*. Los Angeles: Sage.

Sanders, Sam. 2015, November 7. "#MemeOfTheWeek: The Internet vs. Jeb Bush." *NPR*. http://www.npr.org/2015/11/07/455081576/-memeoftheweek-the-internet-vs-jeb-bush.

Schäfer, Mirko Tobias. 2011. *Bastard Culture! How User Participation Transforms Cultural Production*. Amsterdam: Amsterdam University Press.

Schneider, Nathan. 2013. "Breaking up with Occupy." *Nation*, September 11. http://www.thenation.com/article/breaking-occupy.

Schroeder, Audra. 2014. "New 'Beyoncé Voters' Tumblr Perfectly Responds to *Fox News* Sexism." *Daily Dot*, July 12. http://www.dailydot.com/entertainment/beyonce-voters-tumblr/.

Shaw, Frances. 2013. "Still 'Searching for Safety Online': Collective Strategies and Discursive Resistance to Trolling and Harassment in a Feminist Network." *Fibreculture Journal* 22. http://twentytwo.fibreculturejournal.org/fcj-157-still-searching-for-safety-online-collective-strategies-and-discursive-resistance-to-trolling-and-harassment-in-a-feminist-network/.

Shifman, Limor. 2011. "An Anatomy of a YouTube Meme." *New Media and Society* 14 (2): 187–203.

Shifman, Limor. 2013. "Memes in a Digital World: Reconciling with a Conceptual Troublemaker." *Journal of Computer-Mediated Communication* 18 (3): 362–377.

Shifman, Limor. 2014. *Memes in Digital Culture*. Cambridge, MA: MIT Press.

Shifman, Limor, Hadar Levy, and Mike Thelwall. 2014. "Internet Jokes: The Secret Agents of Globalization?" *Journal of Computer-Mediated Communication* 19 (4): 727–743.

Singer, Paul. 2012. "Twitter Memes Go Viral with Help of Big Media Tweeters." *USA Today,* October 21. http://www.usatoday.com/story/news/politics/2012/10/21/twitter-media-invisibleobama-binders/1641967/.

Society for Cinema and Media Studies. 2010. "Society for Cinema and Media Studies' Statement of Fair Use Best Practices for Media Studies Publishing." *Cinema Journal* 49 (4): 179–185.

Solon, Olivia. 2013. "Richard Dawkins on the Internet's Hijacking of the Word 'Meme.'" *Wired* (June 20). http://www.wired.co.uk/news/archive/2013-06/20/richard-dawkins-memes.

Sottek, T. C. 2014. "Ben Affleck Is Sad Batman." *Verge* (May 13). http://www.theverge.com/2014/5/13/5714096/ben-affleck-is-sad-batman.

Sperber, Dan. 2000. "An Objection to the Memetic Approach to Culture." In *Darwinizing Culture: The Status of Memetics as a Science,* ed. Robert Aunger, 163–173. Oxford: Oxford University Press.

Steele, Catherine Knight. 2013. "Shaking off the 'Other': Appropriation of Marginalized Cultures and the 'Harlem Shake.'" *Selected Papers of Internet Research* 3. http://spir.aoir.org/index.php/spir/article/view/838.

Tannen, Deborah. 2007. *Talking Voices: Repetition, Dialogue, and Imagery in Conversational Discourse.* (1989). 2nd ed. Cambridge: Cambridge University Press.

Time Staff. 2012. "Erik Martin—2012 *Time* 100 Poll." *Time,* March 29. http://content.time.com/time/specials/packages/article/0,28804,2107952_2107953_2109626,00.html.

Toelken, Barre. 1996. *The Dynamics of Folklore.* Logan: Utah State University Press.

Van Dijk, Teun A. 1995. "Discourse Analysis as Ideology Analysis." In *Language and Peace,* ed. Christina Schäffner and Anita Wendon, 17–33. Amsterdam: HAP.

Van Dijk, Teun A. 1997. "The Study of Discourse." In *Discourse as Structures and Processes,* ed. Teun A. van Dijk, 1–34. London: Sage.

Van Dijk, Teun A. 2009. "Critical Discourse Studies: A Sociocognitive Approach." In *Methods of Critical Discourse Analysis,* ed. Ruth Wodak and Michael Meyer, 62–86. Los Angeles: Sage.

Van Leeuwen, Theo. 2004. "Ten Reasons Why Linguists Should Pay Attention to Visual Communication." In *Discourse and Technology: Multimodal Discourse Analysis,* ed. Phillip LeVine and Ron Scollon, 7–19. Washington, DC: Georgetown University Press.

Van Zoonen, Liesbet. 2005. *Entertaining the Citizen: When Politics and Popular Culture Converge*. Lanham, MD: Rowman and Littlefield.

Vie, Stephanie. 2014. "In Defense of 'Slacktivism': The Human Rights Campaign Facebook Logo as Digital Activism." *First Monday* 19 (4). http://firstmonday.org/ojs/index.php/fm/article/view/4961/3868.

Walker, Rob. 2011. "Recognizably Anonymous." *Slate*, December 8. http://www.slate.com/articles/arts/design/2011/12/guy_fawkes_mask_how_anonymous_hacker_group_created_a_powerful_visual_brand.html.

Watercutter, Angela. 2013. "The 10 Best Memes of 2013." *Wired*, December 13. http://www.wired.com/2013/12/best-memes-2013/.

Wiles, Rose, Jon Prosser, Anna Bagnoli, Andrew Clark, Katherine Davies, Sally Holland, and Emma Renold. 2008. "Visual Ethics: Ethical Issues in Visual Research." *Economic and Social Research Council National Centre for Research Methods*: 1–43. eprints.ncrm.ac.uk/421/1/MethodsReviewPaperNCRM-011.pdf.

Wodak, Ruth, and Michael Meyer. 2009. "Critical Discourse Analysis: History, Agenda, Theory, and Methodology." In *Methods of Critical Discourse Analysis*, ed. Ruth Wodak and Michael Meyer, 1–33. Los Angeles: Sage.

Zittrain, Jonathan L. 2008. *The Future of the Internet: And How to Stop It*. New Haven: Yale University Press.

Zittrain, Jonathan L. 2014. "Reflections on Internet Culture." *Journal of Visual Culture* 13 (3): 388–394.

Index